IMAGES
of America

Cortland and Bazetta Township

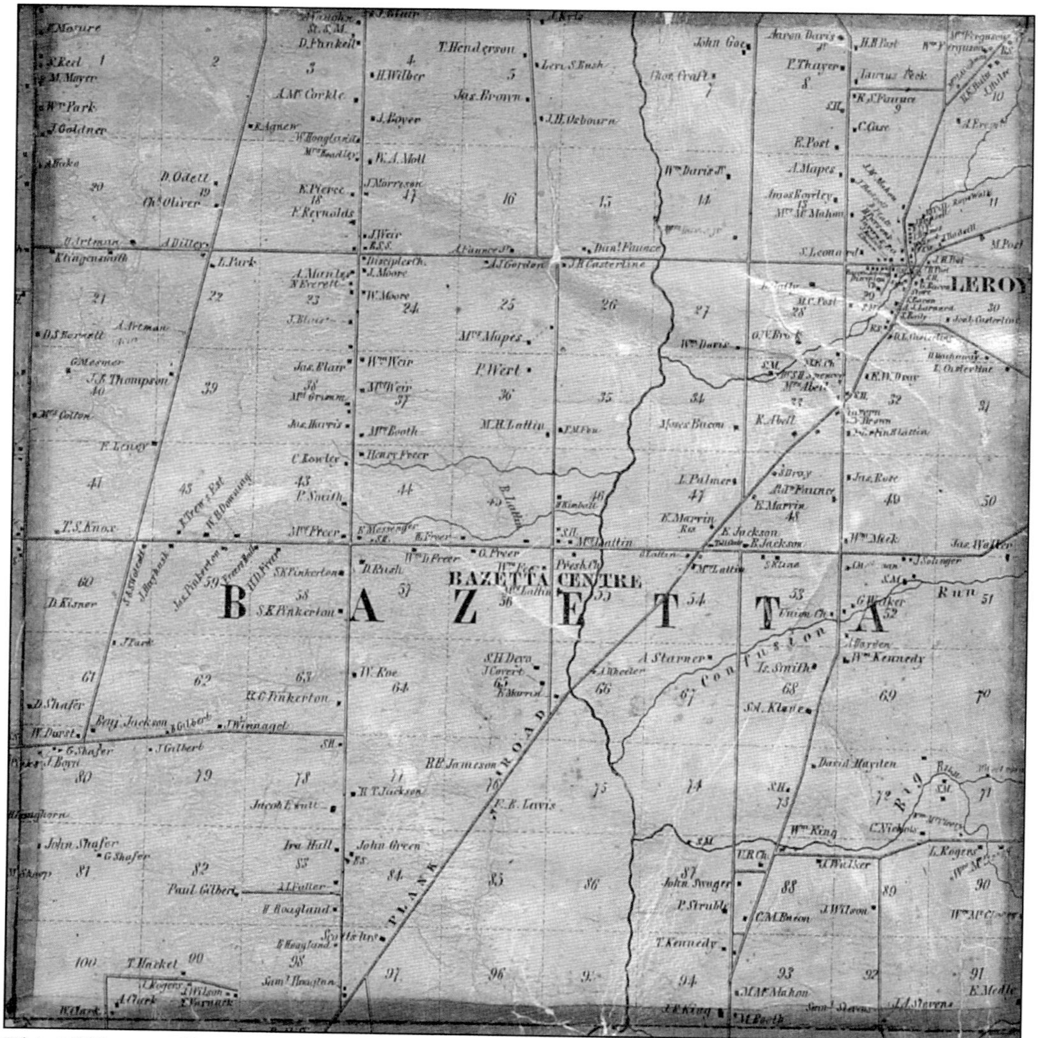

This 1856 map of Bazetta Township shows where roads, houses, farms, mills, churches, cemeteries, blacksmith shops, and major streams were located. The owners' names are included, which makes this a valuable reference to the time period. The straight north–south road, about one third of the way into the west side of the township, is Hoagland-Blackstub Road (Bazetta Road). State Route 305 runs east–west across the middle. These roads were choice locations for early settlers who wanted large farms. Cortland, then noted as "Leroy," is in the northeast section. A close-up of that area is included later in this book. (Courtesy of the Newton Falls Public Library.)

On the Cover: The Oatley Hotel, also known as Hotel Cortland, was located on the southeast corner of Main Street and Railroad Avenue (now Erie Street) near the train station and business district. It provided lodging for travelers and meeting space for businesses and parties in town. The Oatley family owned the hotel for many years. A livery and blacksmith shop was adjacent to the hotel. The building burned in 1930. (Courtesy of the Gessner family.)

IMAGES
of America

CORTLAND AND BAZETTA TOWNSHIP

Sally Lane

ARCADIA
PUBLISHING

ISBN 978-0-7385-9393-7

Published by Arcadia Publishing
Charleston, South Carolina

Printed in the United States of America

Library of Congress Control Number: 2012934602

For all general information, please contact Arcadia Publishing:
Telephone 843-853-2070
Fax 843-853-0044
E-mail sales@arcadiapublishing.com
For customer service and orders:
Toll-Free 1-888-313-2665

Visit us on the Internet at www.arcadiapublishing.com

Dedicated to the people of Cortland and Bazetta,
who so generously shared time, photographs, and memories
to help preserve local history for future generations

Contents

Acknowledgments		6
Introduction		7
1.	Early Years to 1860	9
2.	Churches and Schools	19
3.	Growth of the Town	49
4.	Richards Milling	69
5.	New Century, Many Changes	81
6.	Mosquito Lake	99
7.	Fires and Wrecks	107
8.	Government, Post Offices, and Libraries	111
9.	People, Homes, and Fun	117
About the Organization		127

Acknowledgments

A lifelong interest in local history led me to membership in the Cortland-Bazetta Historical Society, where Dorothy Klein, Grace Allison, and Mary Case, all prolific writers, convinced me to help research and write histories of local homes for a house tour years ago. They became my mentors and inspired me to keep writing for publication, which ultimately led to this book. Dorothy and Grace are now both deceased.

I will be forever grateful to James Woofter, publisher of the *Cortland News*, who offered the use of his scanner for the duration of the project. He also photographed some of the items that were too big to scan and provided some vintage photographs. A huge thank-you to William Hallett of the Cortland Bazetta Historical Society, who patiently located, scanned, and delivered many unique photographs when frequently needed.

Among the many people who have generously shared memories, photographs, and clippings from their private collections are George Gessner and his mother, Evelyn. Their photographs were the beginning of this book. Flo Hutton offered several albums, as did Mary Case, Alvin Mizner, Robert Greenwood, Carol Harrison, Don Jones, William Harned, Mary Lou Reese, Don and Eileen Hazel, James and Nancy Finley, Randy Reel, Louise Hadley, Peggy Mellott, and Walter Richards from Estes, Colorado.

Cortland Christian, Cortland Methodist, and Nazarene Churches opened their archives, as well as Bowers Insurance Group and Wollam Insurance for information on old, thriving businesses in the community. The Bazetta Fire Department also allowed me to copy their photographs. The US Army Corps of Engineers provided many photographs of the building of Mosquito Lake.

My husband, Ralph, has endured months without complaining and listened to me obsess about the book while answering the phone, taking messages, handling the housework, and eating fast food. Thank you, more than I can say.

A special thank-you goes to Sandy Shalton from Arcadia Publishing, who approached me with the idea of writing a book for her company, and Simone Williams, who became my book editor.

Many images in this volume appear courtesy of the Cortland-Bazetta Historical Society (CBHS).

Introduction

History is all around us, especially in Cortland and Bazetta. Buildings, places, and things that we see every day often have a link to the past of which we are unaware. Did you know that Sparkle Market was a theater? That R-B Market has roots to the earliest grocery stores in Cortland? And, what about that creek under the bridge on High Street? What significance does that have in the history of our town and township?

When Edward Scofield, John Budd, Henry Hulse, and a few others entered the township with the purpose of starting a settlement in the winter of 1804, Ohio had been a state for over a year, and boundaries had been established for townships. The five-mile square that would be named Bazetta by Scofield was known only as "township 5, range 3." They soon located the creek; waterpower was the technology of the day, so these early settlers knew they had found something very important. Settlement began with Scofield, when he built a log house on a knoll by about a half-mile south of that creek called Walnut Run. The first order of business was to build a mill for grinding corn and wheat. About 10 families arrived by the time the mill was built in 1811.

The War of 1812 interrupted settlement for a time, but the trickle of settlers increased after it ended. The next step was a school, which was completed in 1813, and then churches. The Bacon family arrived in 1816 and soon parceled out their property with the vision of a town.

About the time of the Civil War, canals had passed their peak, and the railroad began grading and laying tracks for the next move up the technology ladder. Business boomed in the newly incorporated town of Cortland in the 1870s. Over the next 50 years, the area began to change from agrarian to industrial in the town itself, while the township remained mainly rural. It should be pointed out, though, that as a rural area Bazetta was a leader in the farming business. The Experimental Farm, where the Trumbull County Fairgrounds is today, brought many innovations to crops and cattle breeding for the entire country. These innovations helped the United States feed the country during World War I and II and helped change agriculture forever.

In town, there were broom factories, canning factories, a spoke and handle factory, and even one that made bicycle rims besides grocery stores, grist and feed mills, cheese factories, hotels, and liveries.

People with vision, such as Edward Scofield, Nelson Cowdery, Lewis Oatley, the Post family, the Bacon family, and the Wollams, Greenwoods, Bowers, Dursts, Biggins, Richards, Parsons, and Huttons, worked very hard to make the area a good place to live, and the list of people who have done so goes on and on to this very day. Where would we be without the mayors who pushed for water lines, sewers, and electricity?

After Mosquito Lake was created, industry grew in the township, bringing more people to the area. By 1970, both the town and township were the fastest growing areas in Trumbull County. Businesses all along State Route 5 sprang up as quickly as they could be built. Lordstown opened a General Motors plant, Packard Electric expanded into Bazetta, and a K-Mart distribution center arrived.

The last chapter includes a few of the people, homes, and hometown fun. I wish there were more room—and more pictures—to tell the many stories of swimming holes, sled-riding hills, school sports, and of course the Street Fair and the Trumbull County Fair. Maybe that will be another book.

This book attempts to tell the story of Cortland and Bazetta through the photographs culled from residents' albums, the historical society, archives at the library, and other books written about the area, most notably Mary Case's *Cortland-Bazetta Remembered: Personal Reflections of Yesterday*, many of Grace Allison's local writings collected over the years, Thomas Kachur's *Historical Collections of Bazetta Township, Cortland, Ohio*, historical atlases of Trumbull County, and many newspaper collections.

The story, because it is mostly based on available photographs, is incomplete, as images were not found for some parts of the area's history, and memories were not written down. I hope this book will fill in some of the gaps and help the reader to appreciate this special area.

One

Early Years to 1860

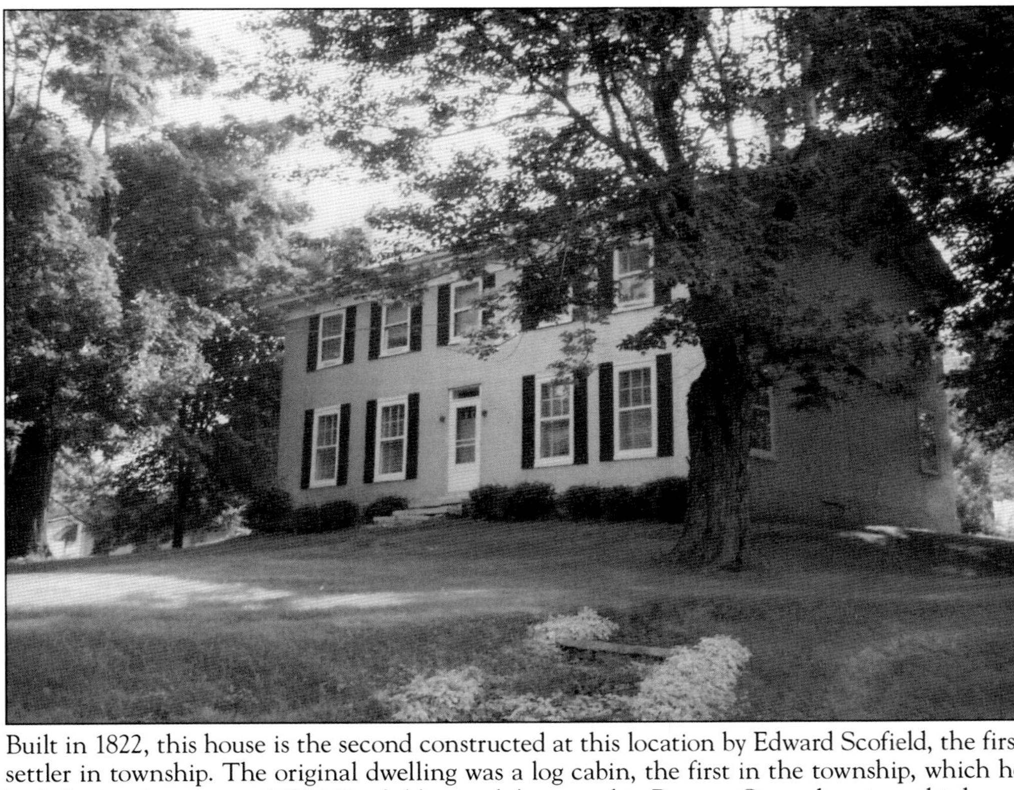

Built in 1822, this house is the second constructed at this location by Edward Scofield, the first settler in township. The original dwelling was a log cabin, the first in the township, which he built during the winter of 1804. Scofield named the township Bazetta. Since that time, this house and farm have been owned by others who were involved in promoting the area. After Scofield, Nelson Cowdery owned the farm in the 1800s. Around 1926, the property was purchased by Natale Pistolozzi and his wife, Margaret. In the 1940s, after Pistolozzi's death, his widow developed lots on the property, which became Natale, Hillman, and Portal Drives. Land for Lakeview High School was purchased in 1960. (Courtesy of Genevieve Pistolozzi Phillips.)

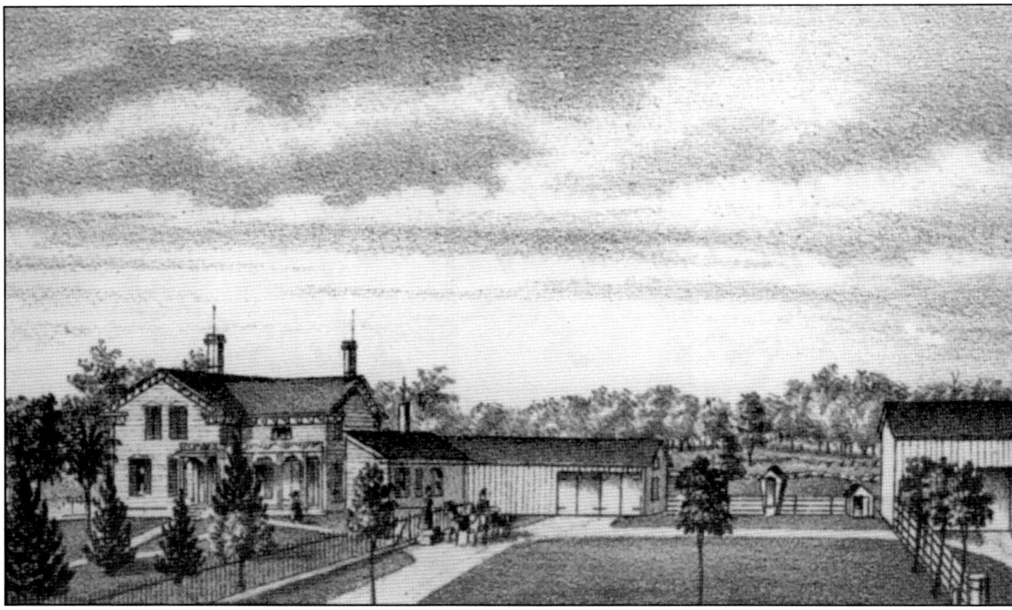

An artist's sketch of the Nelson A. Cowdery property, seen in the previous photograph, was copied from the *Trumbull County Atlas*, published in 1874. Nelson was born in 1826 in Connecticut, and he came to Ohio that year with his parents, who settled in Mecca. In the 1860s, he and his family moved to the former Scofield property. In 1870, he built a cheese factory, which helped the area become a dairy center, and became a county commissioner. He also served as mayor of Cortland from 1898 to 1903. Later, he was one of the organizers of the First National Bank in Cortland and served as one of the first directors and president of the bank. He is pictured below in a cornfield. (Above, author's collection; below, courtesy of Mary Case.)

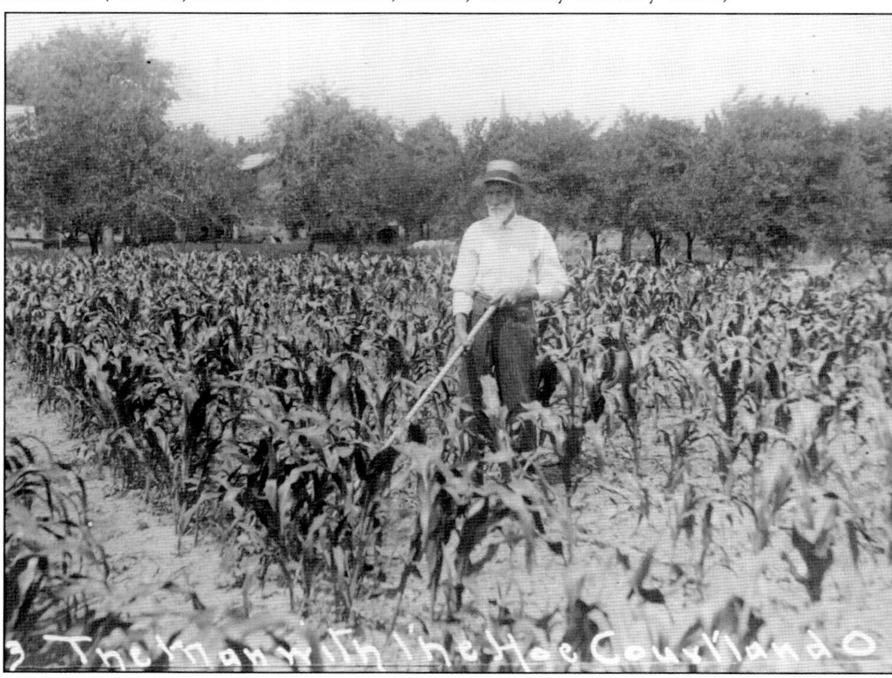

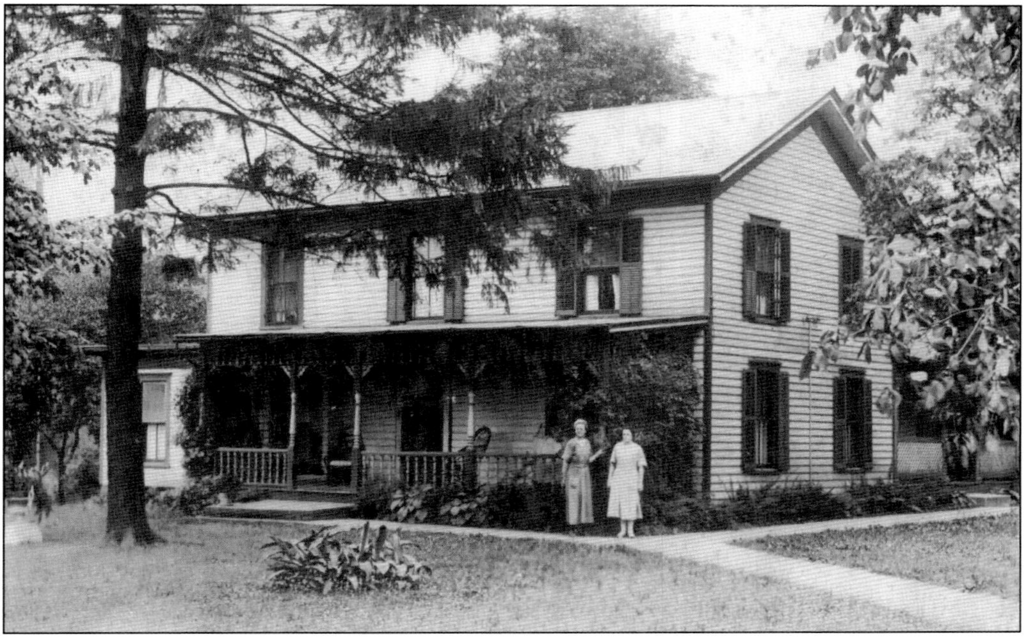

Joshua Oatley, his wife, and two sons, William and Edward, came to Bazetta about 1809 as one of the first half-dozen families to settle in the township. Sometime after the death of his wife, between 1816 and 1819, Joshua left to do some traveling and never returned. William built the house (above) in 1819 that is now located on the southwest corner of West Main and Mecca Streets. His daughter-in-law Minnie Oatley and Neva Shaffer are pictured around 1893. Edward built his house (below) on an adjacent lot on the creek bank, also in 1819. He sold it to George Brock in 1832 and moved to Ashtabula. The house was rebuilt in 1954 by the Rudy family and is now owned by George Gessner. (Both, courtesy of the Gessner family.)

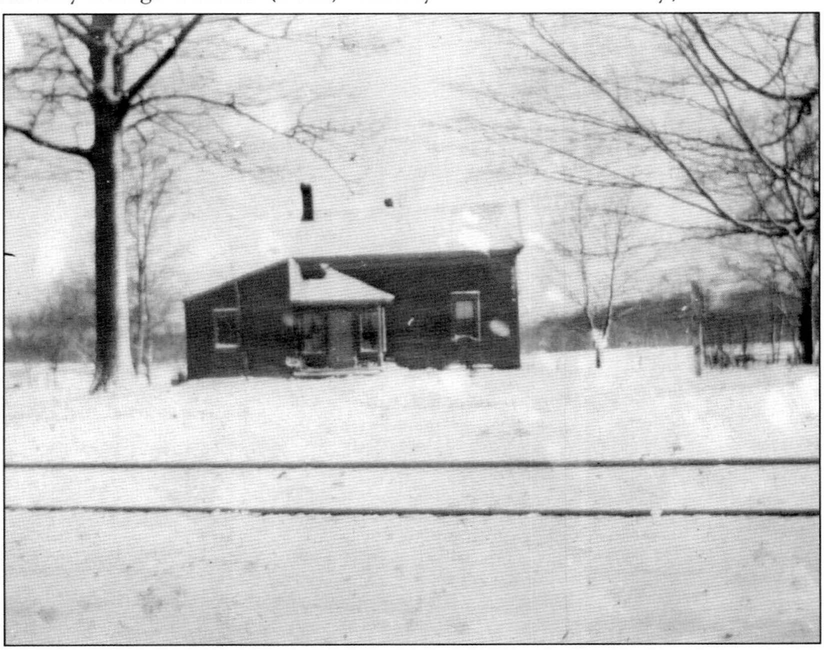

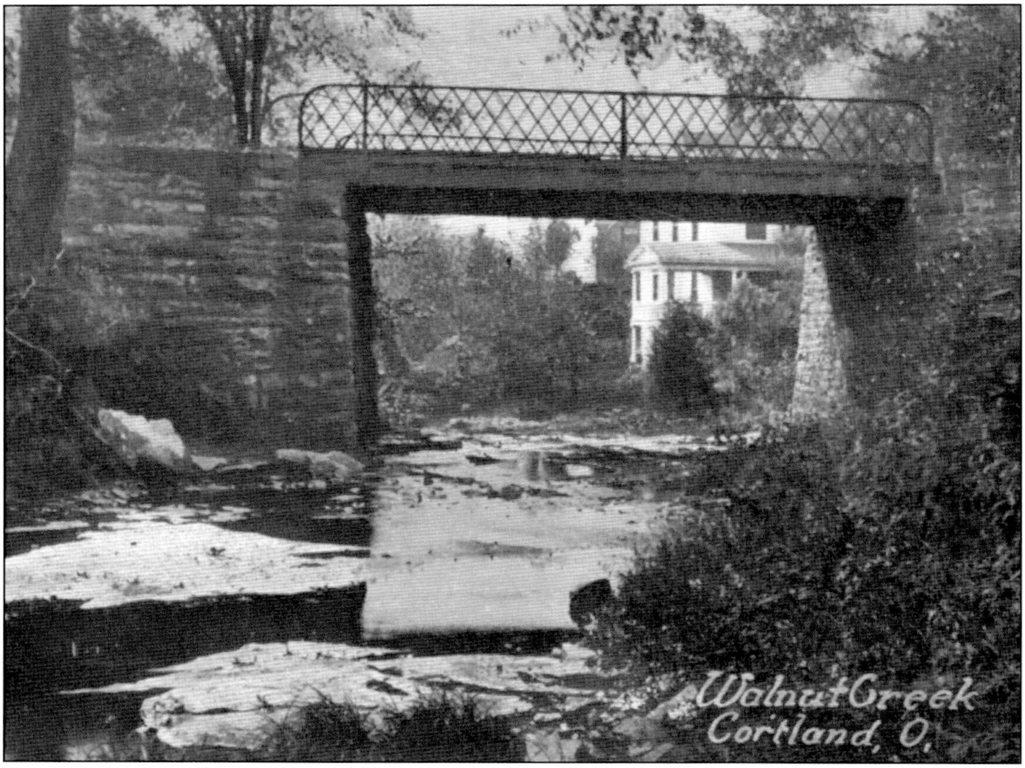

Since 1811, when Edward Scofield and Jeremiah Brooks built the first gristmill on Walnut Run, there has been a building near the southwest corner of Main and High Streets. This house is built on the foundation of an old mill, constructed by J.H. Post in 1846. Until the mill burned in 1890, there were several other mill owners. Ward L. Bacon, great grandson of Samuel Bacon, who owned the mill in 1816, built the house pictured above in 1898. Ward died in 1905. In 1919, the house became the Brookside Inn, a very popular eatery owned by Alex Flanagan. From the late 1970s, the building has been a decorating business owned by Joyce and Richard Masters. The creek and High Street Bridge are pictured below. (Above, courtesy of Don Jones; below, CBHS.)

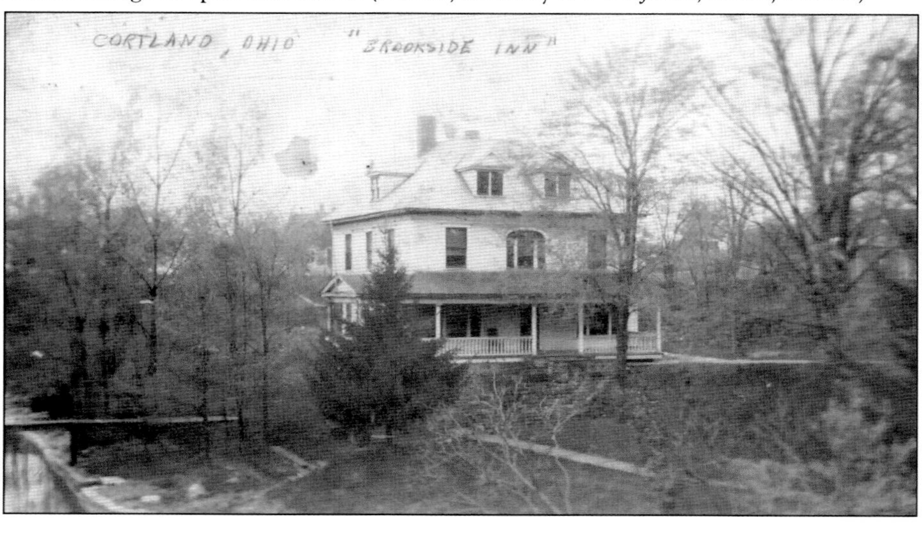

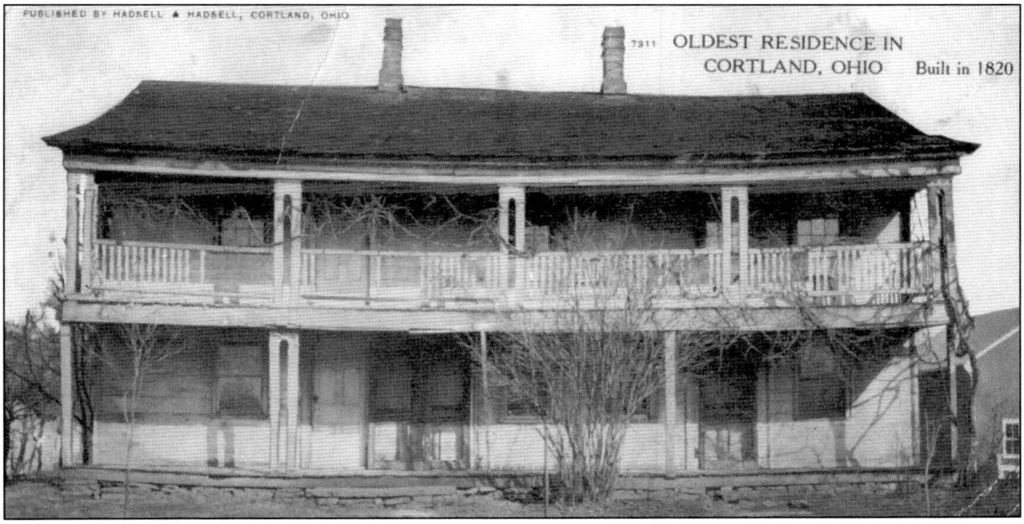

This house stood on West Main Street on the north side, opposite where Grove Drive enters the street; it was built in 1820. Frank Burrows bought it in 1909, tore it down, and built a new home. The Enos Bacon family lived in this building for many years, but sources say they did not build it. (Courtesy of the Gessner family.)

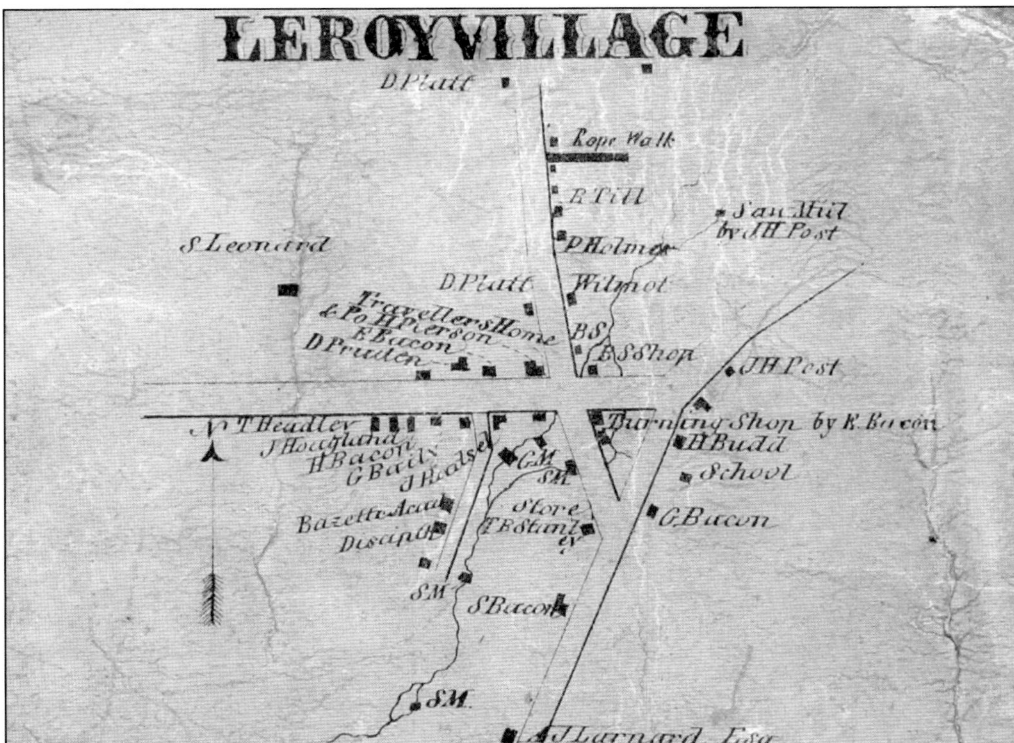

Leroy was the name supposedly given by Edward Scofield for the area around the mill. However, after the large Bacon family arrived, it soon was unofficially called Baconsburg, and sometimes East Bazetta, but the post office was officially called Bazetta. The box labeled "E. Bacon" represents the location of the house pictured above. (Photograph by Jim Woofter, courtesy of George Gessner.)

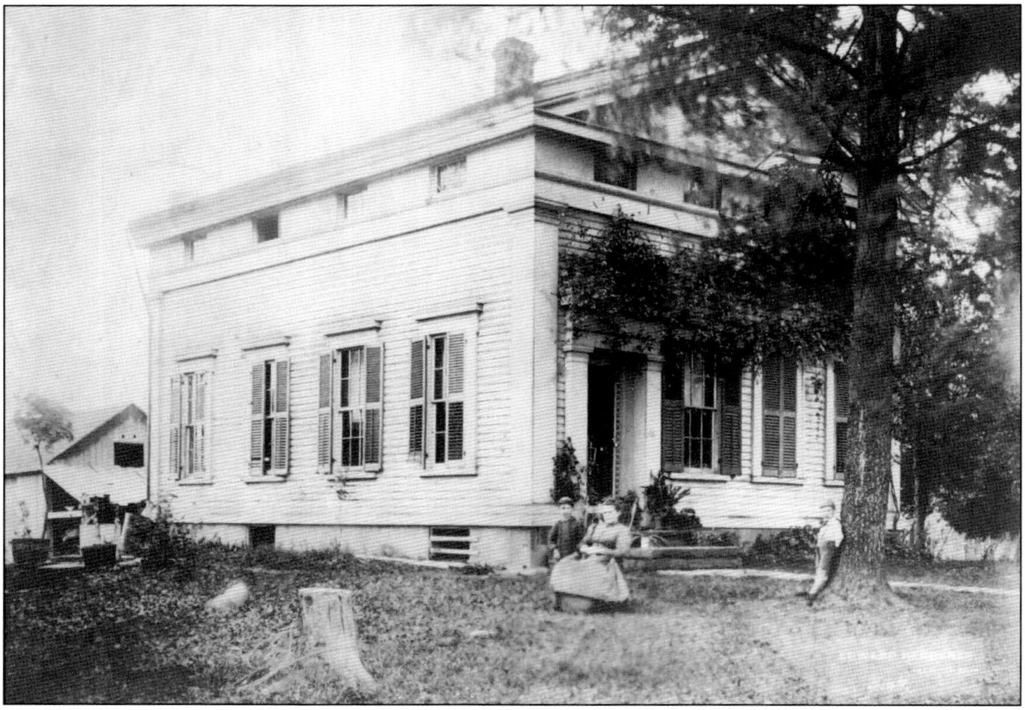

Since before 1860, this house on Warren-Meadville Road was a local landmark. It is the third house built by the Marvin family since 1821, when Joseph Marvin brought his large family from Connecticut. Joseph was the first settler on the west side of Mosquito Creek. The Marvin family figured prominently in the history of both the township and the county. Mother Alicia Marvin is shown with sons Henry Lee and Ezra Marvin. (Courtesy of CBHS.)

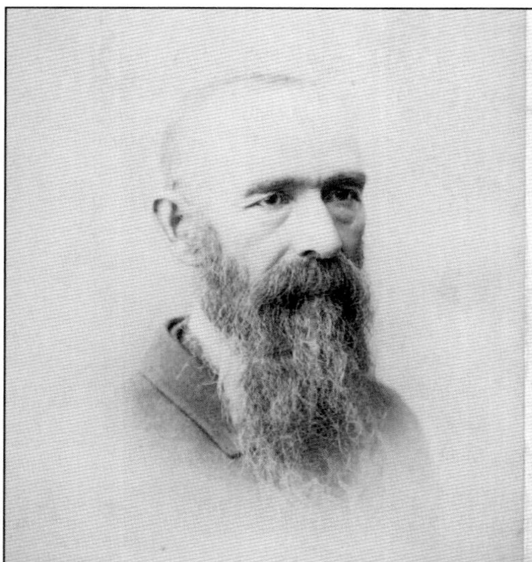

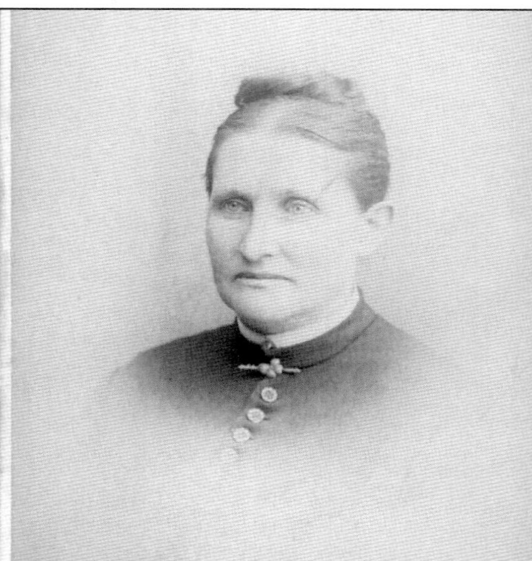

David Deming Marvin was born in 1826 in Bazetta on the Marvin property, the son of Ezra and Lucinda Hall Marvin. He married Alicia Tuttle (born 1845) in 1867, and they had six children: Frederick, who died as an infant, Bessie, Lorane, Grace, Henry Lee, and Ezra. David, a justice of the peace for many years, died in 1910; Alicia died in 1933. (Courtesy of CBHS.)

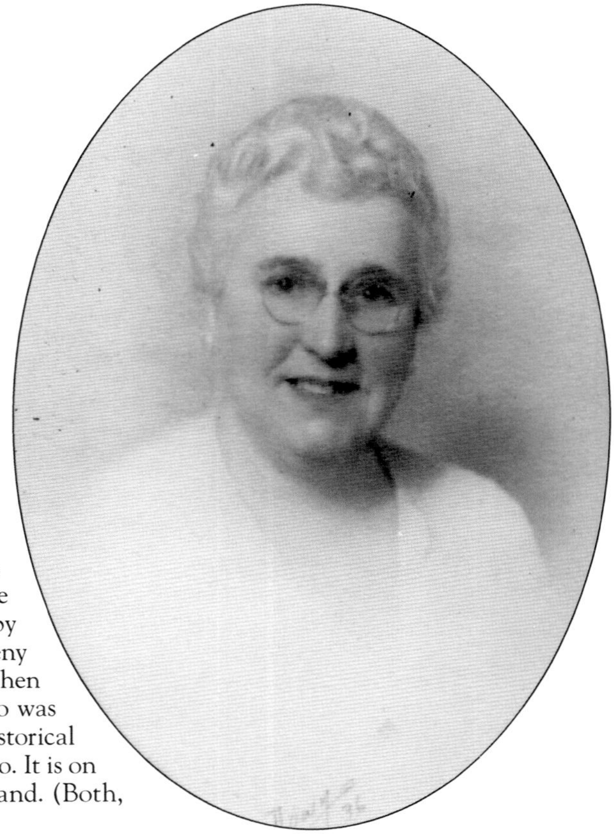

Bessie Marvin, daughter of David and Alicia Marvin, was born in 1875 in the house on the previous page. She was a talented musician, choir director, and popular piano teacher for over 55 years. She lived in the home for 92 years and died just a few months short of the age of 100. Her piano was brought by oxcart from Boston, over the Allegheny Mountains, for her seventh birthday. When the house was sold in 1967, the piano was placed in an outbuilding. The local historical society obtained and restored the piano. It is on display at the Opera House in Cortland. (Both, courtesy of CBHS.)

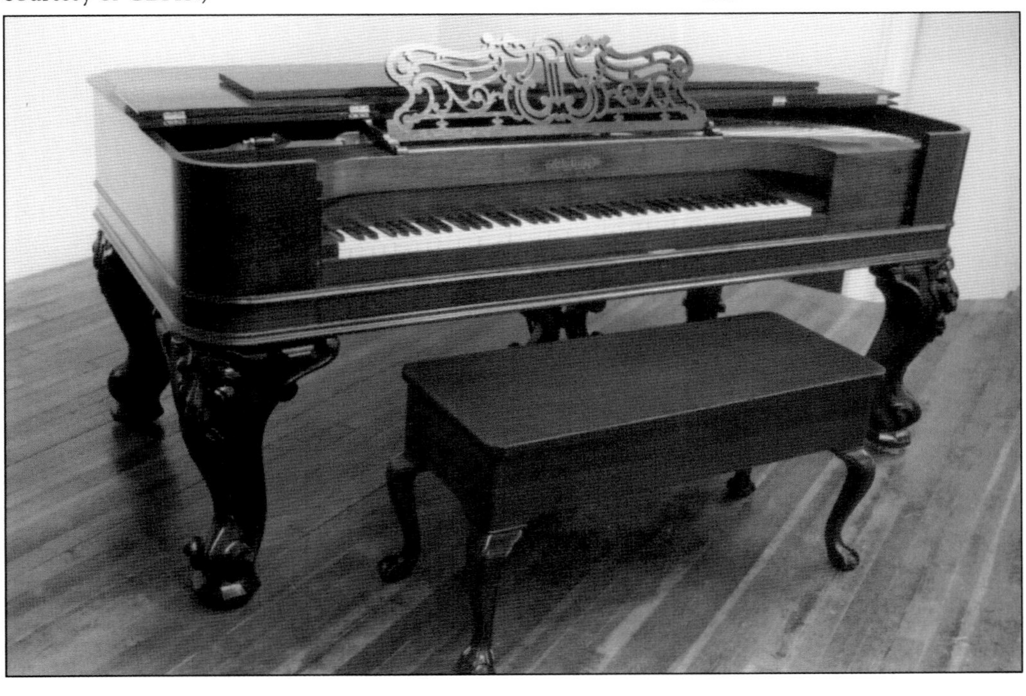

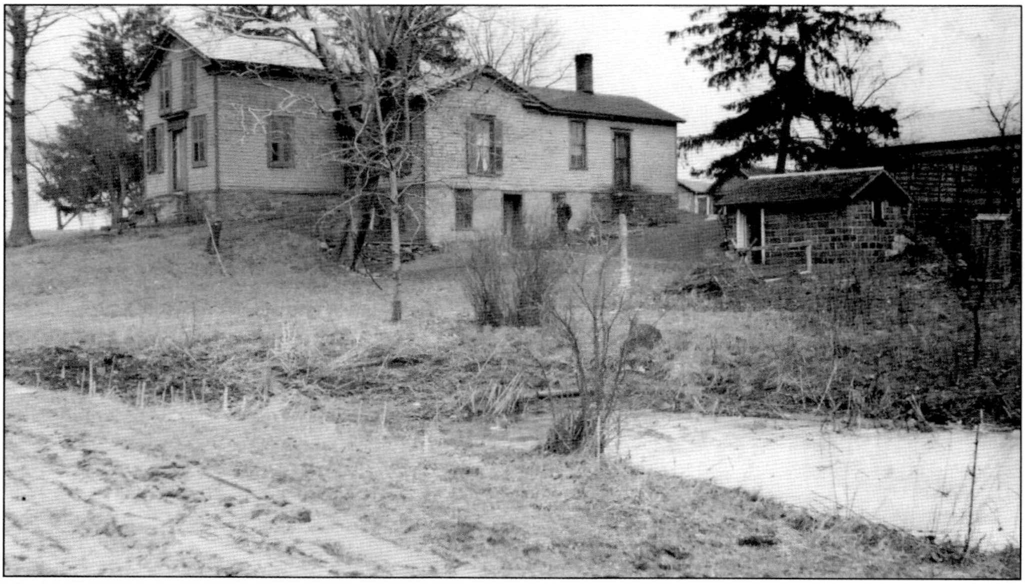

Nathaniel Lattin came to Bazetta in 1831 with his wife, Laura, and children. They settled on lot no. 55 in the center of the township. He replaced the first house that he built with this one in 1840. Nathaniel was a cabinetmaker and farmer, while his wife was a tailor who made gentlemen's clothing and trained apprentices for a store in Warren whose customers were prominent doctors and lawyers. (Courtesy of CBHS.)

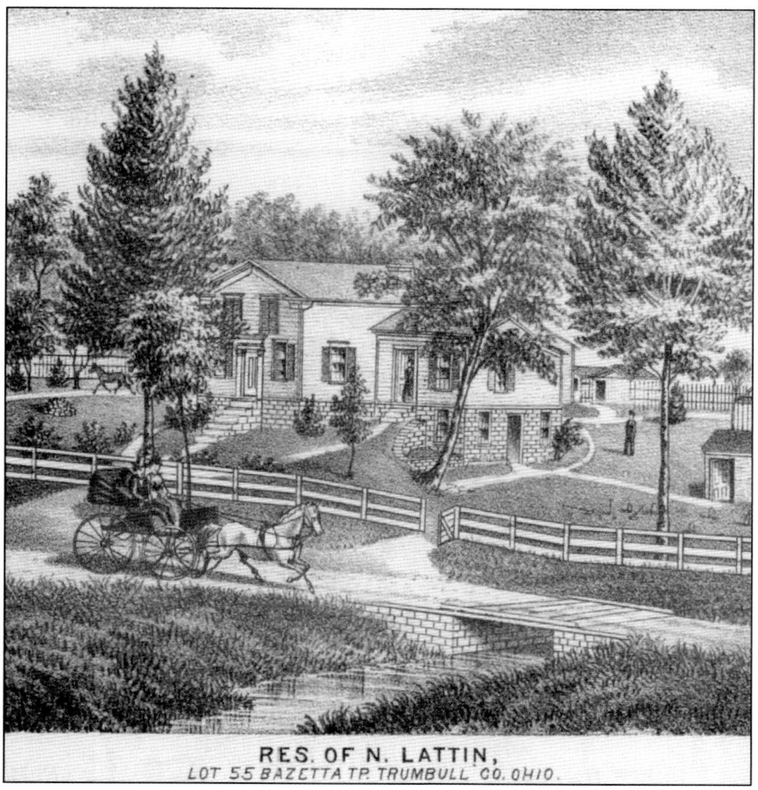

The photograph of the house on this page may have been taken before or after this lithograph from the 1874 *Trumbull County Atlas*. Both are the same house, from the same angle, and even have a person standing near the same spot. This house was razed, and Mosquito Lake was created. A Presbyterian church was also built on this land in 1855 after moving from its first location adjacent to the Casterline Cemetery on South High Street; however, the church disbanded in the 20th century. (Courtesy of CBHS.)

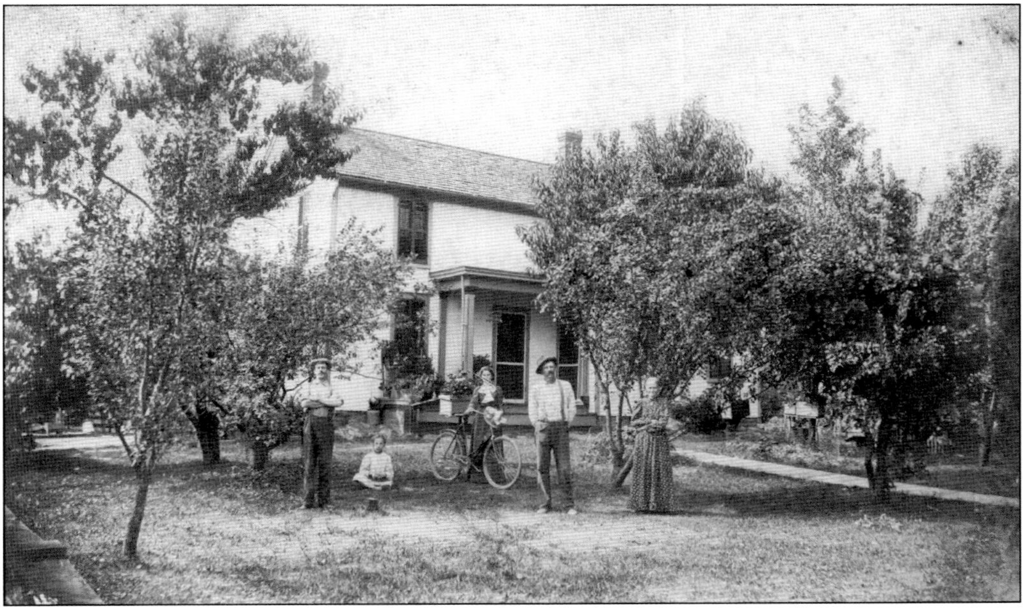

Frank G. Murphy arrived in Bazetta in 1855. The homestead on Durst Clagg Road, seen above, has been in the family ever since and is now the home of great-grandson Donald and his wife, Grace Murphy. This 1893 photograph shows, from left to right, Frank's sons George and William, daughter Alice, Frank, and his wife, Delilah. Below, in front of the barn that has since been torn down are, from left to right, George, Frank, Delilah, and children William and Alice. Many family reunions have been held here for over the last 100 years. (Both, courtesy of Donald Murphy.)

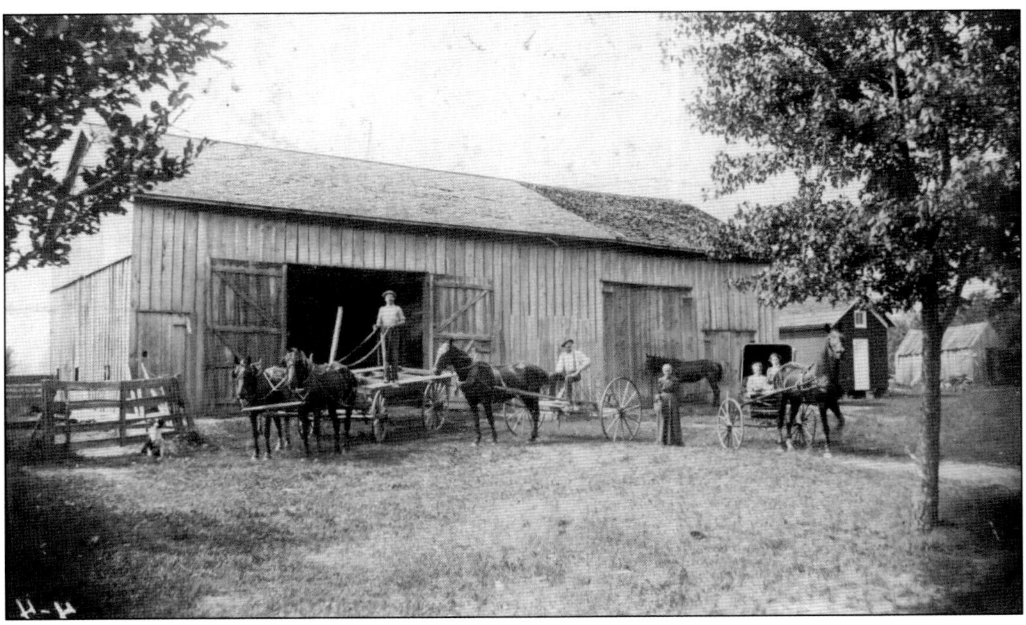

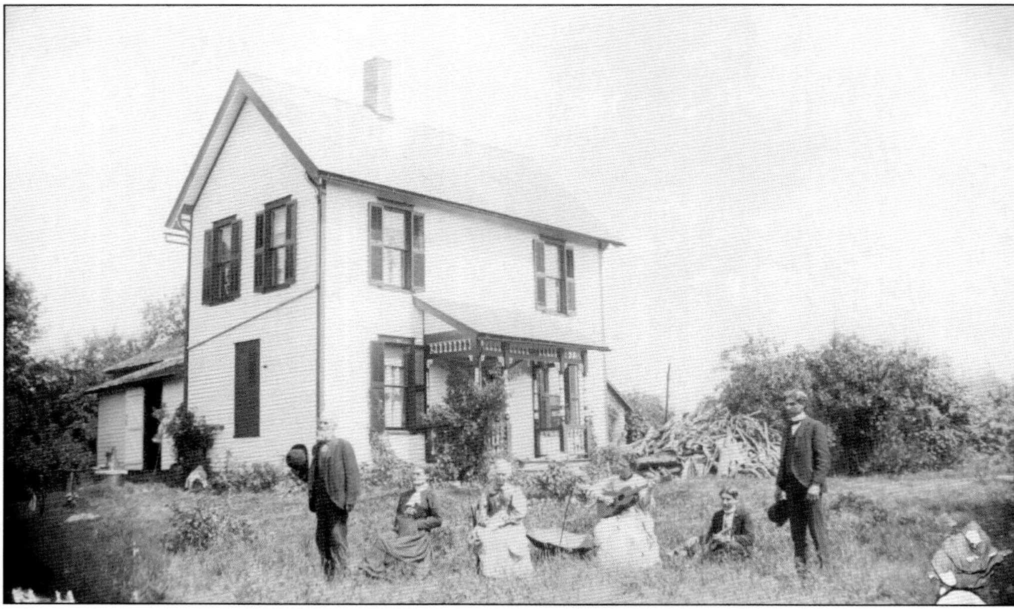

The Byron Winnagle house, on Johnson Plank Road in Bazetta, was built prior to 1856 by Byron's parents, Jonathon and Caroline Risely Winnagle. Pictured here in 1900 are, from left to right, Byron, born in 1842, his wife Eunice Hall Winnagle, Eunice's sister, daughter Effie with the guitar, son Homer who died at age 26, and son Roscoe. (Courtesy of CBHS.)

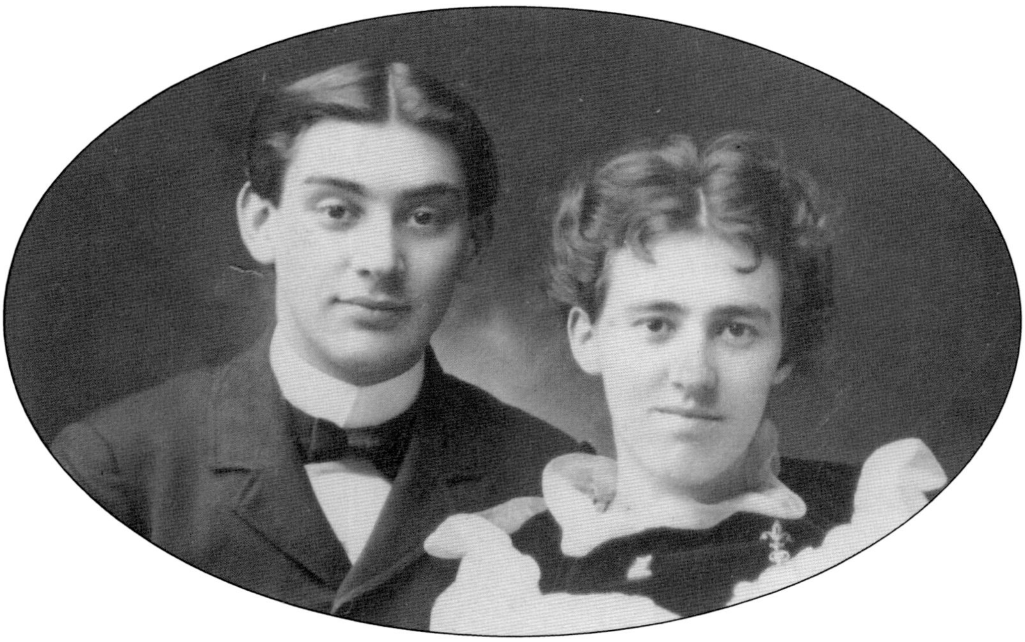

Effie and Roscoe Winnagle are pictured here. Effie was born on January 31, 1877, and died June 17, 1944. She was married to David William Reese. Her brother Roscoe was born in Bazetta on February 4, 1881. After graduation from the University of Kansas Law School and Hiram College, he began practicing law in Warren in 1918. He married Grace Alicia Marvin in 1911, daughter of David and Alicia Marvin. Grace was a noted genealogist in Trumbull County. (Courtesy of CBHS.)

Two

CHURCHES AND SCHOOLS

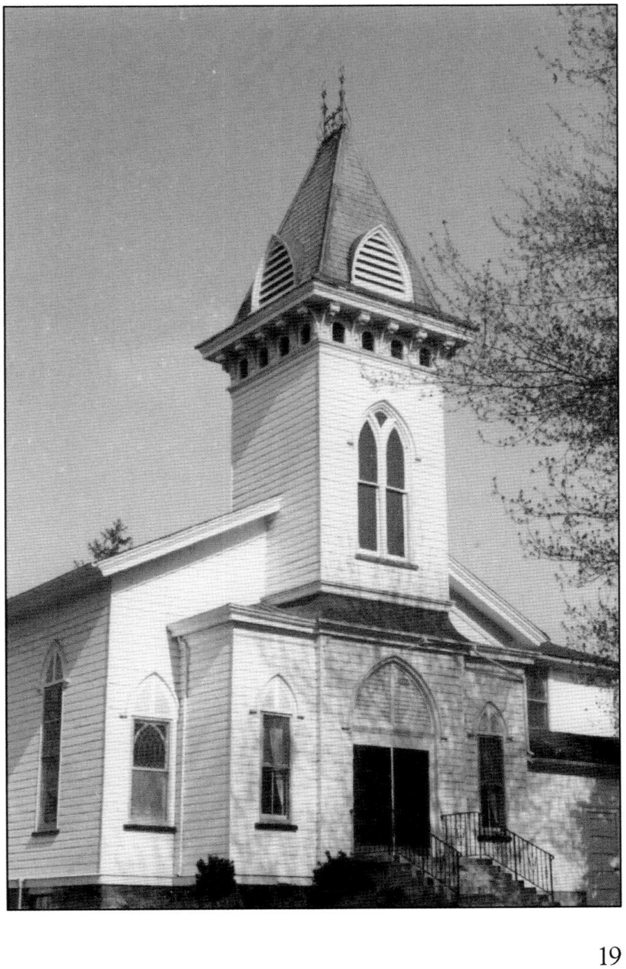

Cortland Christian Church, built in 1853 and located on Grove Drive, had the largest congregation in the county in 1848. The land and adjoining cemetery was donated by Samuel Bacon. The steeple was added to the church when it was remodeled in 1874. After the remodeling, almost 500 people were present at the dedication. In 1860, it was the site of Trumbull County's first spelling bee. Over the years, the church has had numerous additions, yet the simple structure is still evident. Music from the carillon continues to be heard throughout the community each day today as it has for many years. (Courtesy of Cortland Christian Church.)

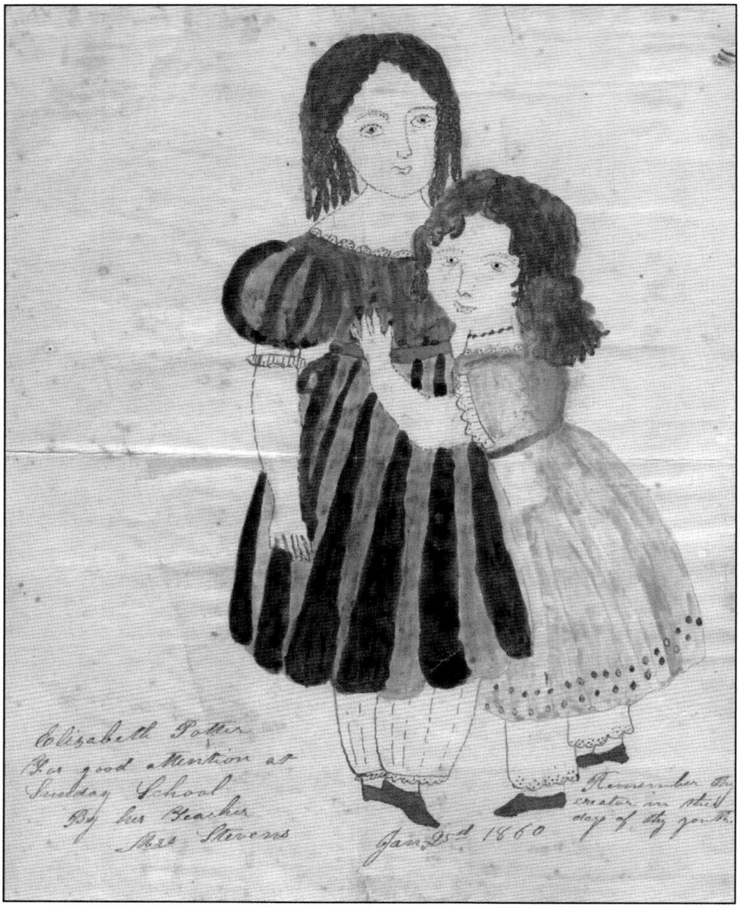

This image was drawn and painted by a Cortland Christian Church Sunday school teacher for Elizabeth Potter in 1860. It reads, "For good attention at Sunday school, by her teacher, Mrs. Stevens." Elizabeth was a relative of Don Jones's mother, May Jones, and is a treasured family item from the past. (Courtesy of Don Jones.)

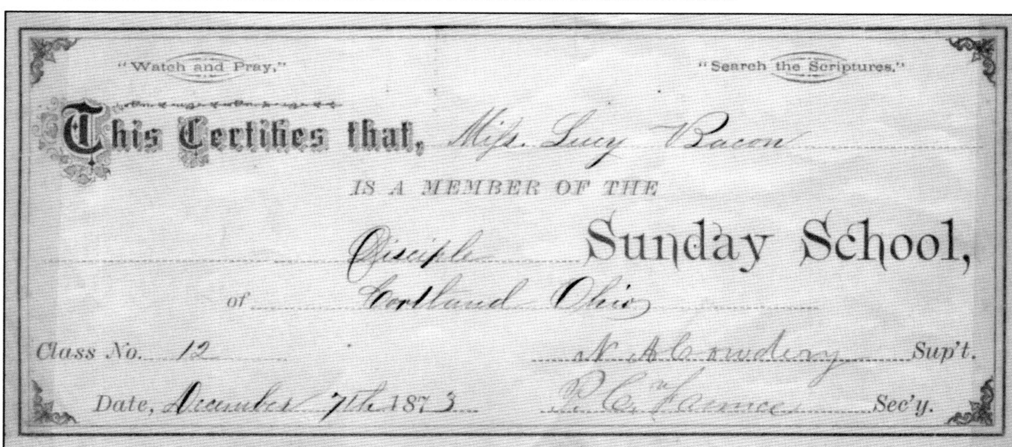
"Watch and Pray." "Search the Scriptures."

This Certifies that, Miss Lucy Bacon

IS A MEMBER OF THE

Disciple Sunday School,

of Cortland Ohio

Class No. 12 N. A. Cowdery Sup't.

Date, December 7th 1873 P. C. Faunce Sec'y.

Lucy Bacon, daughter of Moses and Ruth Tomlinson Bacon, was age seven in 1873 when she was a member of the Disciple Church (now Cortland Christian Church) Sunday school class. Nelson Cowdery, the Sunday school superintendent, and Parmenus Faunce signed her membership receipt. Both businessmen were active members of the church. Sunday School classes began in 1868 at the church. (Courtesy of Lucy Athya.)

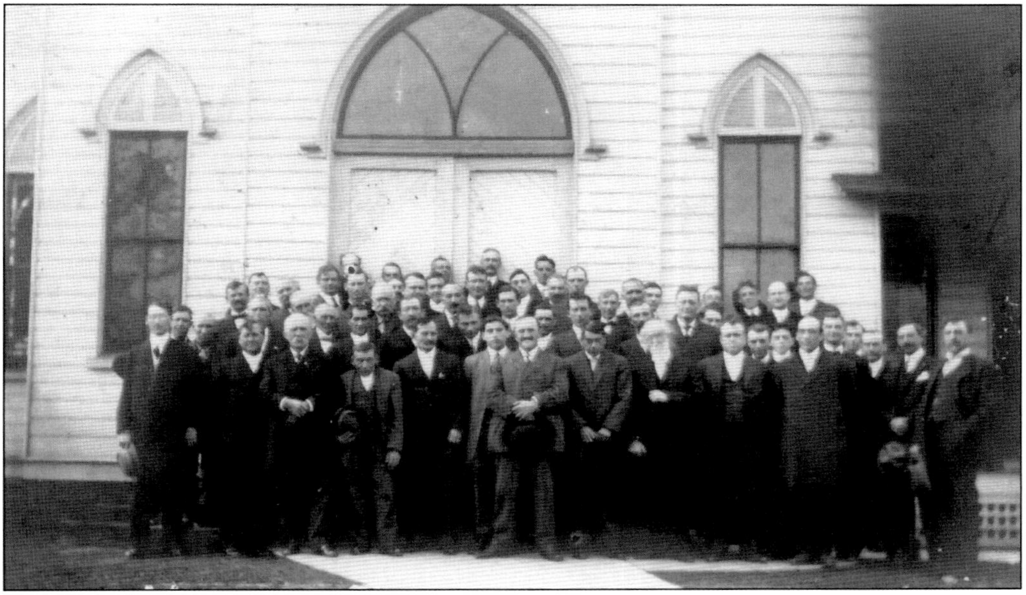

The men's Bible class of the Cortland Disciples Church consisted of a large group of men who worked very hard in the church, doing everything from fundraising to maintenance. They made decisions about the operation of the church. When the Congregational church dissolved, many of those members began attending the Cortland Disciples Church, and it was this men's group that voted to relax rules about immersion baptism to embrace these fellow Christians. (Courtesy of Cortland Christian Church.)

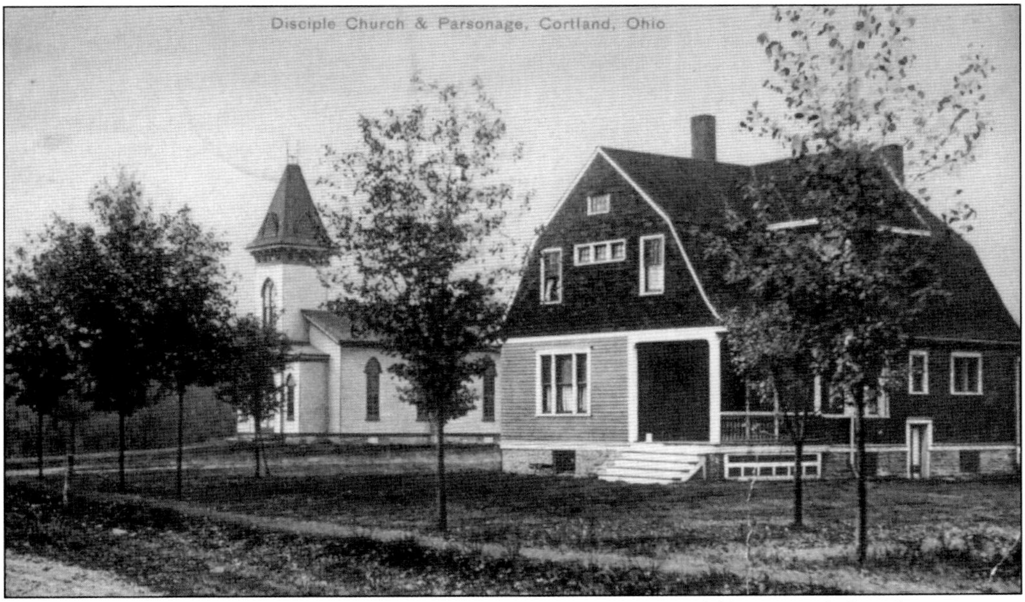

Sometime around 1887, property was exchanged so that a street could be extended to the cemetery next to the church; the street became Grove Drive. On the curve across from the church, a much-needed parsonage was built in 1898. It housed ministers for many years, including a minister of the Church of the Nazarene in 1970, and still can be seen with the date on the cornerstone of the house. (Courtesy of CBHS.)

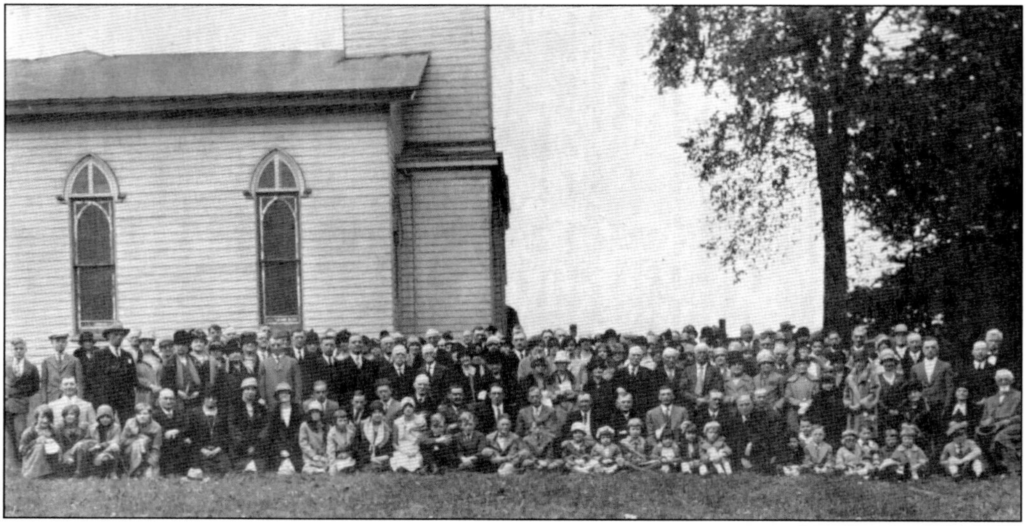

In 1928, the Cortland Christian Church celebrated 100 years. Members of the congregation are seen gathered on the lawn outside for a group photograph. This has become a tradition, and the pastoral archives contain group pictures over the years, as well as many church directories with individual church members pictured. (Courtesy of Cortland Christian Church.)

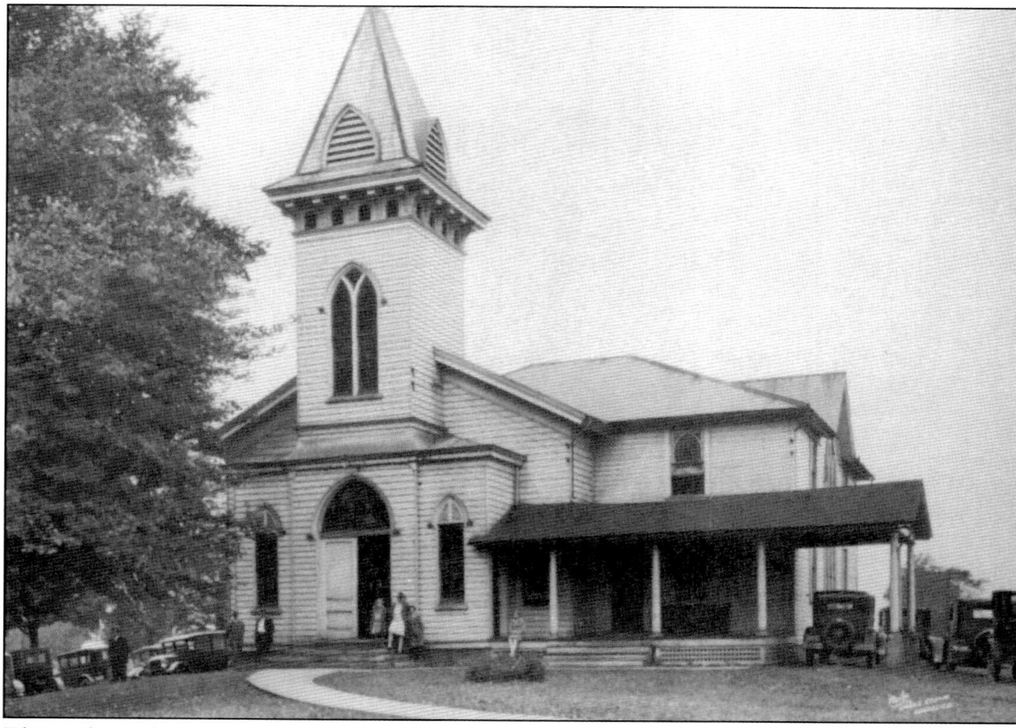

This is how the church looked in 1930. Note the open porch and the large addition on the north side of the building, which gave the church room for Sunday school classes. At one time, horses were tied to hitching posts along the edge of the cemetery and parking lot, but by 1930 automobiles were the preferred method of transportation, as can be seen. (Courtesy of Cortland Christian Church.)

On the west side of Mosquito Creek, at the crossroad named Klondike, another group of disciples began meeting in 1848. Their church was built in 1849 on the southeast corner of Everett Hull and Bazetta Roads but later moved diagonally to the northeast corner. A row of long pews down the center of the church had a rail through the center separating men and women. In 1973, this church was moved and became part of the Historical Village at the Trumbull County Fairgrounds. The new church (below), constructed in 1972, gathered more pledges for the building than expected. In 2012, the church offers a free meal each month and has a day-care center for children of working parents. (At right, courtesy of CBHS; below, photograph by Sara Baxter of the Bazetta Christian Church.)

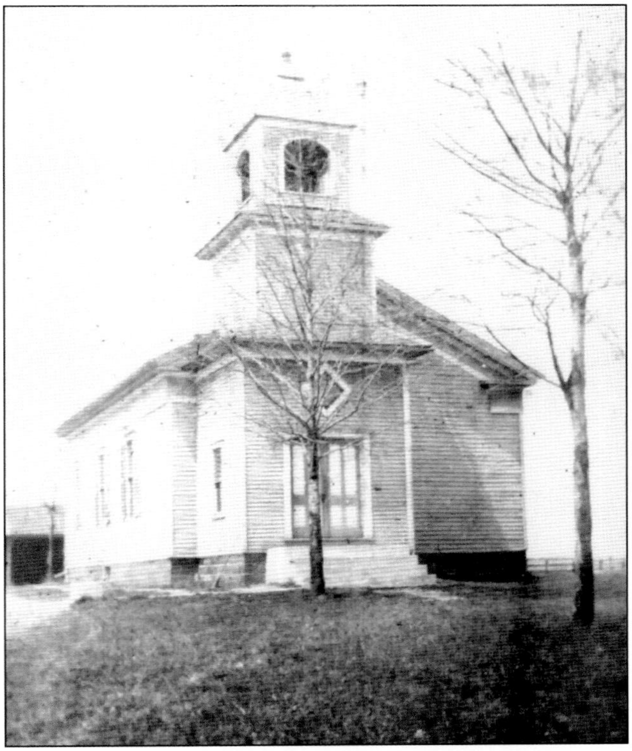

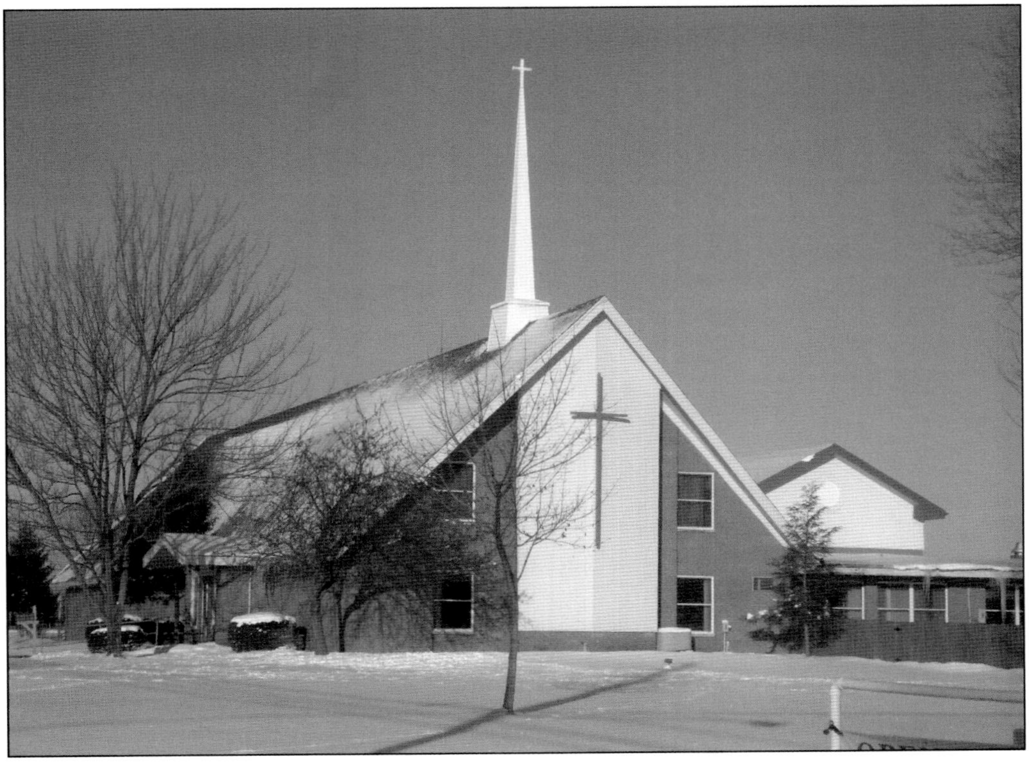

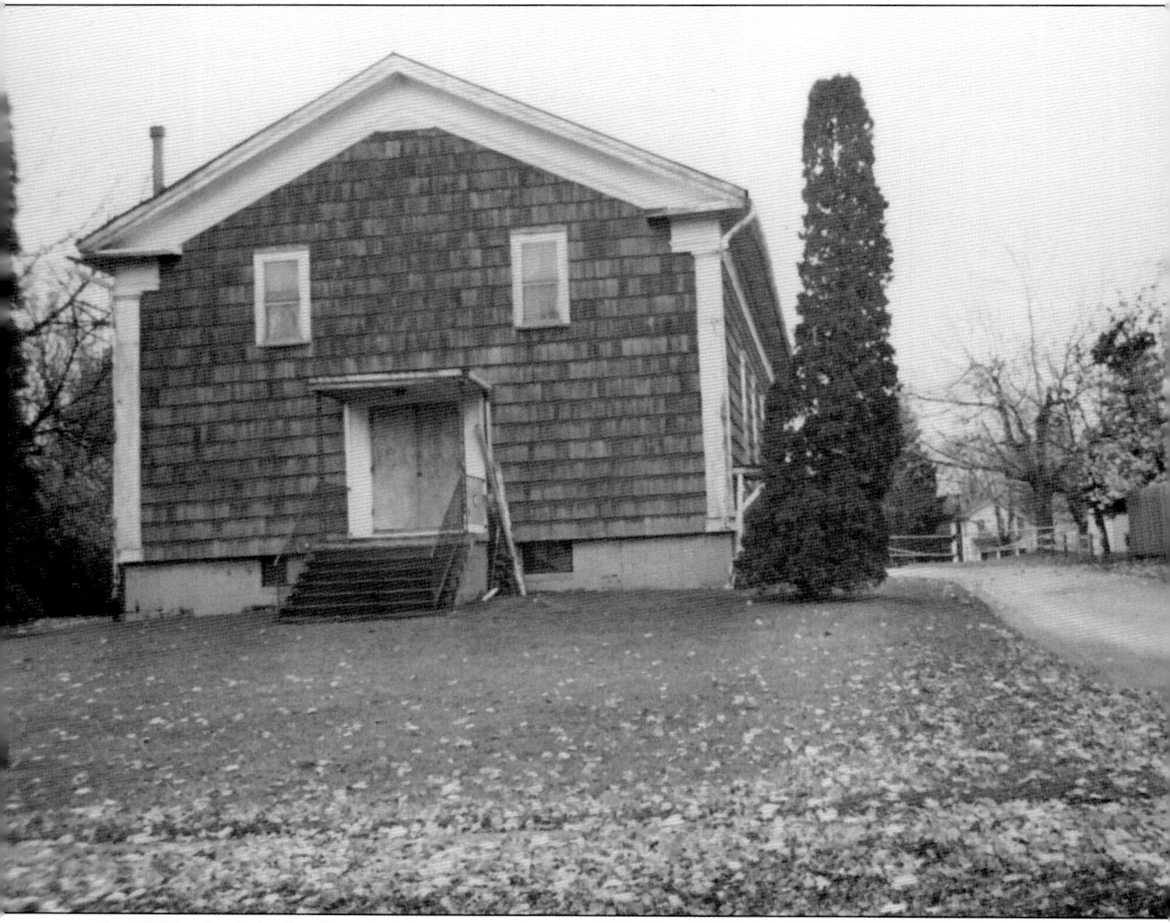

In 1835, the Methodists began to organize and built this church in 1841 on the south side of Walnut Run west of State Route 46. At that time, there was no road to the church from town, and inclement weather prevented worshippers from getting to services. In 1860, the building was put on skids and moved to the site of the present Methodist church on North High Street. In 1879, the building was purchased, moved, and turned to face Park Avenue, where it became Kline's Hall, better known as the Opera House. Later, it was sold and became the Grange Hall. Finally, it returned to the Methodists as a Sunday school annex for a few years. The Cortland Bazetta Historical Society purchased it in 1987, as it appears in this photograph, and restored it. (Courtesy of CBHS.)

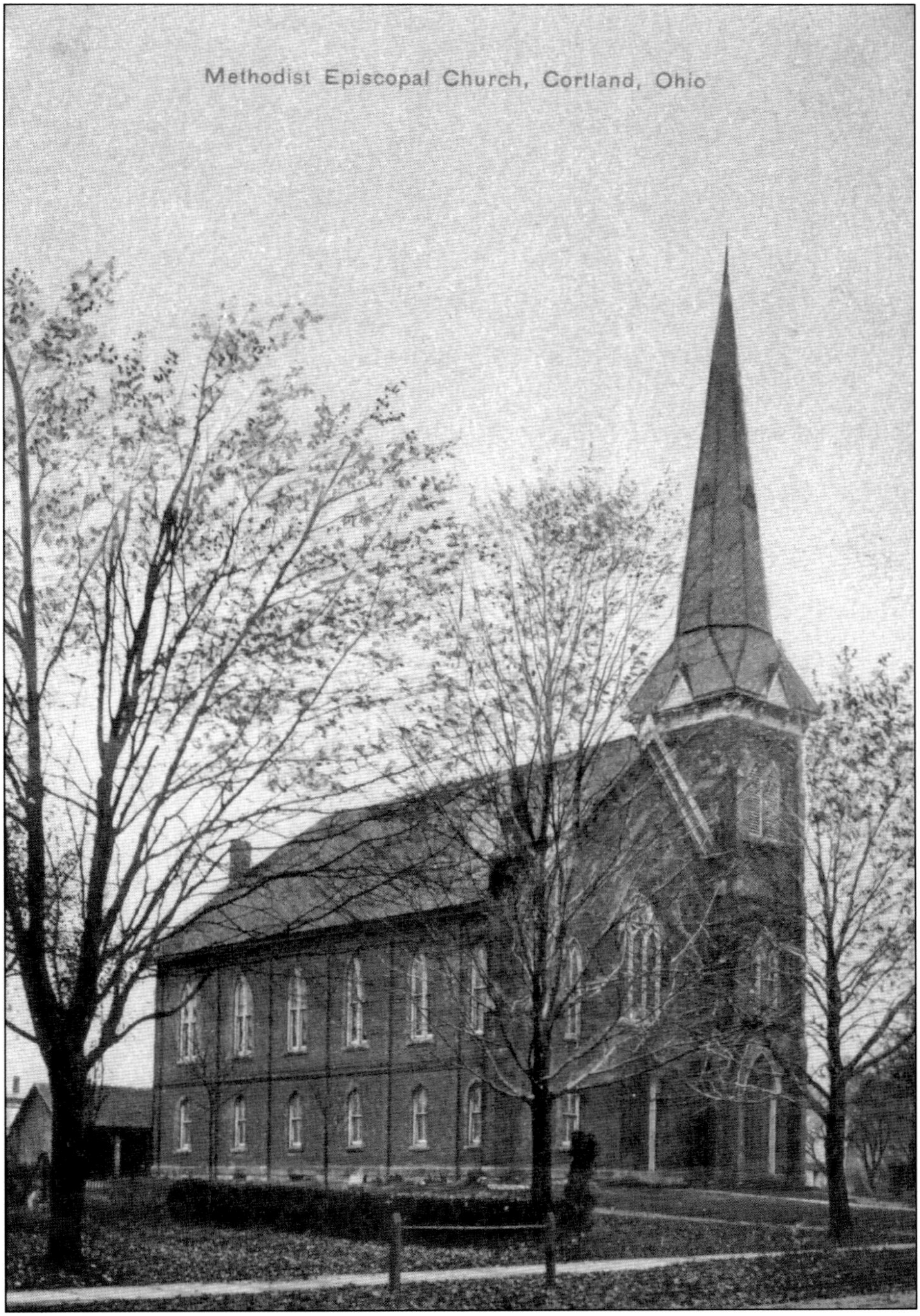

A 50-foot-by-70-foot brick building with a tall steeple replaced the old church at a cost of $10,000. Construction started in 1880, and the building was dedicated in 1881. In 1898, lightning struck the tall steeple and severely damaged the building, with pieces of the ceiling falling down in the sanctuary. Fortunately, no one was injured, even though it happened during evening services. The church was repaired and rededicated a few months later. The steeple was removed in 1927 because of deterioration. (Courtesy of CBHS.)

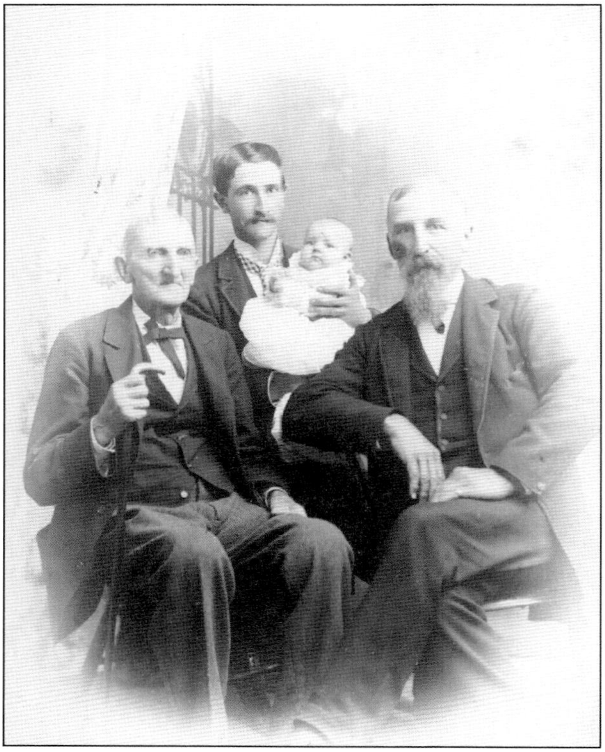

This rare photograph includes Solomon Kline (left). George E. Lynn (right) was married to Kline's adopted daughter, Mary J. Bole. The younger man is one of George's sons, only identified as "Betty's dad," while the infant is identified as one of his two daughters, Betty or Jenny Lynn. Solomon and George were two of the wealthiest men in town. Solomon died in 1884. (Courtesy of CBHS.)

A stained-glass window in the narthex of the Cortland United Methodist Church was placed there in appreciation of Solomon and Elizabeth Kline, who donated $5,600 of $10,000 for the construction of the church in 1879. Besides the donation, Kline purchased the old building, moved it, and remodeled it as a community building called Kline's Hall. (Courtesy of CBHS.)

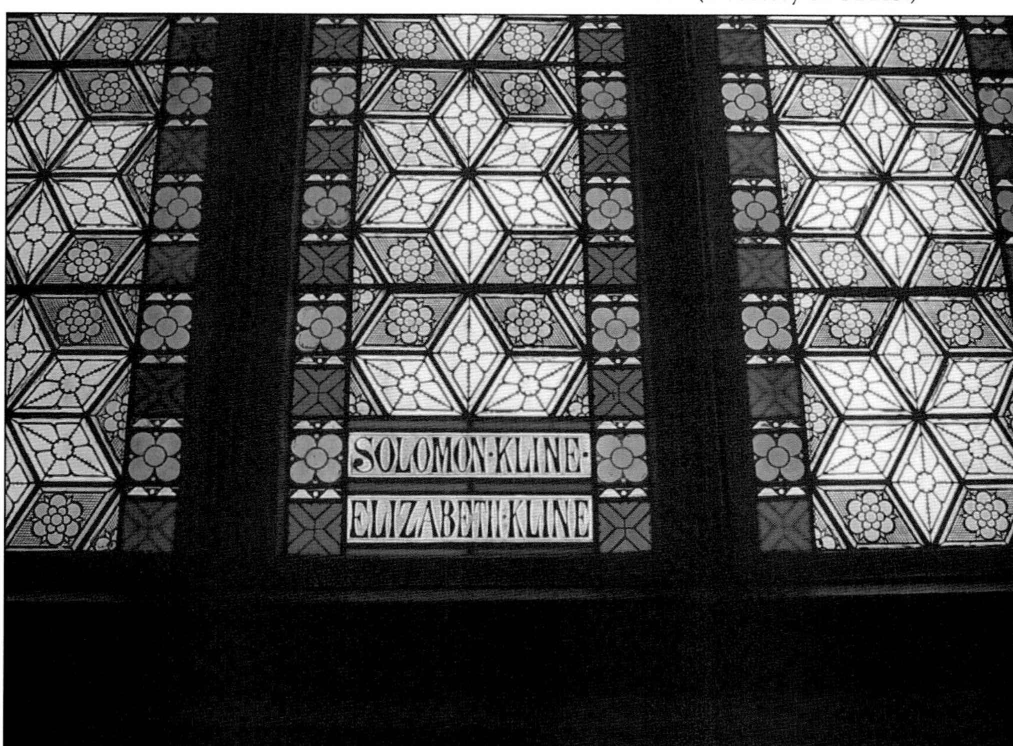

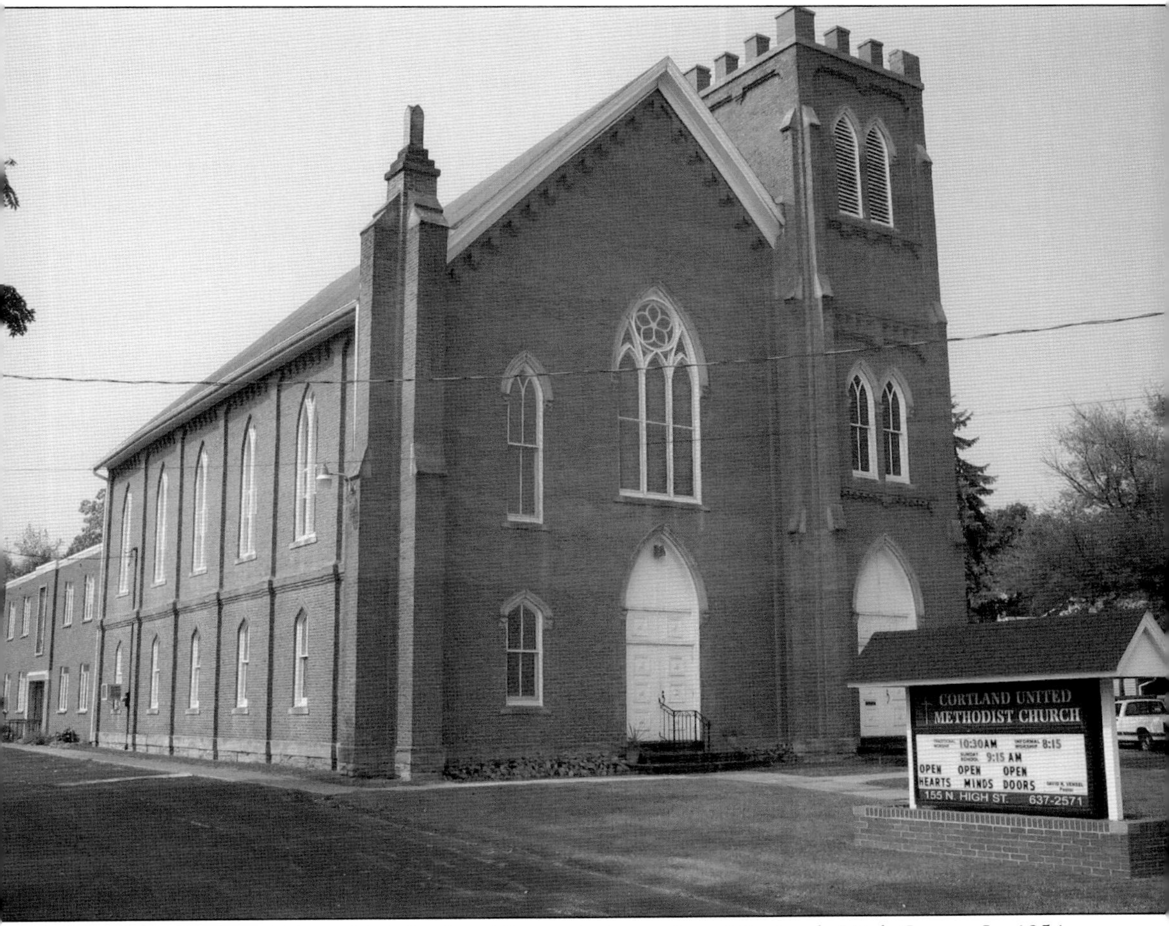

Today, the Cortland United Methodist Church is located at 155 North High Street. In 1954, additions made space for Sunday school classes and offices, and the interior was remodeled and updated. In 1910, funds raised by the church, and matched by philanthropist Andrew Carnegie, paid for the church's first pipe organ. The Christian church and the Methodist church are the two oldest buildings in town. At one time, there was a Congregational church and a United Brethren church. Now, in 2012, these two churches are among several of many denominations throughout the city and township. (Courtesy of William Hallett.)

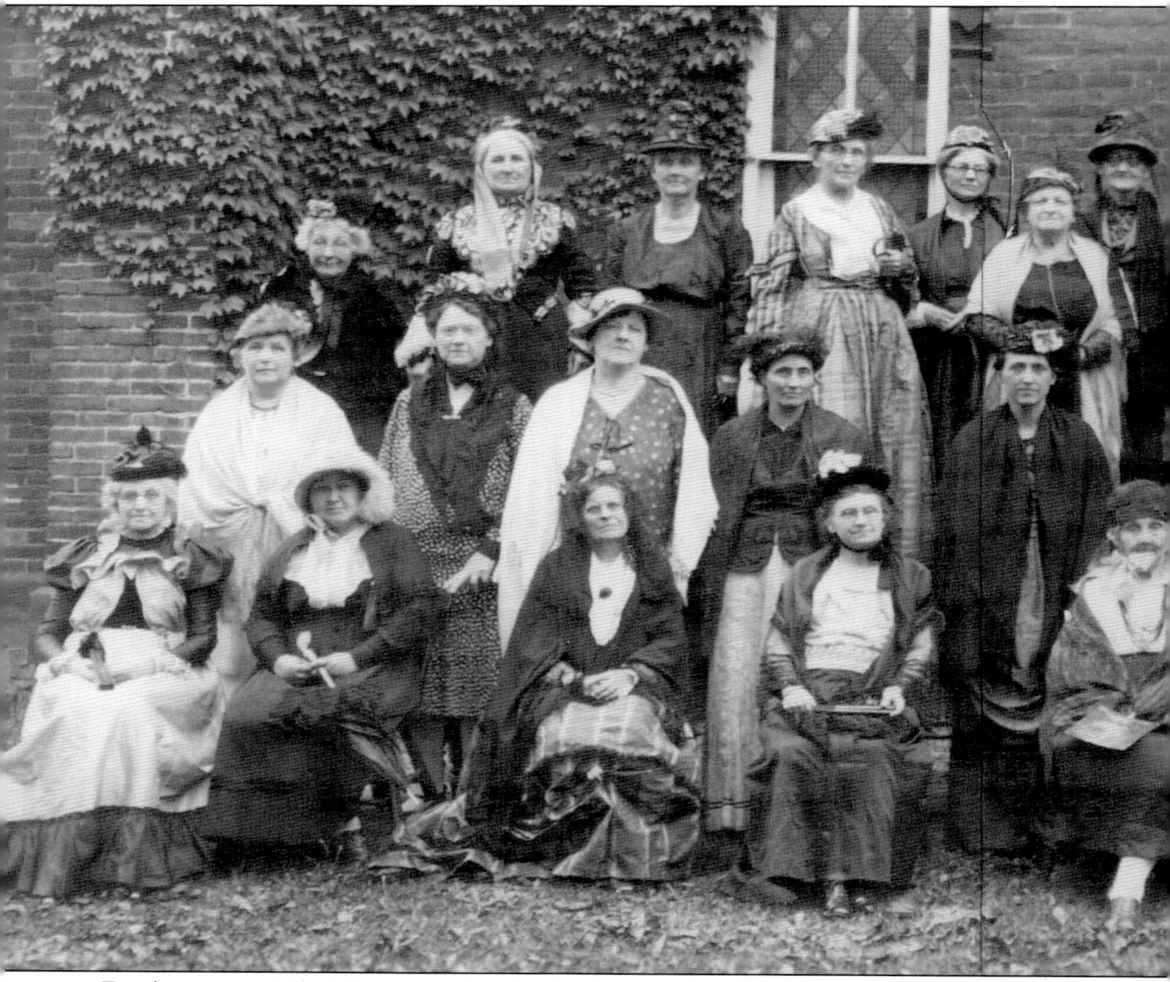

For the centennial celebration of the Cortland United Methodist Church, a meal was served in the old church, and ladies dressed up in 19th-century clothing. This c. 1935 photograph shows, from left to right, (first row) Clara McKean, Madge McKelvey, Minnie Trumbull, Mary Sigler, ? Jones, Minnie Knight, Albertine Freer, Mary Bowers, Addie Paden, and Jennie Love; (second row) Blanche Viets, May Richards, Alice Sigler, Bessie Ruiter, Grace Churchill, Lizze Johnson, Rena

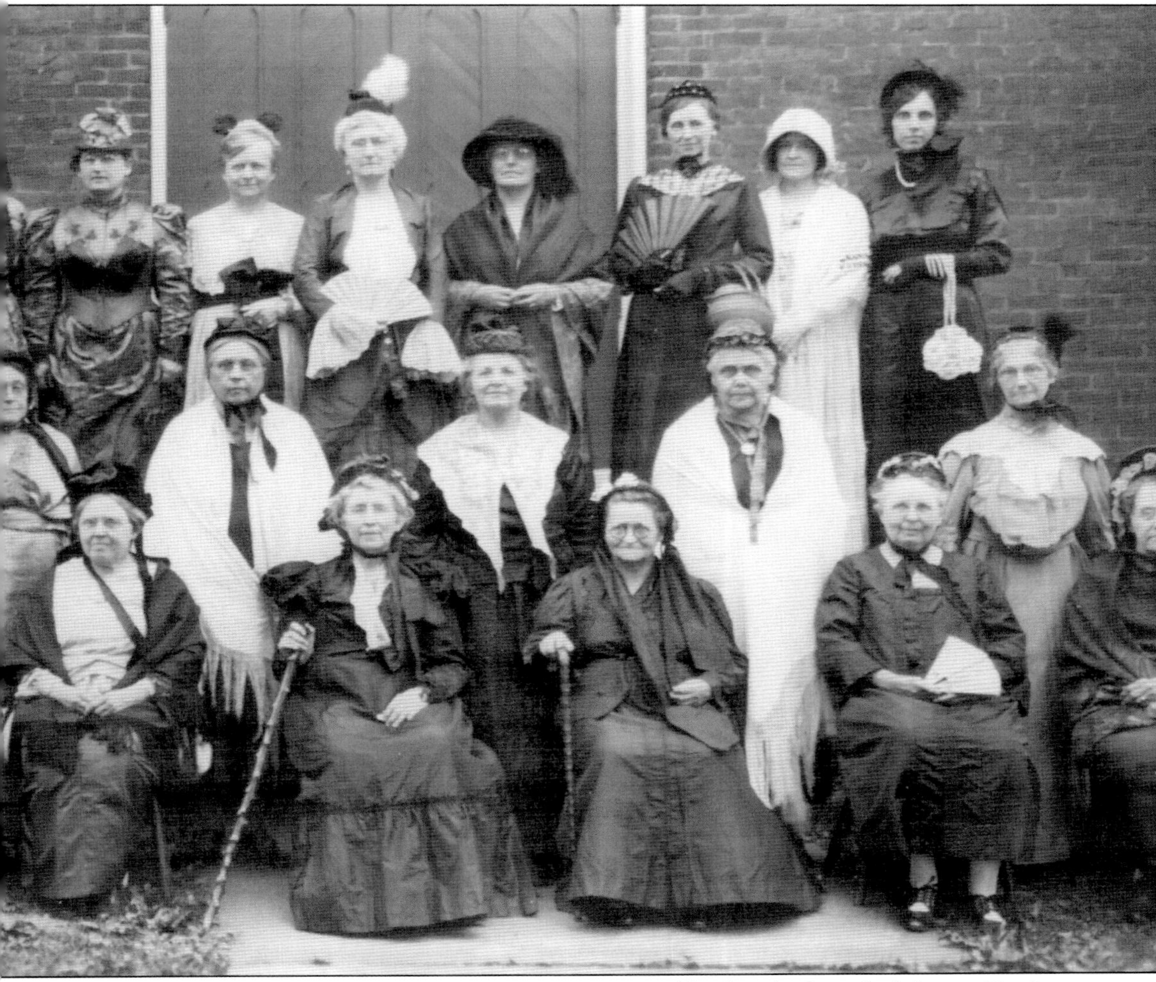

Fitch, Mildred Mahan, Ida Lemmerou, and Inez Gretzinger; (third row) ? Staniford, Jennie Hayden, May Churchill, Rinna Casterline, Alta Ainsley, Jessie Adams, Ella Rice (in front of Jessie), Lydia McClellan, Ruth Weir, Zelma McLaughlin, Margaret Miller, Gertrude Nesbitt, Mildred Sipps, Gertrude Richards, and Clara Love. (Courtesy of Cortland United Methodist Church.)

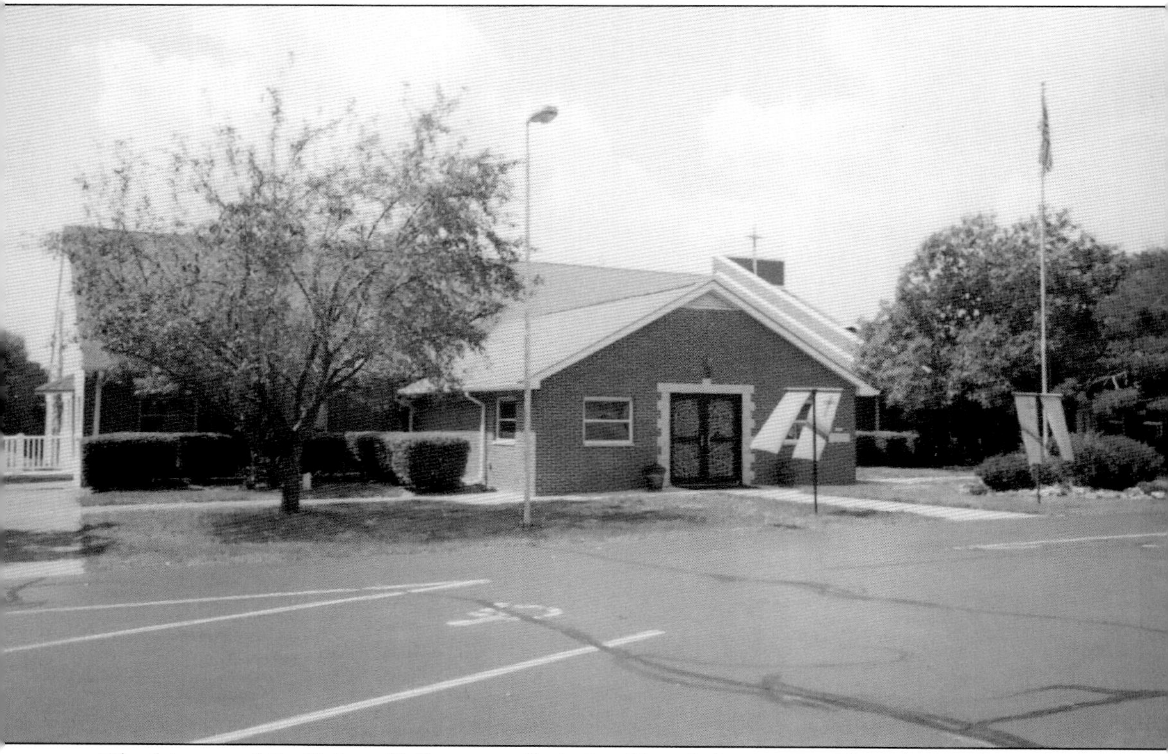

The history of St. Robert Bellarmine Catholic Church began in 1952, when Isabel Williams organized a meeting of area Catholics to discuss having Sunday Masses in Cortland. The first Mass was held at the Cortland Theater (now Sparkle Market) in 1952. Early in 1954, a 30-acre tract of land was obtained about a half mile north of the Cortland village limits. The property, which extends from State Route 46 to Mosquito Lake, includes a 500-foot frontage on the lake shoreline. Ground was broken for the church on March 13 of that year. Thirty members volunteered to do the construction, and donations of materials and funds came from Catholic churches from Cleveland, Warren, Boardman, Mantua, Youngstown, and other cities. (Courtesy of Carol Hunter Harrison.)

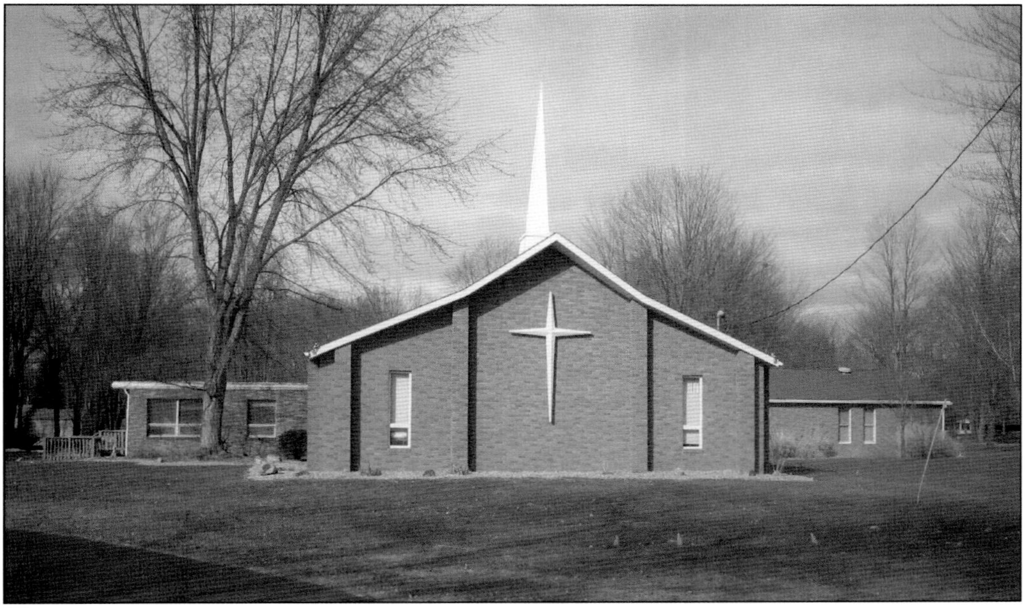

Cortland Church of the Nazarene was founded in 1963. Like many churches, members first met in other buildings: barns, stores, homes, the Opera House, and even theaters. This congregation met in a storefront on Mecca Street. By the next year, they had purchased land on East Main Street from the Viets sisters, Vivian Vera and Wilhemien, and had broken ground for the church. The congregation grew, and by 1978 an addition was needed. Shown below are those celebrating the ground-breaking ceremony for the addition. From left to right are Rev. Ronald Panos, the pastor; George Frost, representative of the church's building committee; Gene Frye of Cogan Industries of Boardman, the builder; and William Roush, the mayor of Cortland. (Above, author's collection; below, courtesy of the Cortland Church of the Nazarene.)

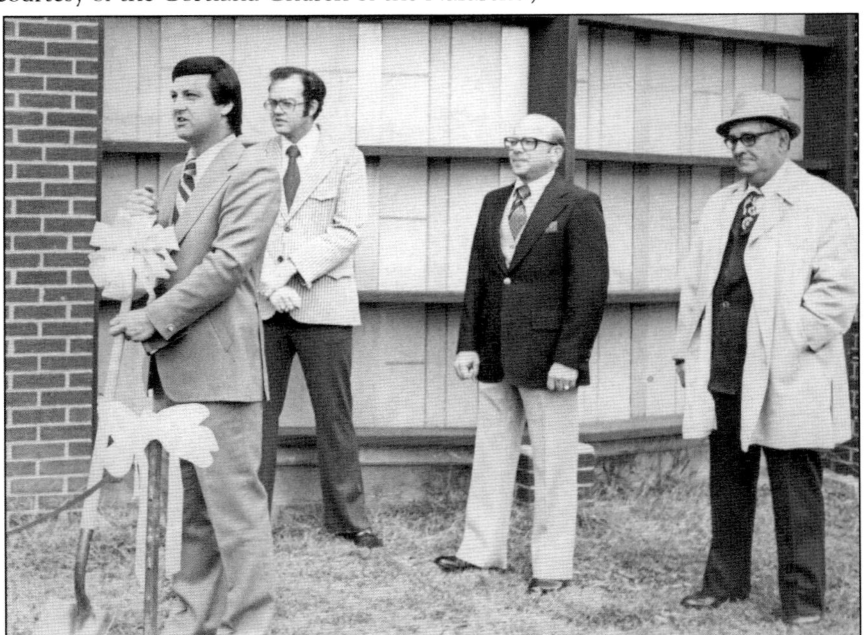

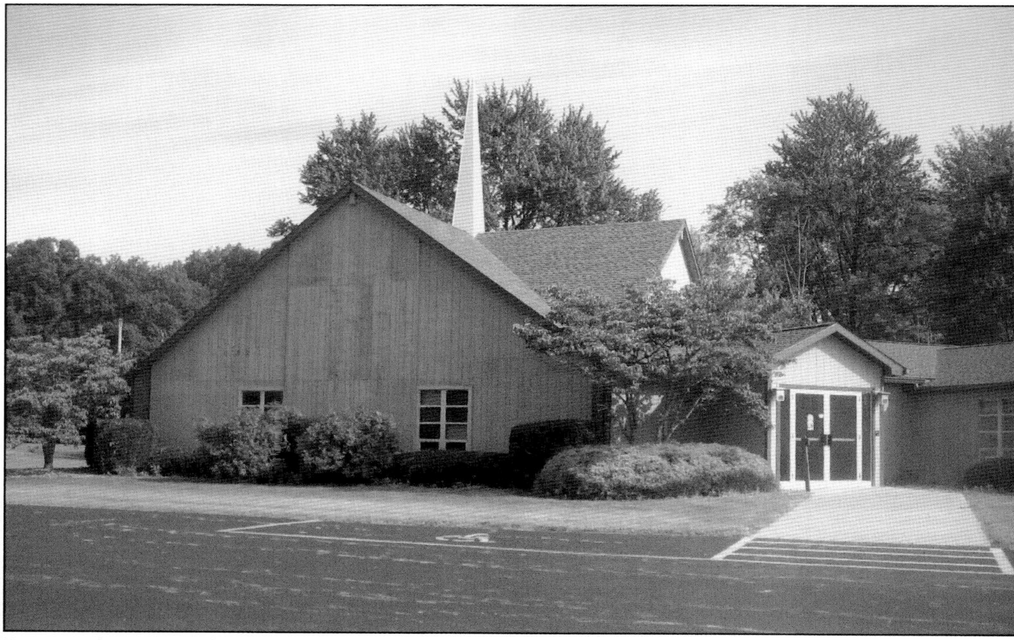

Prince of Peace Lutheran Church started as a mission under the American Lutheran Church in September 1974. Its first worship service was held at Bazetta Township Hall, with 100 people in attendance. By November 1975, the church was built on land near the northeastern boundary of Bazetta Township. William Yesse became the church's first pastor. Since then, the church has undergone two expansions, in 1983 and 1999, adding southeast and northwest wings, a kitchen, nursery, handicap-accessible restrooms, and a larger fellowship hall among other remodeling. Duane Jesse was the church's fourth pastor from 1997 to 2012. A contemporary worship service at 11:00 a.m. was added in 2001, moving the traditional service to 8:30 a.m., with Sunday school in between services. (Author's collection.)

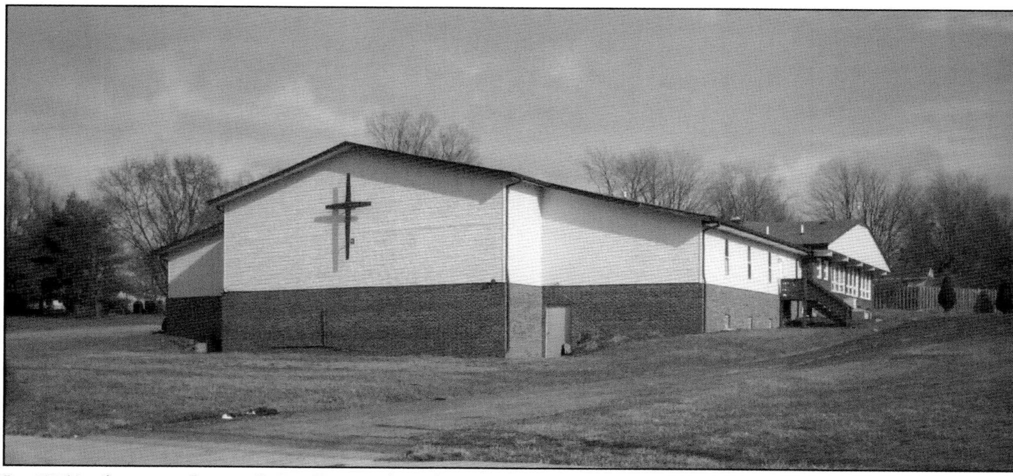

In 1951, the members of the First Church of God met at Grange Hall. In 1955, they purchased four lots on the corner of Hillman Drive and South High Street and broke ground in 1958 for the church that is there today. A parsonage on Hillman Drive was built in the mid-1970s. As members of Lakeview Outreach and Fellowship, they housed the Cortland Area Cares Food Pantry until a larger space was found on Pearl Street. (Author's collection.)

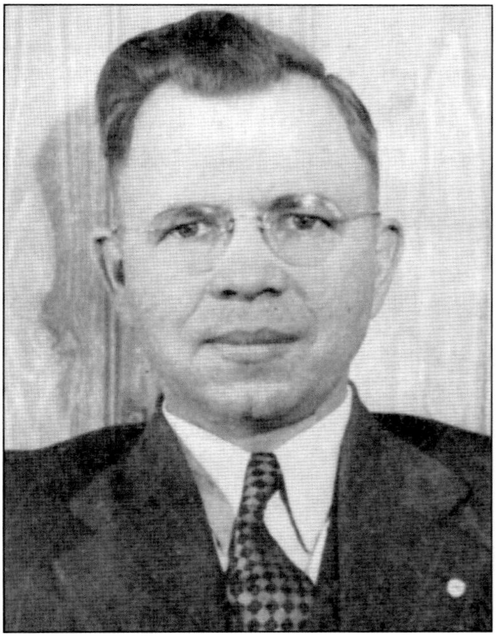

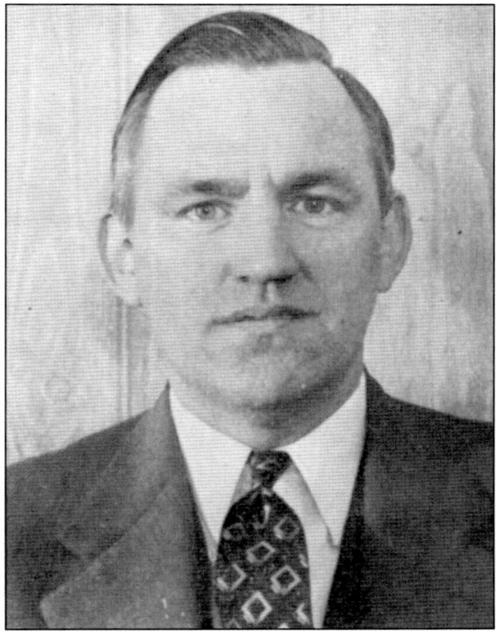

In 1946, when Rev. George VanWingerdon (wearing glasses) of the Cortland Christian Church and Rev. Leonard R. Dittman of the Methodist church joined Walter Richards of Richards Mill and Walter Scott, secretary-treasurer of Cortland Bank, a friendly golf game turned into an extraordinary community ecumenical association, which became known the Lakeview Outreach and Fellowship (LOAF). Now over 65 years old, this organization unites separate groups and churches. There are pulpit exchanges, choir festivals, a joint Vacation Bible School, joint church services on Good Friday, Easter at sunrise at Mosquito Lake, and Thanksgiving Eve. It operates the Cortland Area Cares Food Pantry, sponsors a CROP Walk, and organizes many other activities that benefit the town. The postcard from the 1950s shows four of what are now several churches involved in LOAF. (Above, courtesy of Cortland United Methodist Church; below, Don Jones.)

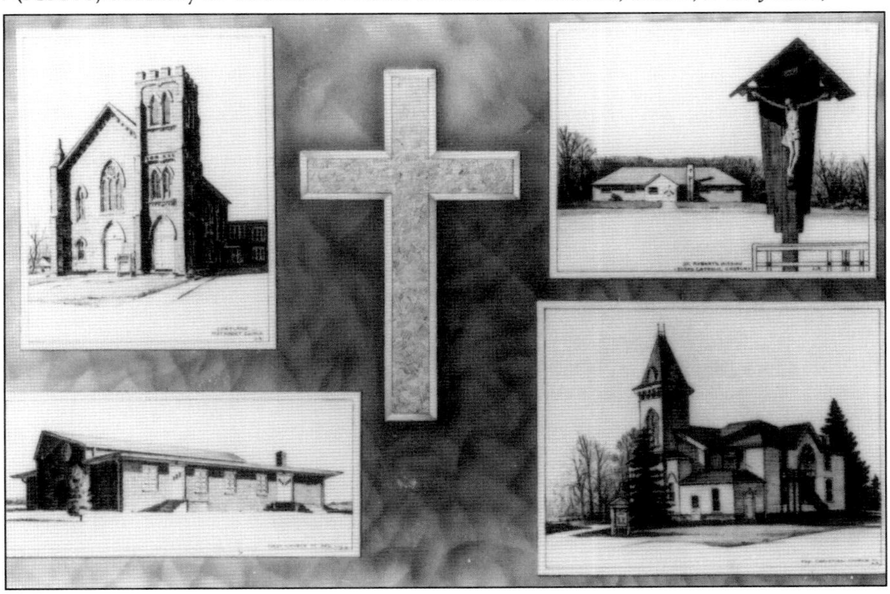

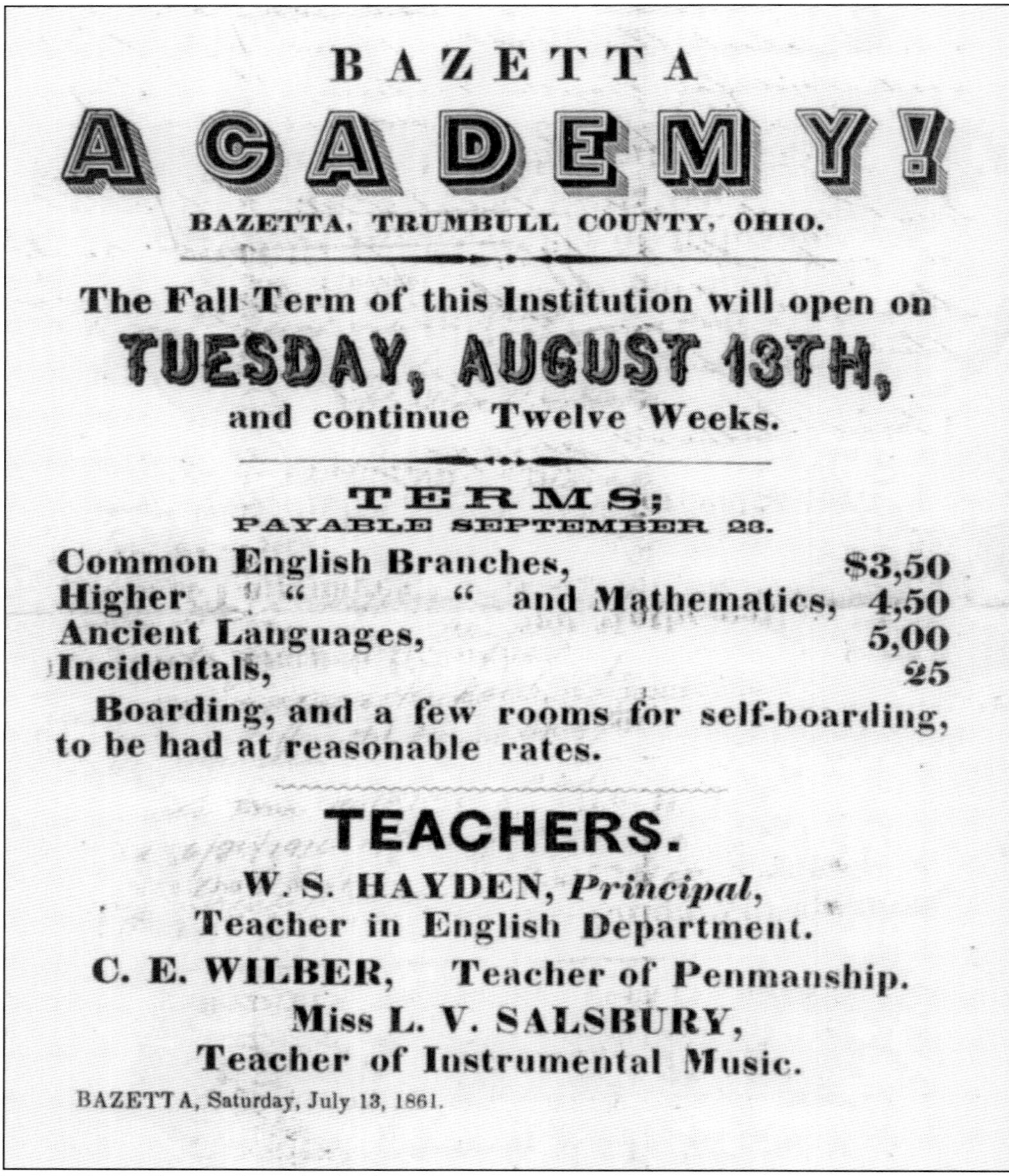

BAZETTA

ACADEMY!

BAZETTA, TRUMBULL COUNTY, OHIO.

The Fall Term of this Institution will open on

TUESDAY, AUGUST 13TH,

and continue Twelve Weeks.

TERMS;

PAYABLE SEPTEMBER 28.

Common English Branches,	$3,50
Higher " " and Mathematics,	4,50
Ancient Languages,	5,00
Incidentals,	25

Boarding, and a few rooms for self-boarding, to be had at reasonable rates.

TEACHERS.

W. S. HAYDEN, *Principal*,
Teacher in English Department.

C. E. WILBER, Teacher of Penmanship.

Miss L. V. SALSBURY,
Teacher of Instrumental Music.

BAZETTA, Saturday, July 13, 1861.

Before the high school was built, there was Bazetta Academy, located at the end of Mill Street before it was extended and renamed Grove Drive. Tuition was charged, and rooms for boarding were available for non-residents. After Cortland Union School was constructed, this building was relocated and used for overflow classes. It was eventually moved to the southeast corner of Pearl and Mecca Streets. (Courtesy of the Gessner family.)

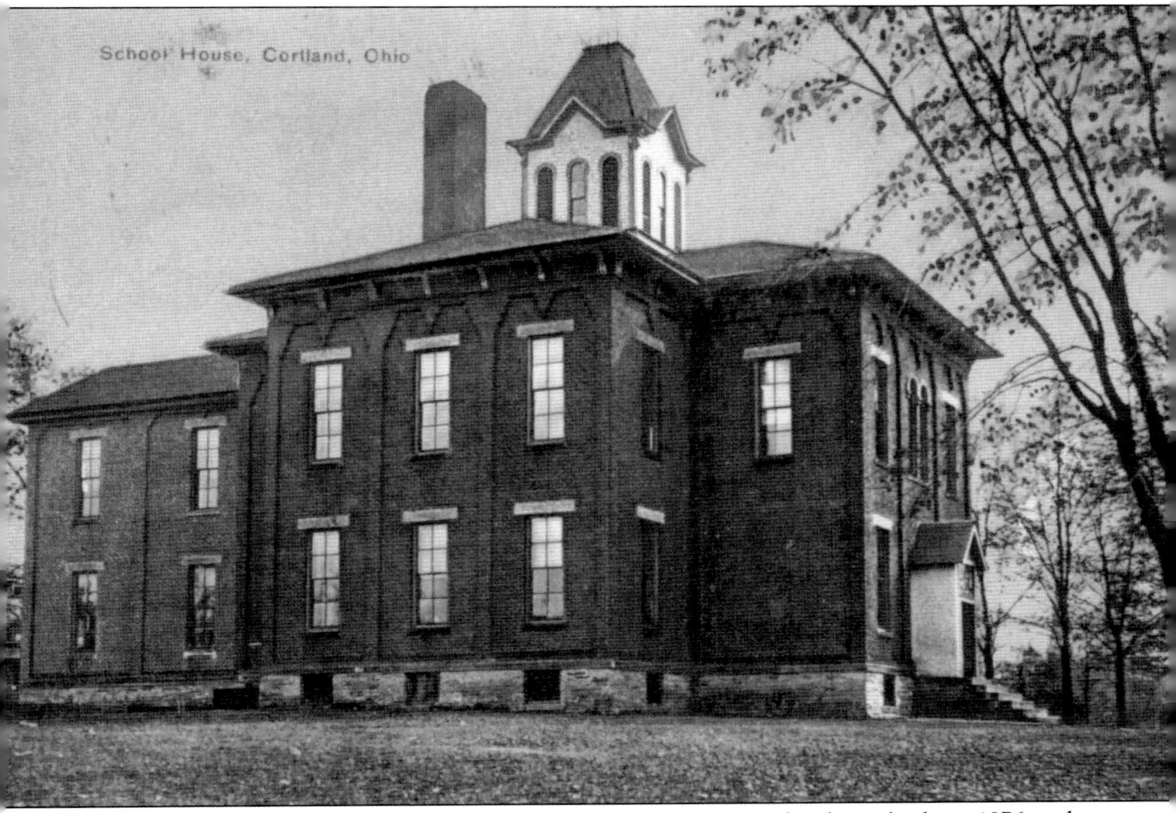

Created by a special act of the state legislature, Cortland Union School was built in 1876 and opened for the 1877 school year. At the time, it had five rooms, but a short time later a wing was added to the first floor. On the first floor, the first and second grades were in one room, the third and fourth grades were in another room, and the fifth and sixth grades were in the wing in the back. On the second floor, the seventh and eighth grades were in the back room, and the high school students used the two front rooms. The Opera House was used for school functions. (Courtesy of CBHS.)

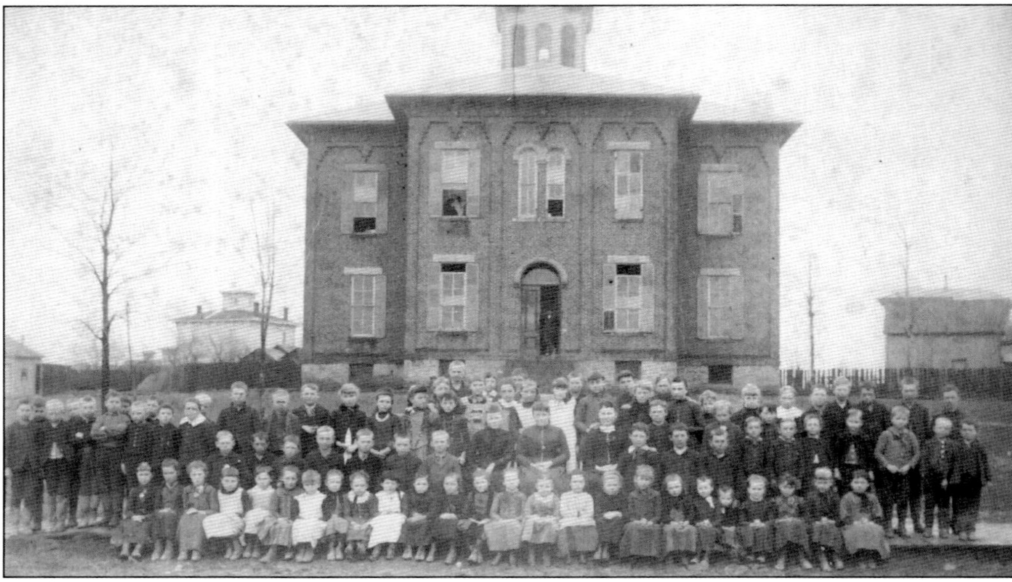

This photograph may depict elementary students at Bazetta Academy, probably in the 1880s. Note that the door does not have a roof and the trees are young. There are about 80 students and teachers in this photograph. Research indicates that between 125 and 165 students attended the school each of the years before 1900. (Courtesy of CBHS.)

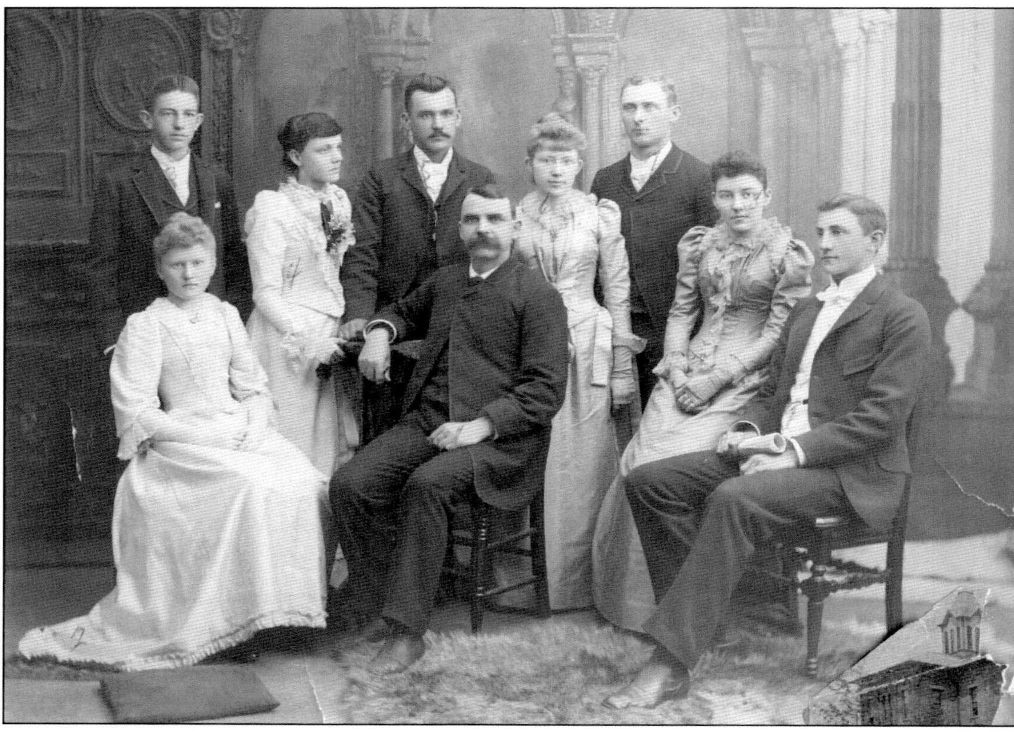

Students of the class of 1892 are, from left to right, (seated) Carson Larnard, Professor Reed, Fred M. Lynn; (standing) Arlie Kennedy, Bertha Fansler, VanBuren D. Viets, Myra Burrows, Frank Nichols, and Alene Hadsell. (Courtesy of CBHS.)

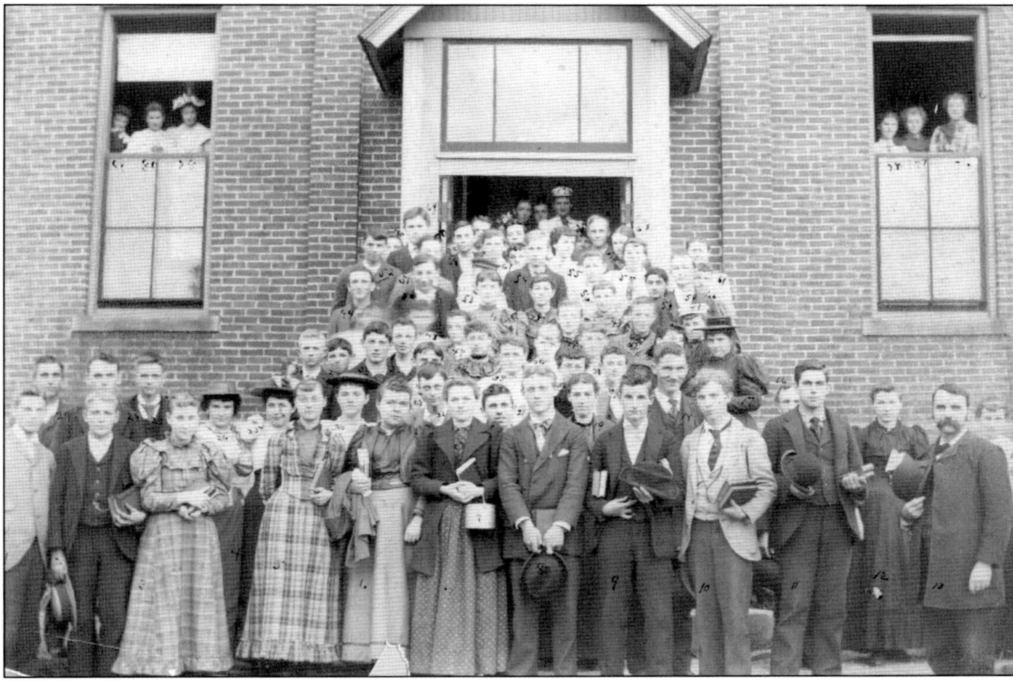

Along with their teachers, about 80 students appear in this 1895 photograph, most likely grades 7 through 12. Sources indicate there was a total of 165 students that year. There were 12 graduates in the class of 1895: Ida Bushnell, Norma Dutcher, Ethel Halsted, Mary Hutchins, James DeNean, Archie Diehl, E. Clyde Hardy, Will H. Meek, B. Frank Parsons, Carlon Rogers, Walter D. Trumbull, and Eason Lattin. (Courtesy of CBHS.)

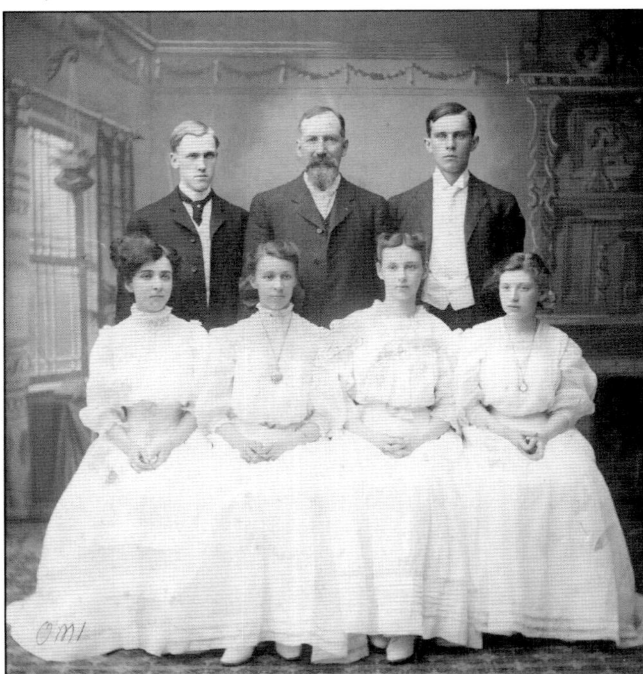

The class of 1906 consisted of two young men and four young women. From left to right are (first row) Fidelia Hart, Cinderella Mott, Edna McCorkle, and Edith Wildman; (second row) O. Mark Richards, Prof. L.W. Mauck, and Mark Dray. Both Richards and Dray belonged to a men's singing quartet as young men, along with the Marvin brothers, Henry Lee and Ezra. Wildman became a well-known artist. (Courtesy of Walter Richards.)

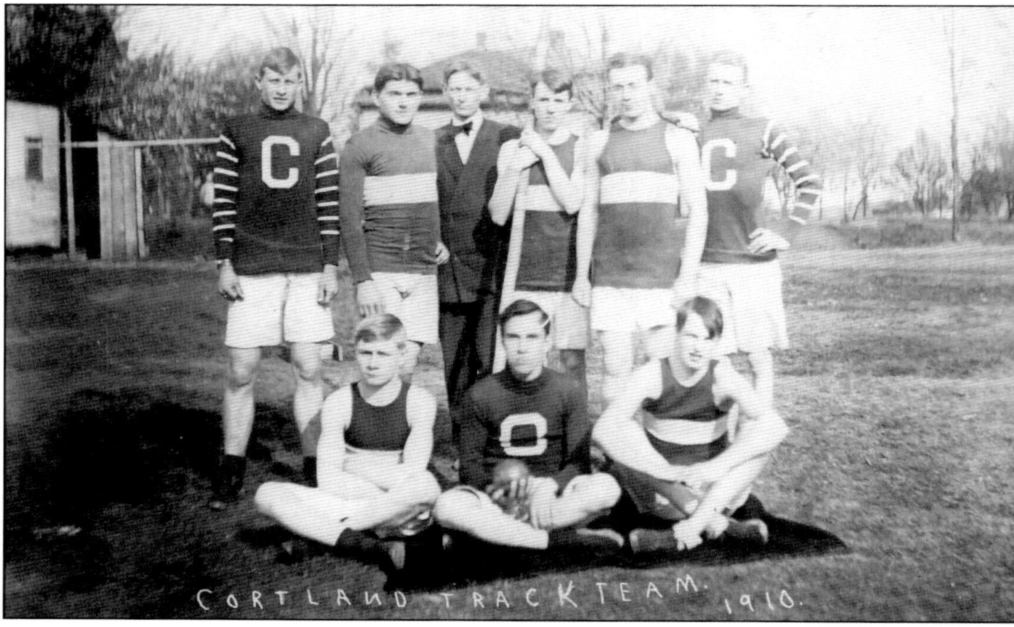

The Cortland High School football team is pictured above in 1913. The players on the 1919 team are seen in the photograph below. From left to right are (first row) Carleton McCurley, George Kyle, and Ivan Frye; (second row) Honus McCormick, Robert McLaughlin, Asa Spencer, and Kenneth Mahan; (third row) Stanley Brown, Parmly Hall, Herbert Hadley, Arthur Bascom (superintendent), Archer Dilley, George Pritchard, and Austin Sigler. (Both, courtesy of CBHS.)

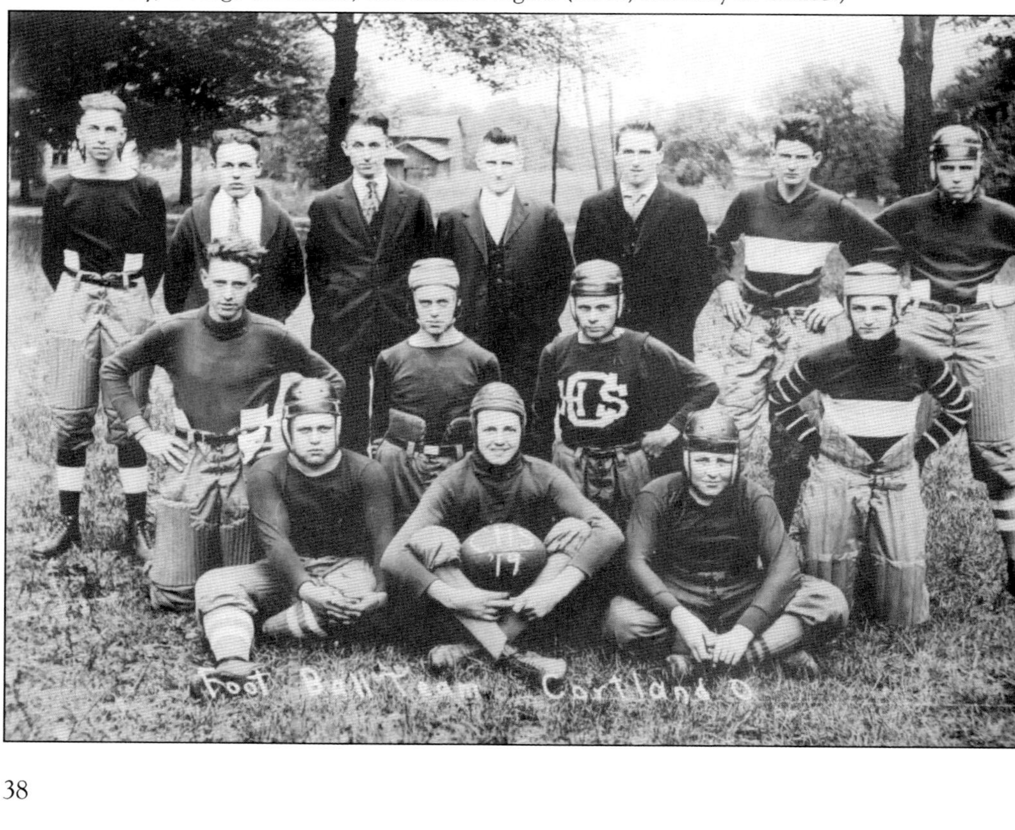

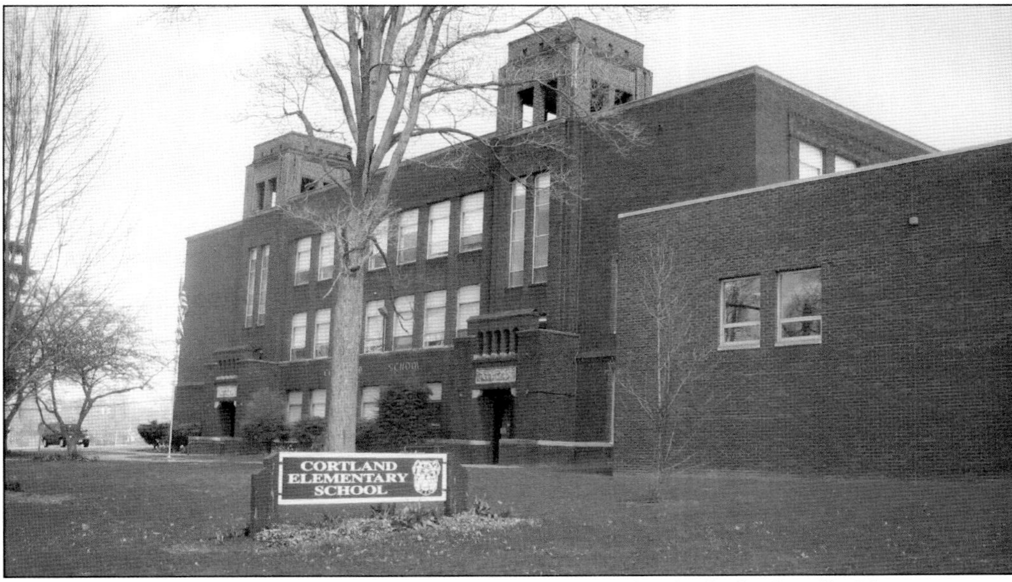

In 1923, a new Cortland School was built "around" the 1876 school. The back wall of the gymnasium and a narrow hallway on the first floor were part of the original school. Until 1961, this building contained all 12 grades before it became one of two elementary buildings until it closed in 2009. Additions in 1939 included a stage, and in 1954 additions on the north and south ends of the building included a cafeteria (that became the library), kindergarten rooms, and a music room. Final additions were made in 1995. (Courtesy of CBHS.)

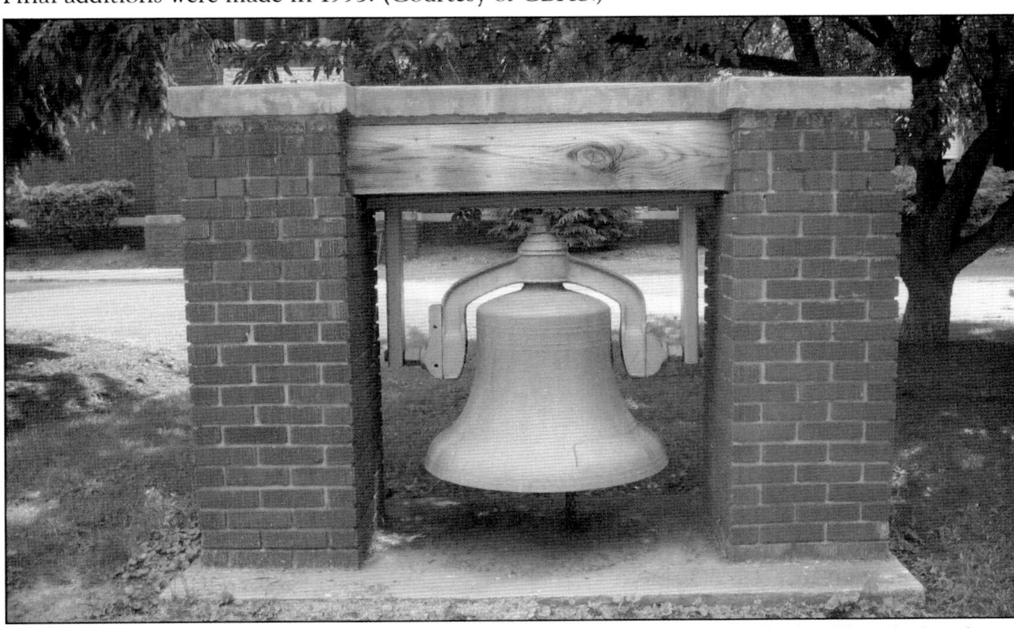

The bell from the old school was hung in a belfry in the north end of the building before being removed in the 1940s when the timber around it deteriorated. In 1971, after students brought in pennies to place the bell on display, it was mounted on timber from Richards Mill and supported by brick columns. It was rung on the first day of school to celebrate 200 years of the US constitution in 1987 and again when the building closed. (Courtesy of CBHS.)

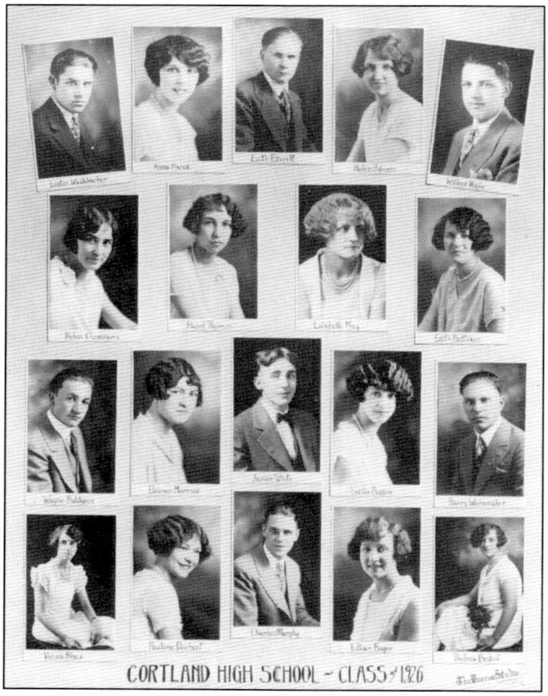

This was one of the first classes to graduate from the Cortland School, which opened for the 1924 school year. Students from the class of 1926 pictured here are, from left to right, (top row) Lester Weckbacher, Anne Marek, Leith Everitt, Helen Adams, and Wilbur Kyle; (second row) Helen Clemens, Hazel Thumm, Lolabelle May, and Edith Bettiker; (third row) Wayne Baldwin, Eleanor Morrow, James White, Luella Biggin, and Harry Wanamaker; (fourth row) Vivian Blair, Pauline Dechert, Charles Murphy, Lillian Boger, and Thelma Brobsl. (Courtesy of CBHS.)

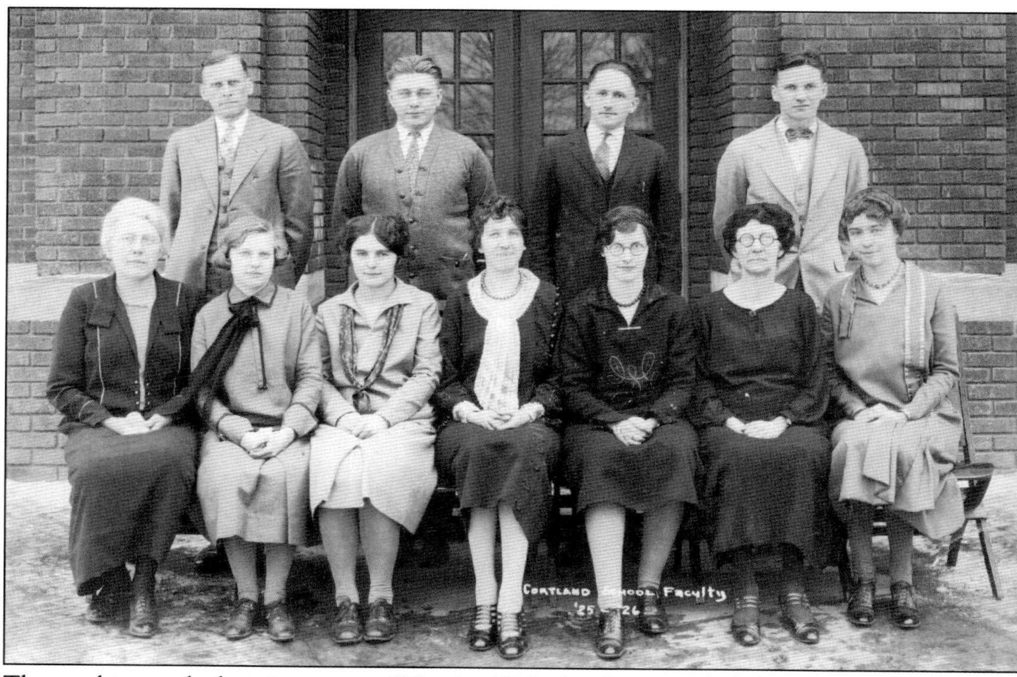

The teaching and administrative staff for the 1925 school year included (first row) Christa Craft (seventh and eighth grades), Edith Rogers (fifth grade), Agnes Carey (fourth grade), Vera Viets, (first grade), Wilhemien Viets (third grade), Mrs. Caldwell (second grade), and Elizabeth Galvin (English); (second row) Stanley Hall (superintendent), Mr. Jerome (sixth grade), Mr. Wagner (principal), and Mr. Slater (music). (Courtesy of CBHS.)

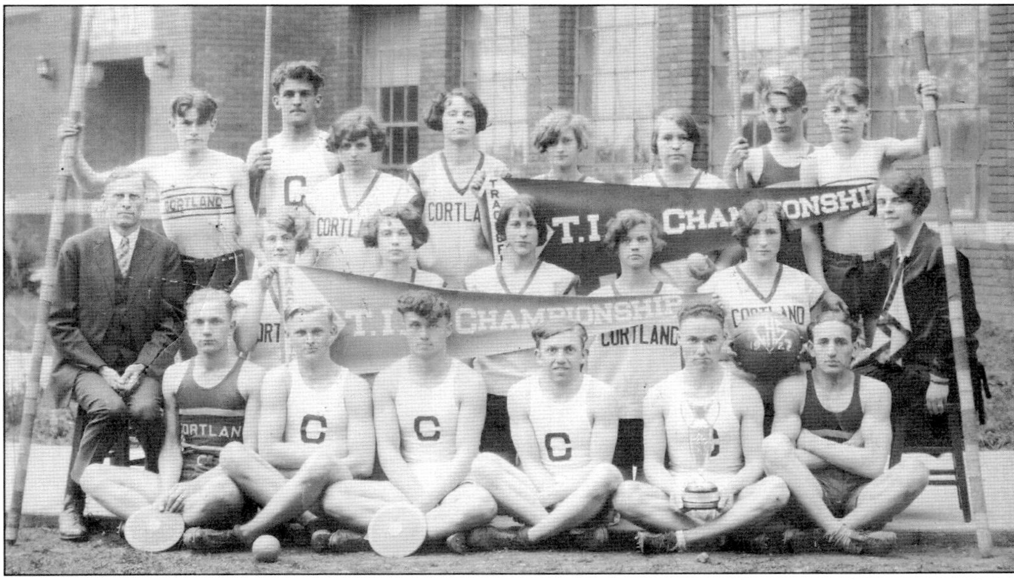

In 1927, both the boy's track and girls' basketball teams were Trumbull County champions. From left to right are (first row) Paul Retterer, Lloyd Parsons, Blaine Yose, Dick Knight, Paul Yose, and Franklin Vorhees; (second row) track coach Stanley Hall (nicknamed "Prof"), Hilda Brobst, Ethyl Yose, Hazel Gauchi, Zola Brobst, Peg Shaffer, and basketball coach Agnes Carey; (third row) Earl Foltz, Bart Cook, Caroline "Red" Canfield, Mariam Simpson, Lucille Rice, Peg Tate, Bill Faulkner, and Don Meek. (Courtesy of CBHS.)

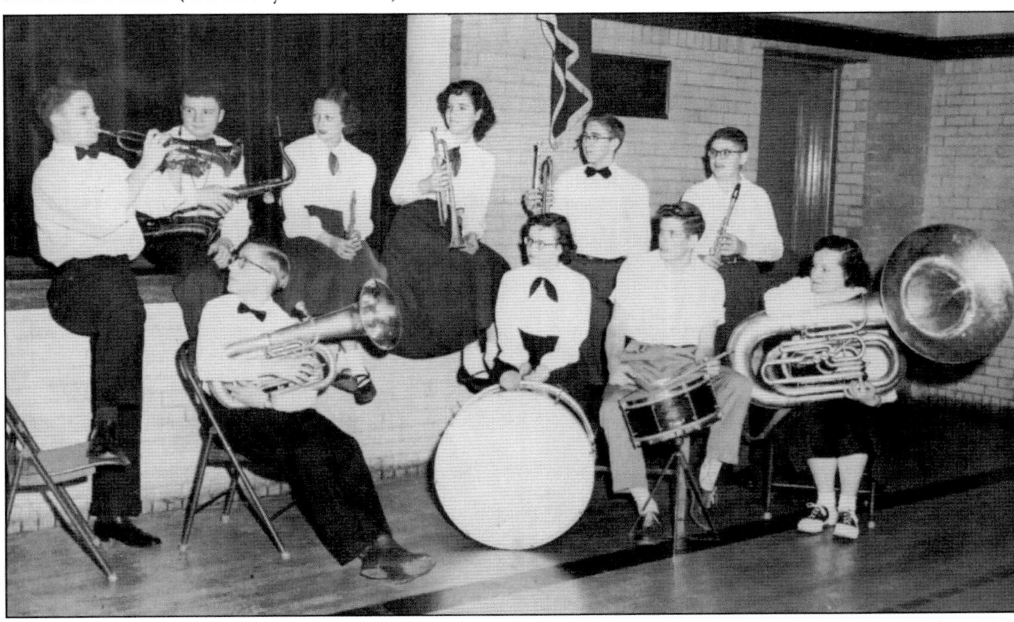

Over the years, many students played in the bands that helped cheer on their teams. This 1953 band performed at home basketball games and assemblies. From left to right are (sitting) Johnny Shilling, Janice Dietz, Carl Wollam, Janice Hargate; (standing) Ronnie Retterer, Harry Croft, Janice Whipkey, Marsha Marsh, Jack Swenehart, and Rodger Foltz. Favorite songs to be played were "Jayhawk" and "Whispering." (Courtesy of CBHS.)

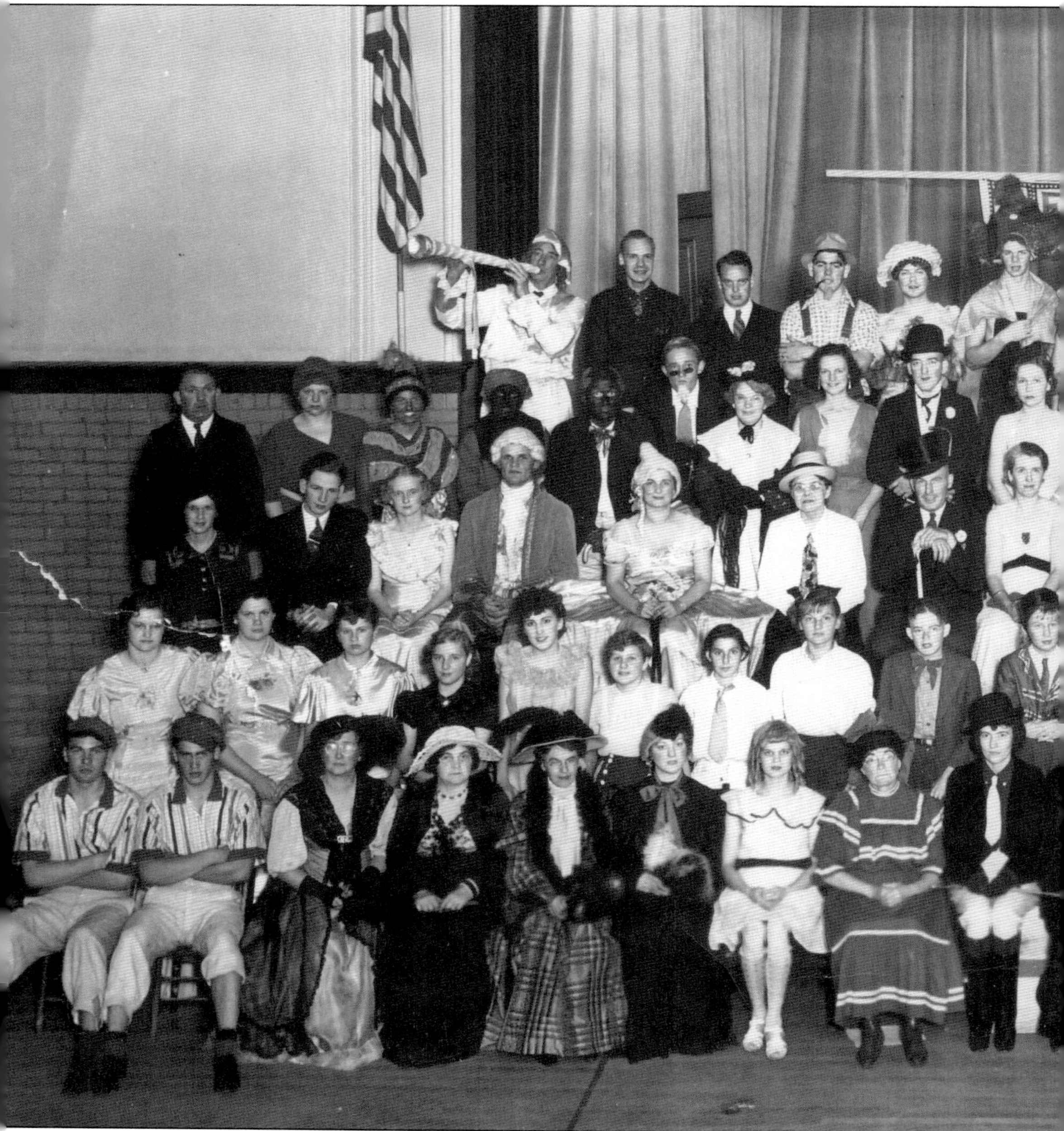

In the 1937 school year, a community play was held in the auditorium of Cortland High School, with many citizens as well as students participating. From left to right are (first row) Wilbur May, Charles Snow, Helen Snow, Mabel Irwin, Adah Hudson, Miss Thelma Brobst, Zeola Retterer, Jessie Morrow, Miss Norton, Gordon Irwin (bear), Mildred Granger, Miss Swink, Louise Biggin, Harold Brobst, Miss Roberts, Wilma Monroe, Kathleen Thumm, Jesse Stevenson, Robert Dilworth, and Ruthe Wollam; (second row) Evelyn Ensign, Louise Payne, Lilla Downs, Beulah Dechert, Jean Davis, Nadine Collins, Margaret Pistolozzi, Dorothy Sala, Billy Gail, Geraldine Goff, Jane Wake, Pauline Miller, Virginia Button, Doris Jones, Lucille Downs, Amelia Smelko, Mary McNaughton, Theresa Sanford, Wilma Baker, Wanda Outland, and Betty Marsh; (third row) Mrs. Knight, Jack

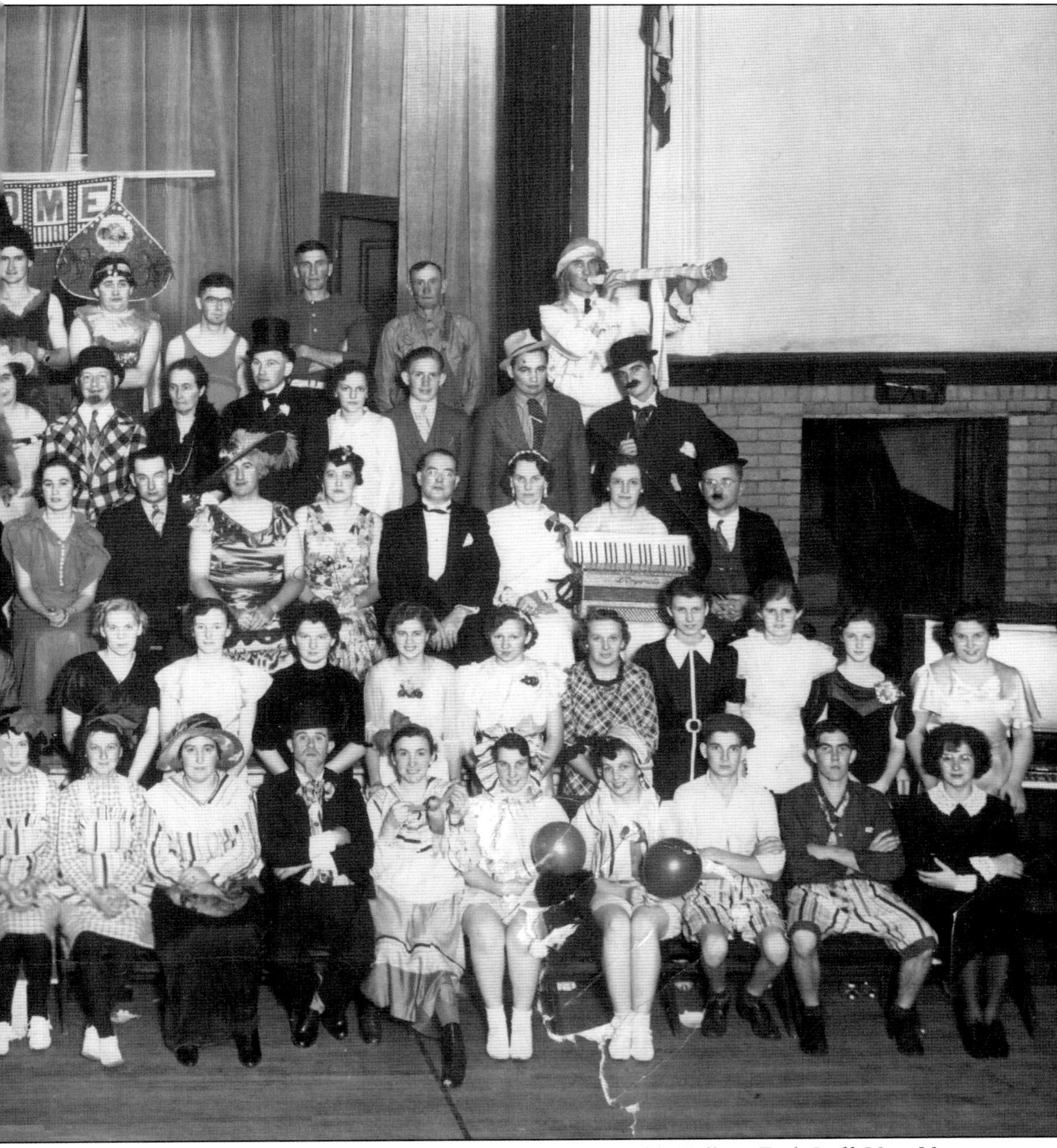

Monroe, Florence McLaughlin, Joe Tresey, Miss Steiner, Hilda Zellers, Earl Goff, Vera Viets, Fred R. Carlile, Lois Tate, Delbert Biggin, Superintendent Pugh, Mrs. Cover, George Kyle, Clara Love, Wilhemein Viets, and Rev. George Van Wingerdon; (fourth row) Richard Knight, Mildred Carroll, Carol Bowers, Mrs. Frank Meek, Frank Bowers, Johnathan Ruiter, Clara Kays, Miss Howe, Edward Van Auken, Mildred Shilling, Ward J. Viets, Jessie Dilworth, Lee Wollam, Bessie Ruiter, Rev. McCutcheon, Betty Hall, Delmar Townsend, Joe Smelko, and Charles Collins; (fifth row) Burt Ruiter, the director (name unknown), Robert McLaughlin, Douglas Wollam, Lewellyn Wollam, Paul Hebner, Jim Brobst, Frank Wall, Mr. Kirk, Sherman Corfman, Howard Snow Jr., Rollie Edwards, and Charles Irwin. (Courtesy of CBHS.)

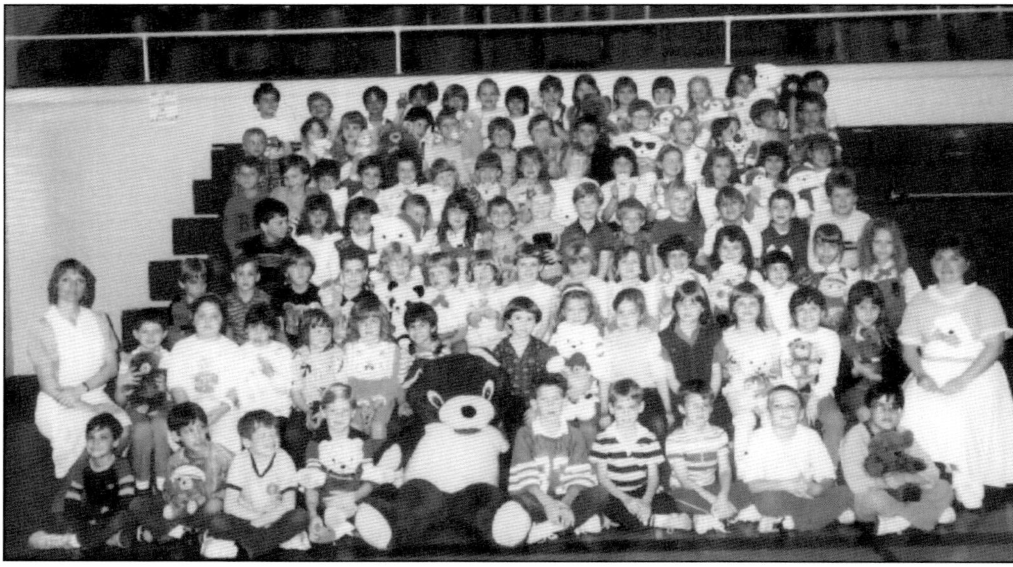

For over 20 years, one of the most popular events for first graders was the Teddy Bear Club, started by teacher Sally Palmer. The end of the school year was celebrated with a Teddy Bear Picnic on the school lawn. This 1986 photograph shows the class of 1998 in first grade. Mary Bumstead is the teacher to the left of the students, and Sally Palmer is on the right. (Courtesy of Sally Palmer.)

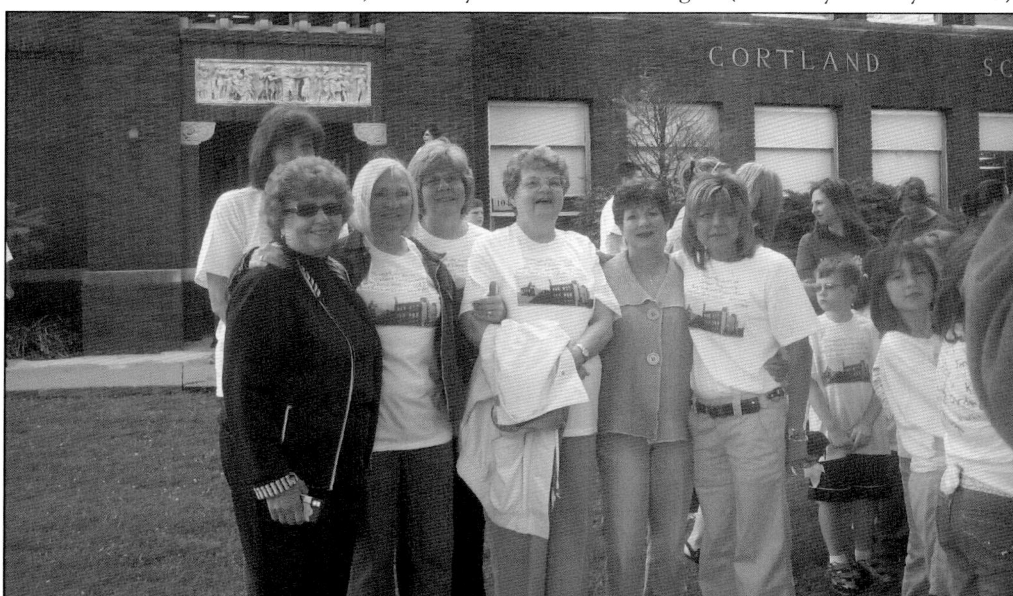

When the Cortland Elementary building closed in 2009, many former students, teachers, and townspeople commemorated the event. T-shirts, with an image of the old school on the front, were designed by custodian Pam Collier. Pictured here are teachers at Cortland Elementary and visiting former coworkers on the school's last day. From left to right are Rosemary Kokor (retired), Anne Herman, Mary Bumstead, Mary Lou Bristol, Donna Lewis (retired), Gayle Johnson (retired), and Sharon Bayus. The closing commemorated 133 years that a school has been on the site. The district presently has three buildings that serve nearly 2,000 students. (Courtesy of CBHS.)

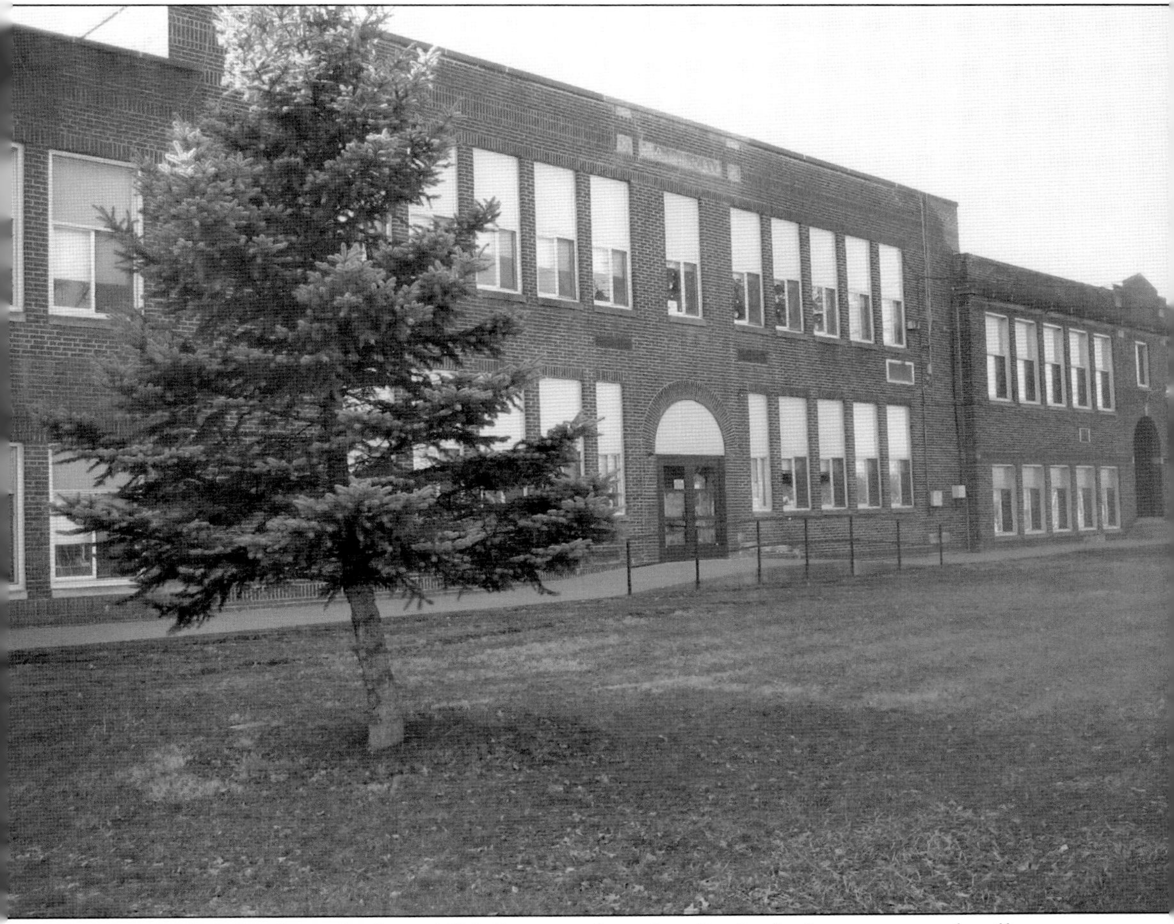

Bazetta High School was built in 1929. Prior to that, the district had one-room schoolhouses on the west side of Mosquito Creek before Mosquito Lake was created; they were the last such schoolhouses in Trumbull County. The first graduation occurred in 1936, with the ceremony held at the Bazetta Christian Church. The following year, the class was able to hold the ceremony in its newly completed gymnasium. Later, in 1956, both Cortland and Bazetta schools were becoming crowded, and thus the districts decided to consolidate. In 1961, a new high school was built, and the district was named Lakeview, a name that satisfied residents on both sides of Mosquito Lake. (Courtesy of CBHS.)

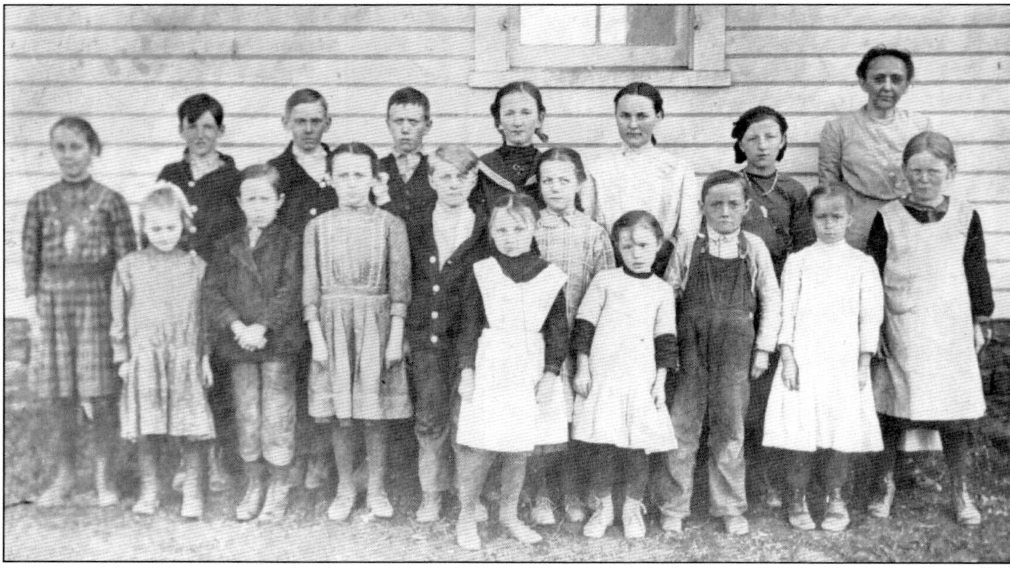

This school was located on the west side of Mosquito Creek near the intersection of Bazetta Road and State Route 305. Pictured here in 1914 or 1915 are, from left to right, (first row) Helen Rising, Poscoe Double, Leona Wilds, James Thompson, Stella Wilds, Cliele Brubaker, Abie Chmitlan, Ward Freer, Abbie Double, and Lucille Thompson; (second row) Ethel Prince, George Pritchard, Chas. Freer, Floyd Double, Bessie Ritchard, Mildred Rising, Leona Chmitlan, and teacher Lottie Oatley. (Courtesy of CBHS from Lucille Rogers.)

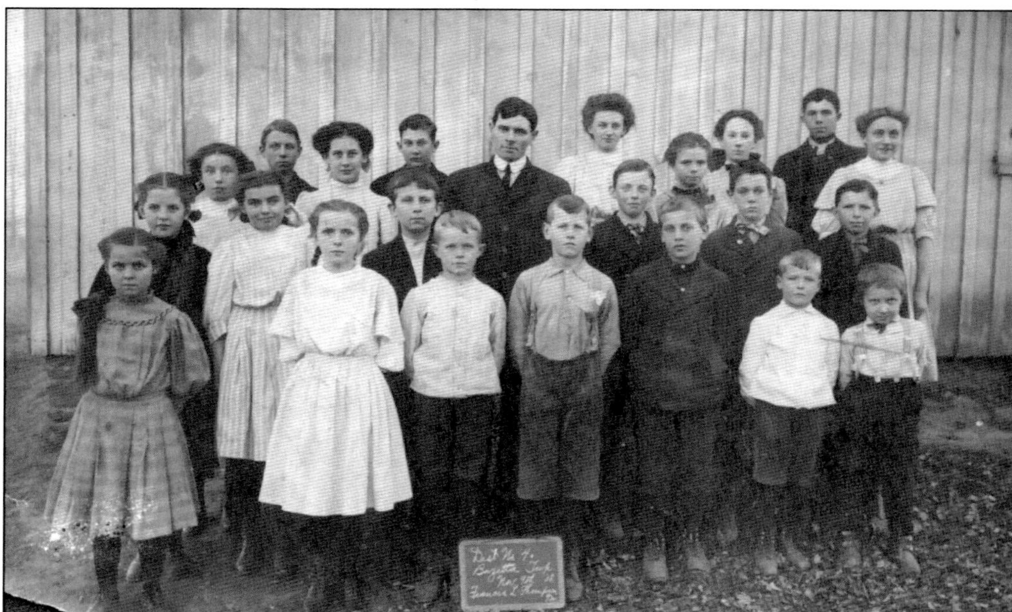

The District No. 4 School was located at the present site of the Lakeview Elementary building. This was also the lot chosen for Bazetta High School in 1929. Francis Thompson was the teacher (center, wearing the tie) in this November 1908 photograph; Fern Planck is in the front row in the white dress, Nellie Planck is the second child from the right in third row, and Mildred Hoagland is the second from the left in third row. The rest of the children are unidentified. (Courtesy of CBHS from Lucille Rogers.)

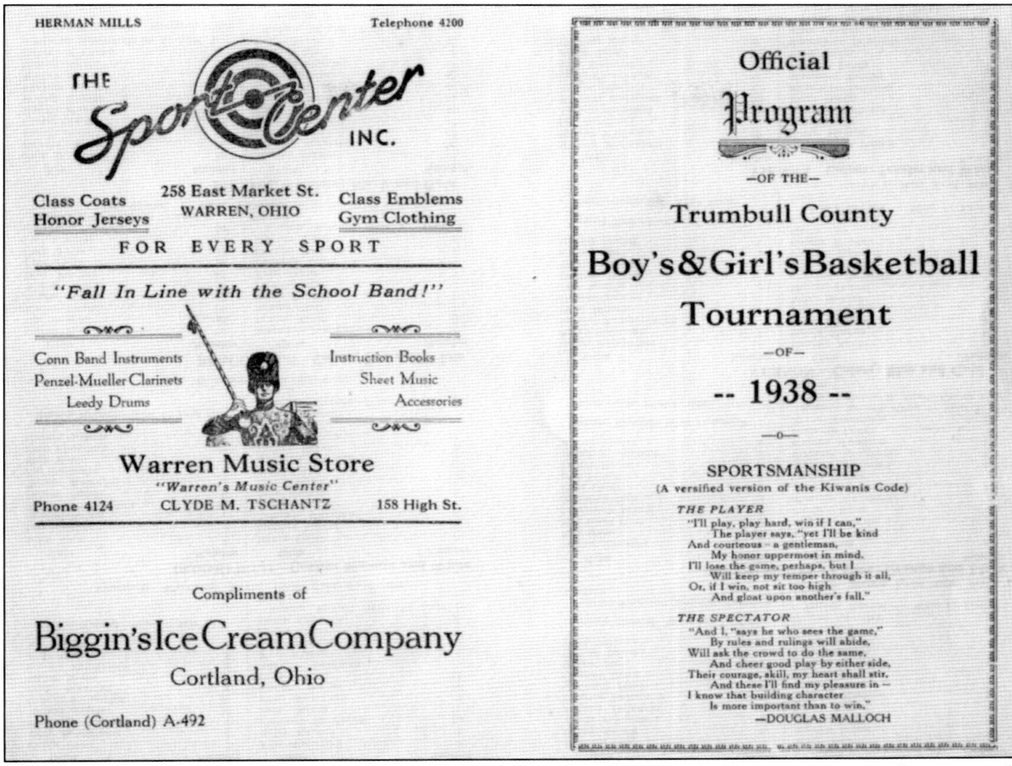

A program from 1938 Trumbull County Boys and Girls Basketball Tournament shows much more than just the teams, as the advertisements give a snapshot of local businesses. Team jackets, like today, were popular. Notice that cones were sold for 5¢ at Biggin's Ice Cream, a Cortland business. The poem on the front of the program about good sportsmanship reflects the ideals of a generation. According to team records, Mineral Ridge boys' team was a leading contender. (Both, courtesy of CBHS.)

BAZETTA — Colors: Blue and White

Boys	Number	Girls	Number
Roger Peck	7	Ann Miscevich	4
Billy Schellhorn	5	Betty Snyder	5
Raymond Yannucci	6	Florence Shellhorn	13
Robert Sando	12	Betty Smith	11
Robert Kilpatrick	10	Edna Mae Culp	10
Louis Santucci	3	Strobie Rector	14
Ralph Durst	11	Ruth Kinney	12
Kanko Tahtivirta	8	Adelaide Santucci	9
Nelo Niemi	4	Marian Jones	8
Joe Buran	9	Irene Swander	3
		Helen Arnold	6
		Elene Swander	7
Season Record—Won 5; lost 12.		Season Record—Won 5; Lost 11; Tied 1.	

Coach—R. Woodford Davis, Ohio State University.

BLOOMFIELD — Colors: Maroon and White

Boys	Number	Girls	Number
John Such	5	Helen Lucik	5
Lee Giddings	4	Lovetta Kollar	8
Roland Kollar	7	Arminta Hoagland	3
Ralph McGrannahan	10	Donna Bowyer	7
Emery Smida	9	Jean Russell	9
Wayne Rosenberry	3	Lottie Sulek	11
Joe Supinski	6	Doris Nicol	11
Nick Bovis	8	Kathryn Applequist	4
Fred Chapman	44	Esther Zakany	7
Robert Gedeon	33	Verna June Nicol	12
		Ora Ennis	
		Wilma Reeves	
Season Record—Won 4; Lost 6.		Season Record—Won 1; Lost 6; Tied 1.	

Coach—W. Robert Titus, Ohio State.

BRACEVILLE — Colors: Red and White

Boys	Number	Girls	Number
Junior Hall	90	Stephana Domyanich	11
Ed. Monroe	80	Louise Shoff	10
Edwin Phelps	70	Wilma Hall	7
James Atkin	40	Irene Kolozd	9
Wayne Wilms	50	Dorothy Nye	3
Dick Fischer	65	Vera Atkin	5
Fred Juris	55	Priscilla Zorca	8
Earl White	45	Evelyn Branson	4
David Moser	30	Marion Zorca	6
Robert Jarklerode	60		
Season Record—Won 2; Lost 8.		Season Record—Won 7; Lost 2; Tied 1.	

Coach—Joseph V. Ross, Fairmont State Teachers College.

BRISTOL — Colors: Black and Gold

Boys	Number	Girls	Number
Paul McDowell	50	Marian Seiple	49
Harold Shorts	54	Mildred Seemann	50
Joe Thomas	55	Marie Barbe	47
Elmer Clark	52	Mary Hoagland	42
Randil Munson	56	Alma Barbe	41
Robert Reavis	57	Marjorie Sutliff	51
Francis Bauer	51	Laura Mae Henry	46
Walter Starck	59	Agnes Brooker	45
Robert Seiple	58	Mary Seemann	44
Robert McClean	53	Eleanor List	4
		Mary Bronk	48
Season Record—Won 8; Lost 5.		Season Record—Won 4; Lost 10.	
Coach—Ramon C. Harmon, Ohio Northern.		Coach—R. E. Thornton, Ohio State.	

MINERAL RIDGE — Colors: Orange and Black

Boys	Number	Girls	Number
William Dray	5	Mary Baker	10
Frank Smith	6	Evelyn Jones	6
Thomas Smuss	7	Lois McMahan	7
Stanley Polanski	10	Leona Seifert	3
Charles Patterson	9	Bernice Keeling	14
Clarence Davis	8	Alice Geibert	8
Charles Lynn	11	Lois Seifert	5
Robert Noel	3	Bonnie Maurer	12
Harold Brooks	4	Venda Carnes	4
David Richards	12	Betty Holt	9
		Lila Bright	11
		Hellen Ludwick	13
Season Record—Won 14; Lost 2.		Season Record — Won 3; Lost 9; Tied 2.	
Coach—Woodrow Shiples, Baldwin-Wallace.		Coach—Marion Lynn, Ohio State.	

SOUTHINGTON — Colors: Orange and Black

Boys	Number	Girls	Number
Junior Baugher	12	Jane Olson	10
Bill Stroup	11	Ann Mae Viets	8
Raymond Hart	6	Virginia Craver	4
Lawrence Libert	9	Pauline Russ	7
Marshall Hall	10	Blanche Wojnarski	5
Paul Clark	5	Marjorie Kusmaul	14
Bill Libert	7	Louise Potter	3
Lester Davis	8	Mildred Mathews	11
Frank Blackshere	3	Virginia Longberry	12
Albert Pinier	4	Martha Huselton	15
		Jeanette Leiby	6
		Helen Harshman	9
Season Record—Won 5; Lost 9.		Season Record—Won 9; Lost 5.	
Coach—Sim Earich, Ohio State.		Coach—Helen E. Reed, Grove City College.	

VERNON — Colors: Blue and Gold

Boys	Number	Girls	Number
Henry Seikkenen	13	Martha Noble	14
Steve Pollander	5	Helen Moran	13
Robert Klingersmith	14	Ruth Winans	11
Paul Wilson	11	Anna Vulanich	15
Harold Tupper	12	Mary Reeder	17
Jim Morris	2	Marian Jewell	16
DeWitt Marsh	15	Angelena Rechedy	10
Wallace Mickle	6	Mildred DeMay	18
Gilbert Orr	4	Pauline Rasesak	6
Harold Jewell	1	Donna Warner	2
		Eloise Orr	5
		Ellen Siekkinen	7
Season Record—Won 5; Lost 7.		Season Record — Won 4; Lost 7; Tied 1.	
Coach—John Elk, Kent State.		Coach—Helen L. Hall, Kent State.	

VIENNA — Colors: Scarlet and White

Boys	Number	Girls	Number
Walter McConnell	51	Donna Mae Pound	11
Robert Williams	52	Betty Martin	8
Lee Bradbury	56	Lois Clower	6
Arthur Sheridan	57	Roselyn Terlesky	9
William Redmond	50	Mary Darig	10
Robert Combos	53	Elizabeth Lathrop	15
Lynn Clower, Jr.	54	Margaret Taiclet	12
Sam Kupensky	58	Eleanor Darig	5
Bruce Scott	55	Vera Viets	7
William Rogos	59	Genevieve Edwards	4
		Alice Clower	3
Season Record—Won 6; Lost 6.		Season Record—Won 5; Lost 8.	
Coach—Charles E. Goforth, Illinois Southern.		Coach—Miss Clara Mehlmann, Ohio State.	

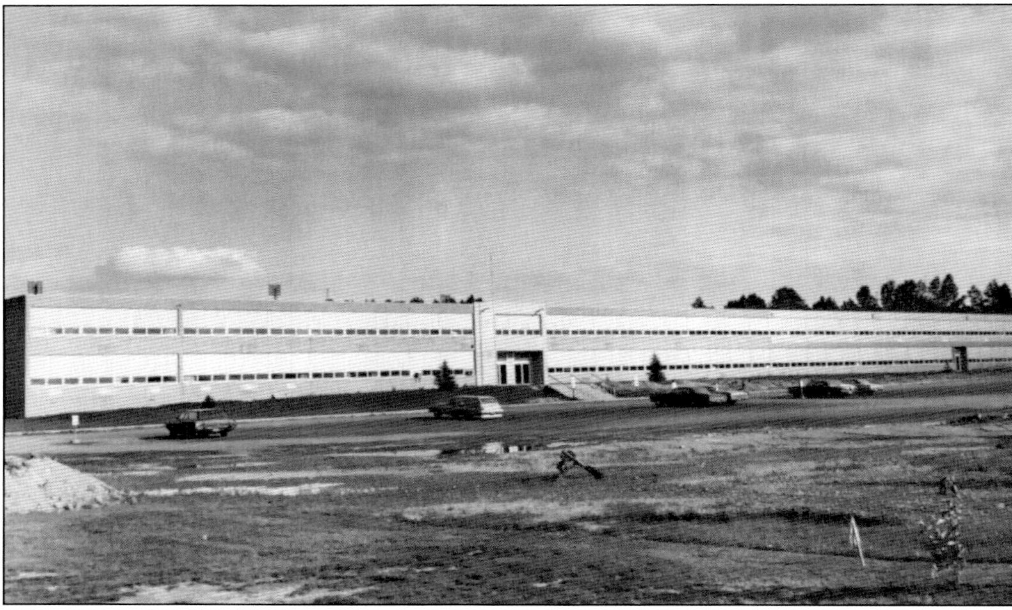

Lakeview High School was constructed as a one-story building in 1961 on property purchased from the Pistolozzi family; in 1971, a second story was added. This is a photograph from the January 9, 1972, dedication program. Besides a second floor, which added classrooms and a library, a new gymnasium was added with seating for 1,500. William Roush was the superintendent, and Frank J. Stocz was the high school principal. (Courtesy of CBHS.)

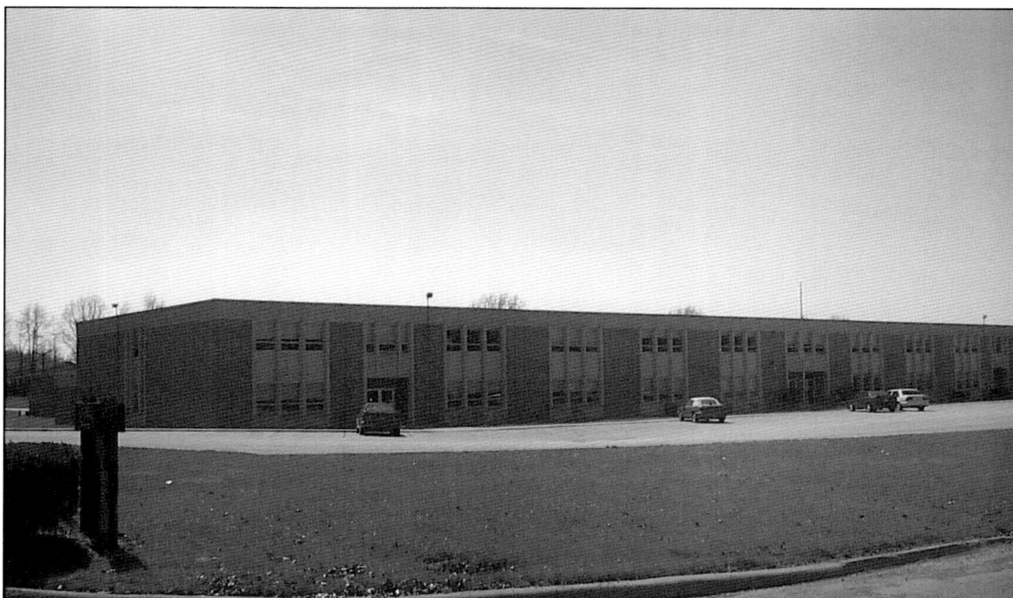

In 1978, when Lakeview Middle School was built on Wakefield Drive, both the elementary school and high school were bursting with students as the population soared. At various times, the building accommodated fourth through eighth grades, depending on the number of students at the different grade levels and space available at the other buildings. Additions were made to the school in 1995. (Courtesy of CBHS.)

Three

Growth of the Town

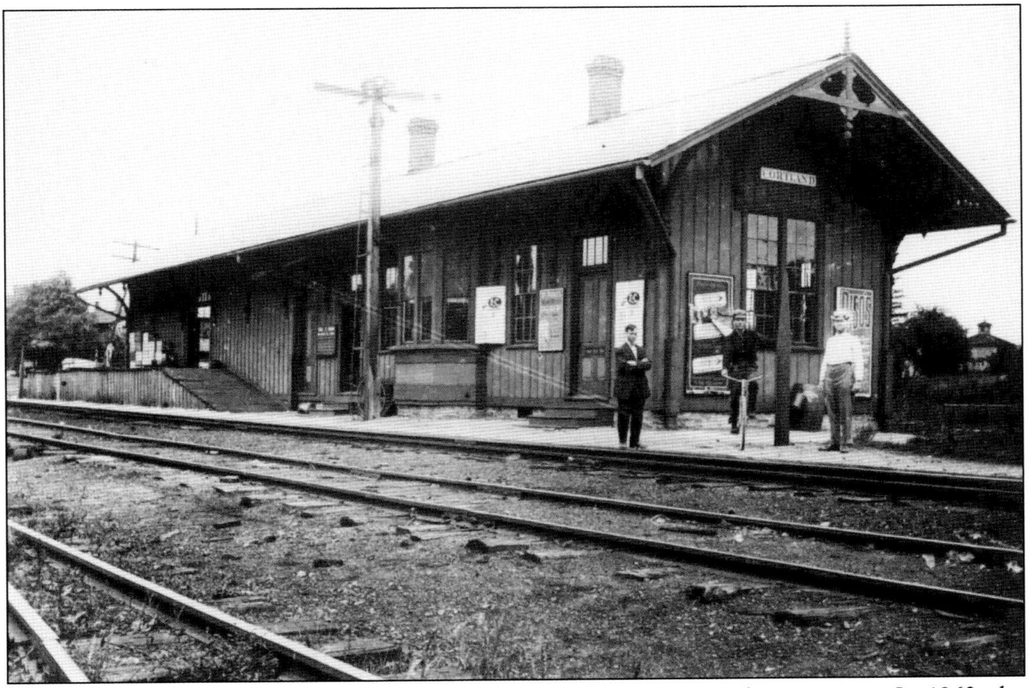

The train station changed the course of the town's history in more than one way. In 1863, the first passenger train on the Atlantic and Great Western Railroad went through Bazetta from Meadville, Pennsylvania, to Warren. Lewis Oatley organized citizens to raise $1,500 to influence the placing of a station and stockyard in Baconsburg. A small station was built first before the one pictured here was constructed in 1872, a then state-of-the-art depot on Erie Street by the tracks off the north end of Main Street. The building was 60 feet long and had separate waiting rooms for ladies and gentlemen; a loading dock was on the north end of the depot. Orrin Gates, who arrived with the railroad as an engineer and minister at the Disciples Church, convinced the town to change its name to Cortland. (Courtesy of CBHS.)

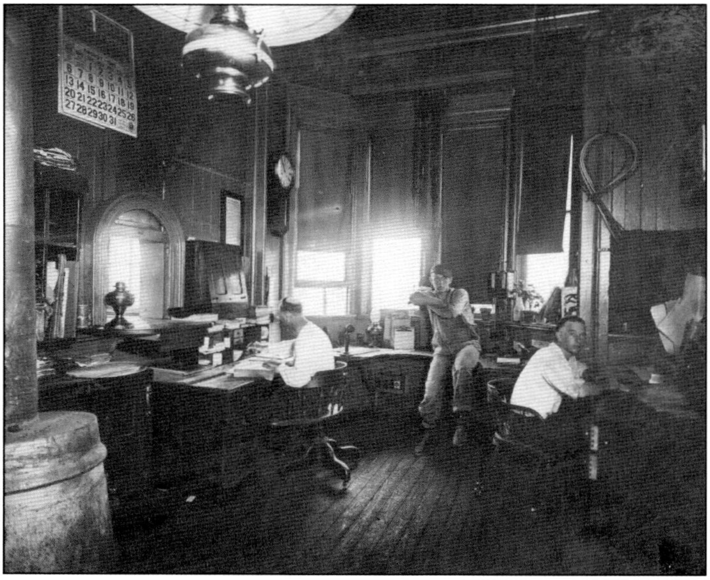

Probably the most important detail in this photograph is the calendar that reads, "August, 1916"; it gives a historical reference point. The writing on the back of the image states that Gaylord Kean is one of the men pictured and that this is the inside of the Cortland Train Depot. The view from the windows of this office would have been two hotels, a livery, and after 1883 a mill. The town was right around the corner. (Courtesy of CBHS from Louise Hadley.)

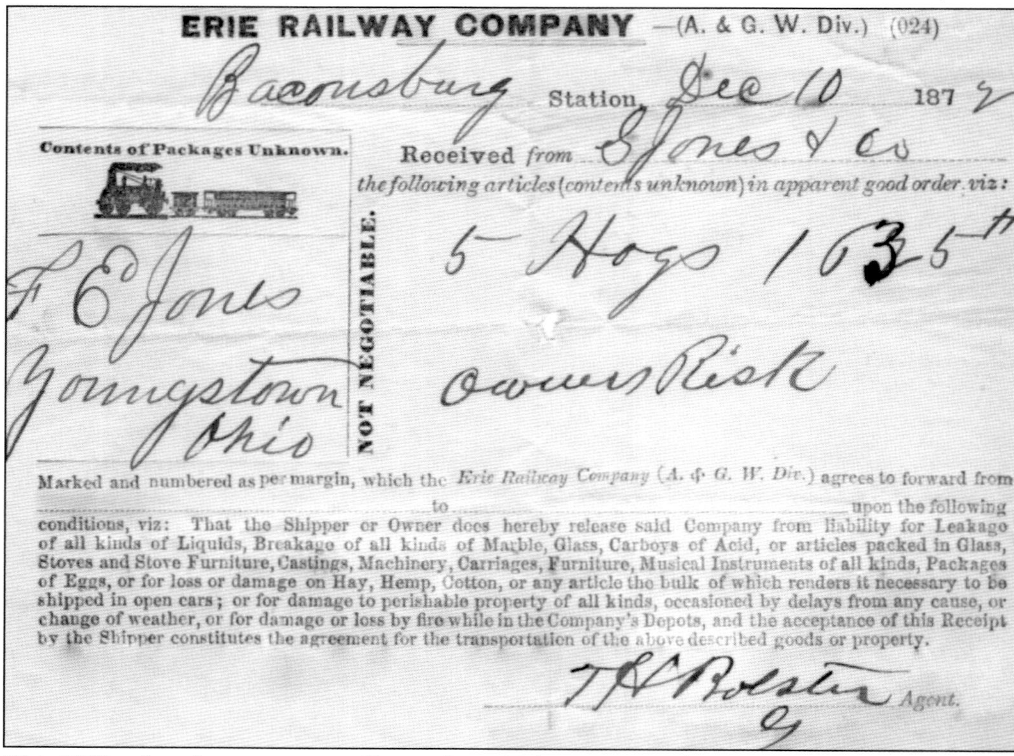

ERIE RAILWAY COMPANY —(A. & G. W. Div.) (024)

Baconsburg Station, Dec 10 1872

Contents of Packages Unknown.

Received from S Jones & Co

the following articles (contents unknown) in apparent good order, viz:

NOT NEGOTIABLE.

F E Jones
Youngstown
Ohio

5 Hogs 1635#

Owners Risk

Marked and numbered as per margin, which the *Erie Railway Company (A. & G. W. Div.)* agrees to forward from .... to .... upon the following conditions, viz: That the Shipper or Owner does hereby release said Company from liability for Leakage of all kinds of Liquids, Breakage of all kinds of Marble, Glass, Carboys of Acid, or articles packed in Glass, Stoves and Stove Furniture, Castings, Machinery, Carriages, Furniture, Musical Instruments of all kinds, Packages of Eggs, or for loss or damage on Hay, Hemp, Cotton, or any article the bulk of which renders it necessary to be shipped in open cars; or for damage to perishable property of all kinds, occasioned by delays from any cause, or change of weather, or for damage or loss by fire while in the Company's Depots, and the acceptance of this Receipt by the Shipper constitutes the agreement for the transportation of the above described goods or property.

T H Rolster *Agent.*

This 1872 railroad receipt states, "Baconsburg." The townspeople attempted to incorporate the village in 1869, but a glitch occurred and the town did not receive the confirmation. In 1873, the people delivered another document to Columbus, and the village finally became officially incorporated as Cortland. The name at the post office changed from Bazetta in 1874. For many years, though, documents often referenced Cortland as "formerly Baconsburg." (Courtesy of Sid Case.)

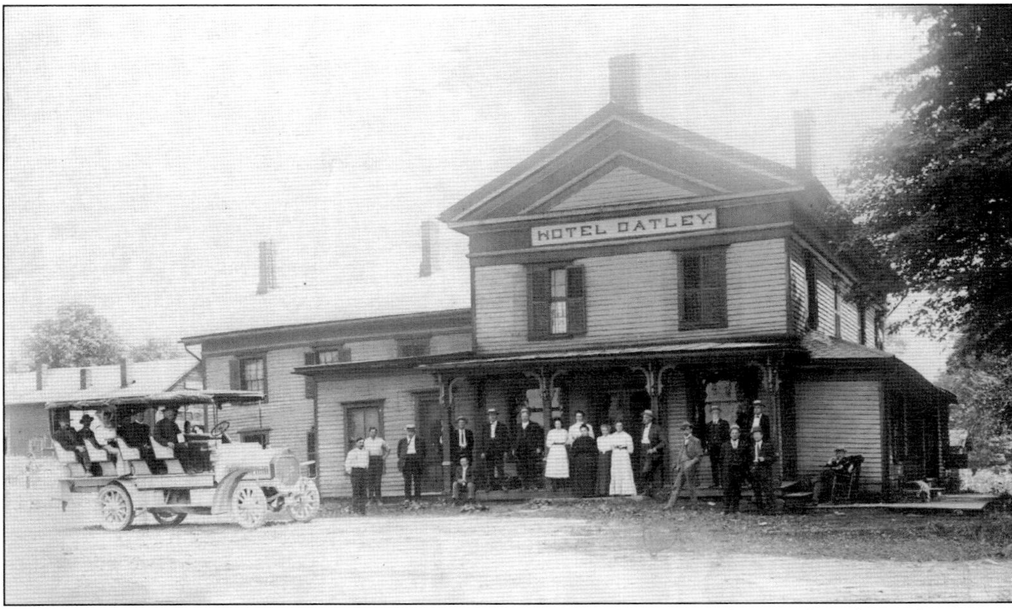

Before it became known as Hotel Oatley around 1893, the town's largest hotel was known as the Sugar Grove Hotel. After the town's incorporation, it became Hotel Cortland for almost 20 years. Some sources say the main part of the building was a dance hall that had been moved from Johnston. It was an important part of the town from about 1857 until it burned in 1930. (Courtesy of the Gessner family.)

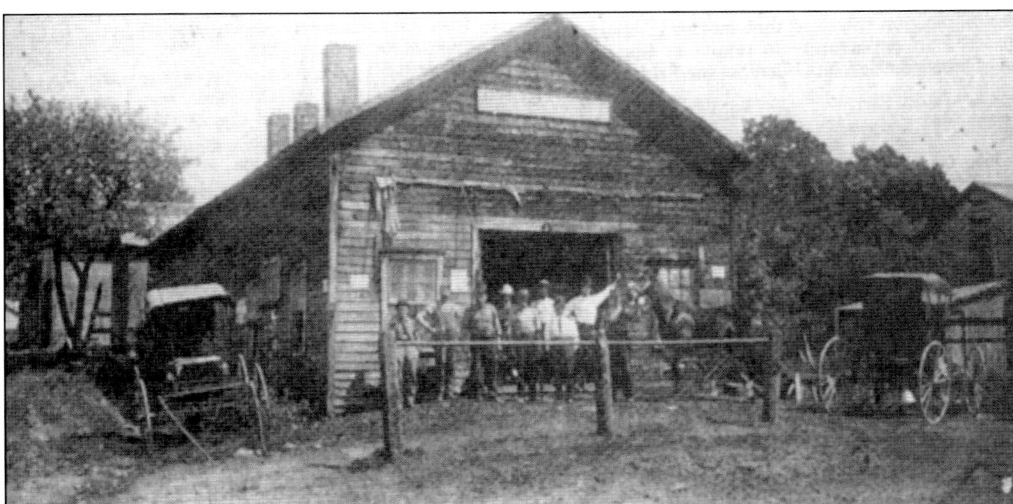

This blacksmith shop and livery was located at the intersection of Main and Erie Streets and was next to the Hotel Oatley. Although the date of this photograph is unknown, the short gentleman with a shirt and tie in the front row is A. Orrin McLaughlin. A fire consumed this building in the 1892, killing 10 horses and destroying all of the carriages and wagons. Only one cow was saved. (Courtesy of the Gessner family.)

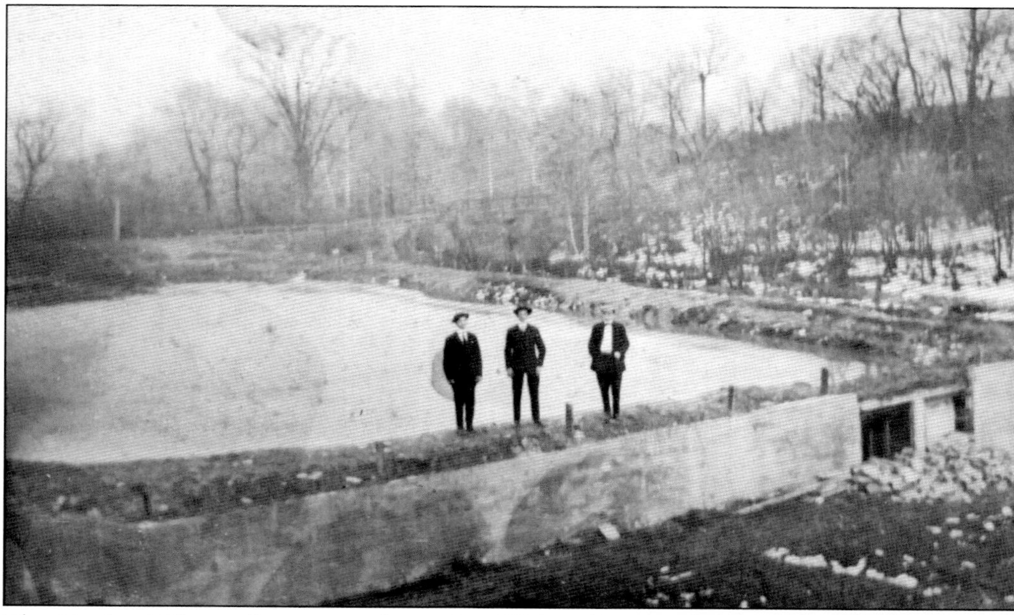

The Cortland Cheese Factory was located on Walnut Run on the west side of State Route 46. Nelson Cowdery and Craft established the company, and Lewis Oatley was the chief agent, which made the area a dairy center. F.G. Kingdom was the manager of the plant. Pictured here are John Oatley and some friends on the foundation of the cheese factory. (Courtesy of the Gessner family.)

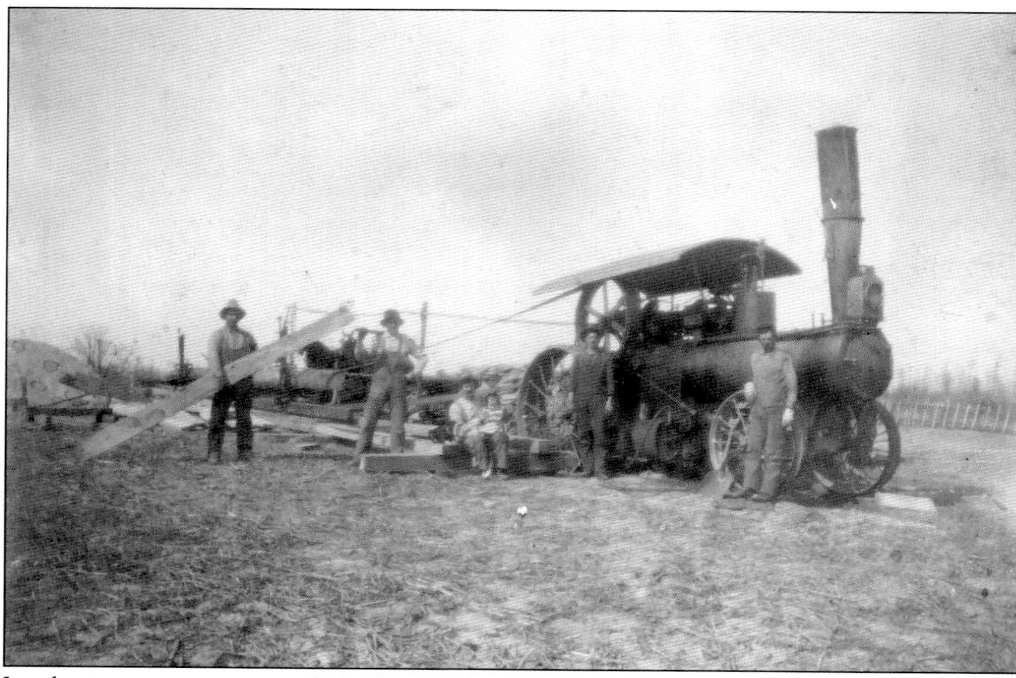

Lumbering was necessary to help clear the land. This machine was a portable type of saw that was used to make planks. Huge logs can be seen in the background, as well as lumber, which look like they may have been made into railroad ties. (Courtesy of the Gessner family.)

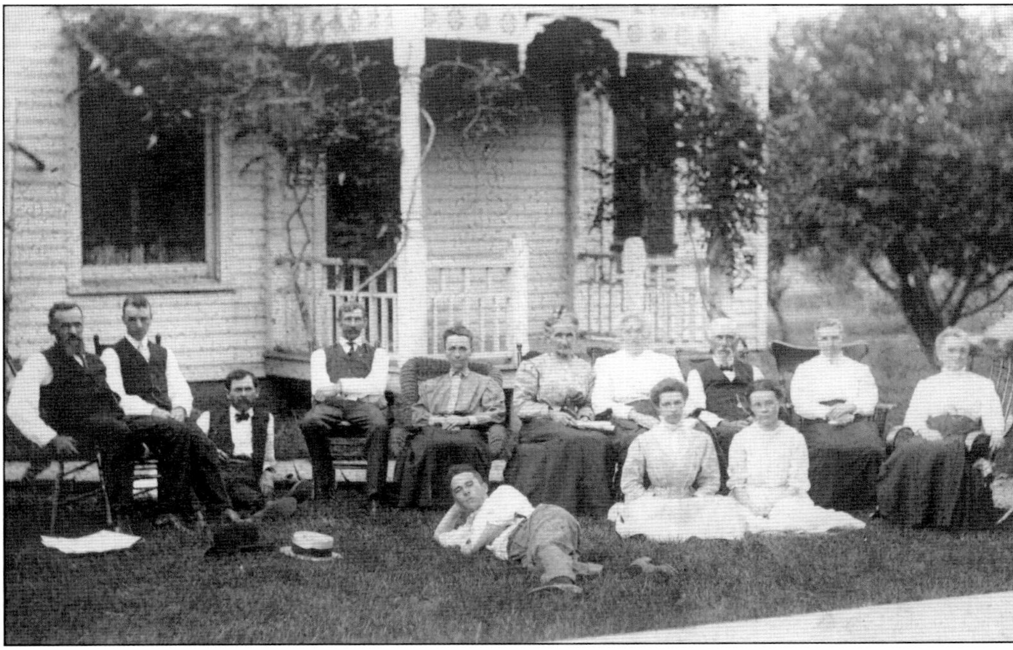

Samuel Bacon was the first to arrive in 1816 with his family when he purchased the mill from Edward Scofield. His son Enos started the first store on the south side of Walnut Run, near the mill, and other family members helped settle the town. The town was unofficially called Baconsburg for over 50 years because of the number of Bacons. The photograph above shows some Bacon family members relaxing on the lawn of one of their homes in town. The photograph below shows some of the family's horses and buggies. (Both, courtesy of Lucy Athya.)

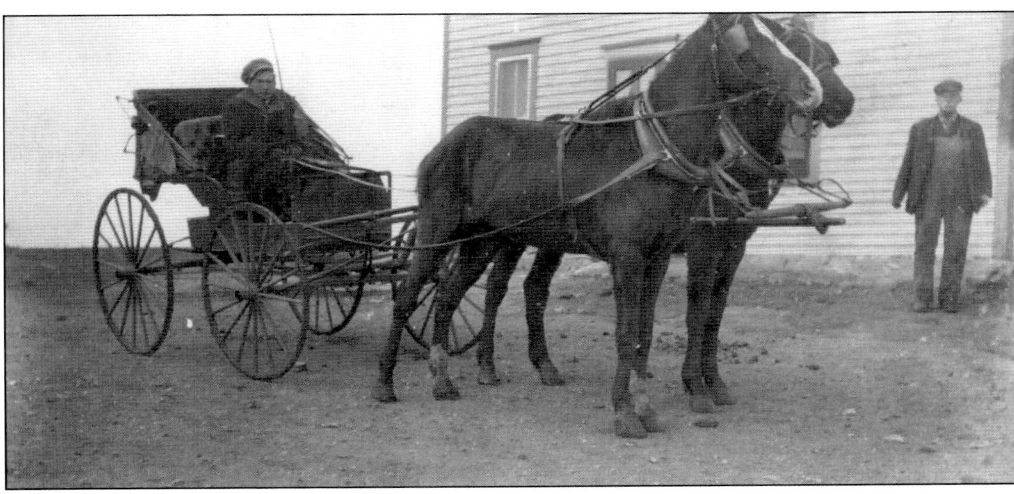

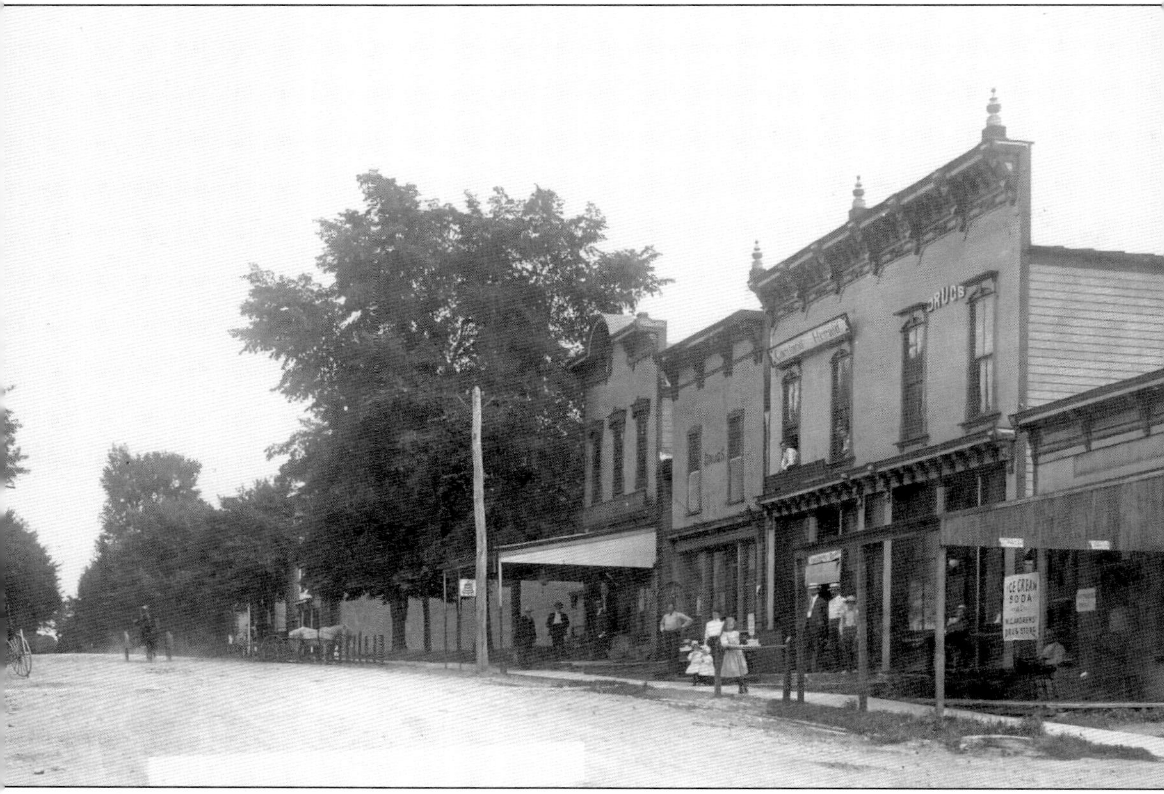

This is what the south side of Main Street looked like from 1873 up to about 1890, when a few telegraph and telephone lines were strung along the road. The town would have been newly incorporated in 1874. Cortland was very proud of its sidewalks, which many towns did not have. A macadam road was paved in 1890 from downtown Main Street to the railroad tracks. The store farthest away on the right is H.G. Bacon's grocery store. Next to it are two drugstores separated by the *Cortland Herald* office; the low building in the front advertises ice cream sodas. Just west of the low building (not visible) was the driveway to the Hotel Oatley livery. These buildings on Main Street all burned in the 1939 fire. (Courtesy of CBHS.)

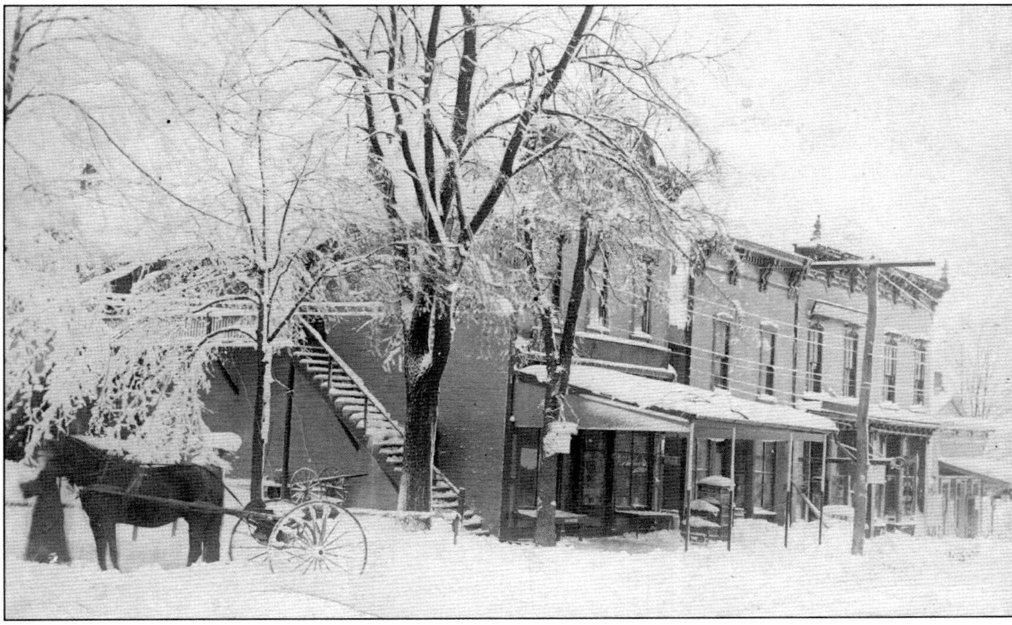

These are close-ups of some of the stores in the previous photograph but at a slightly later date. The first one on the left was the former location of H.G. Bacon & Company, while the center building at one time was operated by Frank Richards, a relative of Nelson Richards Sr. Later, H.J. Gilmore used it for a dry goods store before the Sigler & Gilmore block was built. Richards moved his business to Mecca Street, where Nelson Richards Jr. would establish his feed store and later his mill. This part of town burned down in 1939. The advertisement at right is for H.G. Bacon's store. (Above, courtesy of CBHS; at right, Mary Case.)

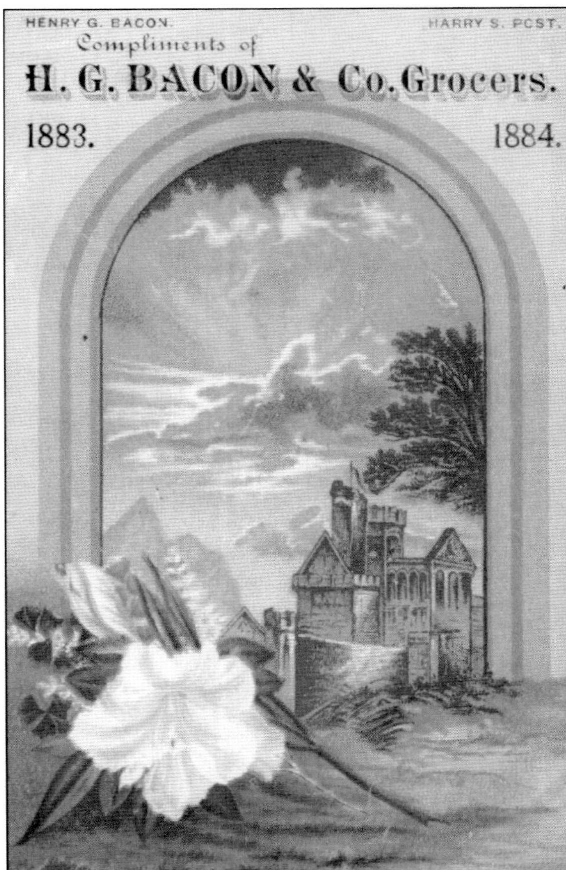

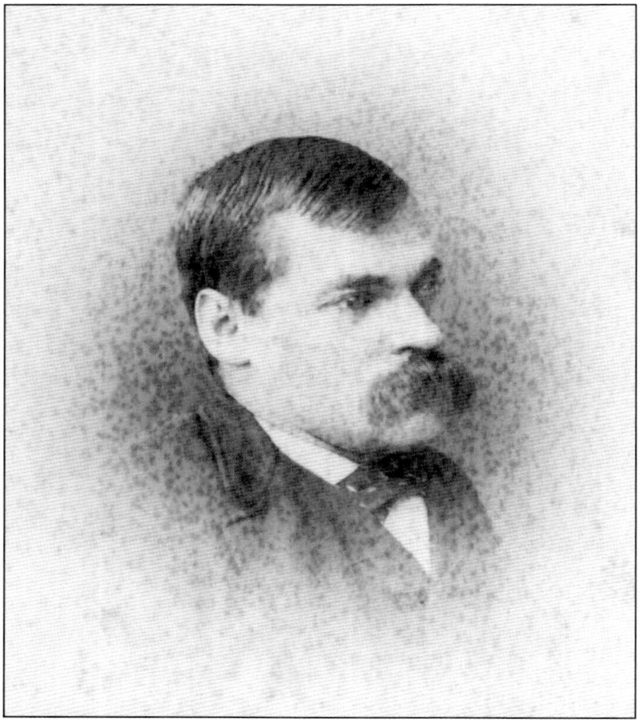

Rufus N. Cowdery, born in 1858, was the son of Nelson A. Cowdery. He opened a stationery and notions store in 1884 on the north side of Main Street and within a few years built a new store on the south side. In 1886, he married Lydie Faus. His home was located on the northwest corner of South Bank and Grove Streets. (Courtesy of CBHS.)

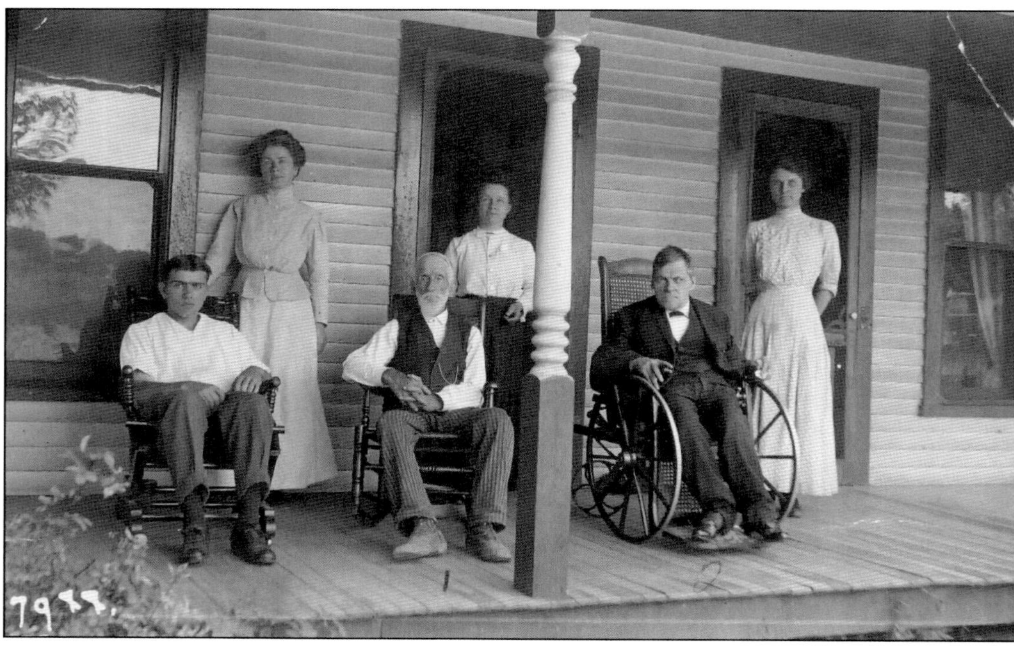

In 1910, Nelson Cowdery (center, with the beard) was a widower and president of the First National Bank (in Cortland). The woman behind Nelson is unidentified. Nelson's son Rufus N. is sitting in the wheelchair, while Rufus's wife, Lydie, stands behind him. The young man to the left is likely Rufus's nephew Clarence Struble, with his mother, Helen Struble (Lydie's sister), standing behind him. (Courtesy of Dave Cover.)

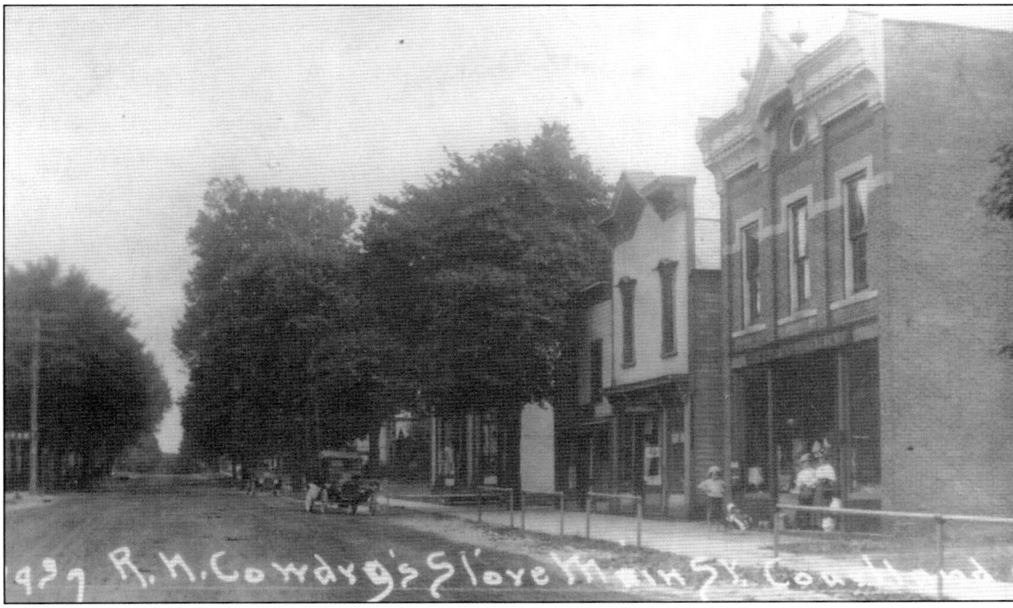

R.N. Cowdery's new store was very popular, attracting customers from nearby townships. It was noted for its top-of-the-line goods, including clothing for men and women, school supplies, stationery, gift items, crockery, and glassware, such as that shown below. It was also the only place in town that sold a variety of newspapers. The building still exists as the second one from the southwest corner of South Bank and Main Streets. (Above, courtesy of CBHS; below, Dave Cover.)

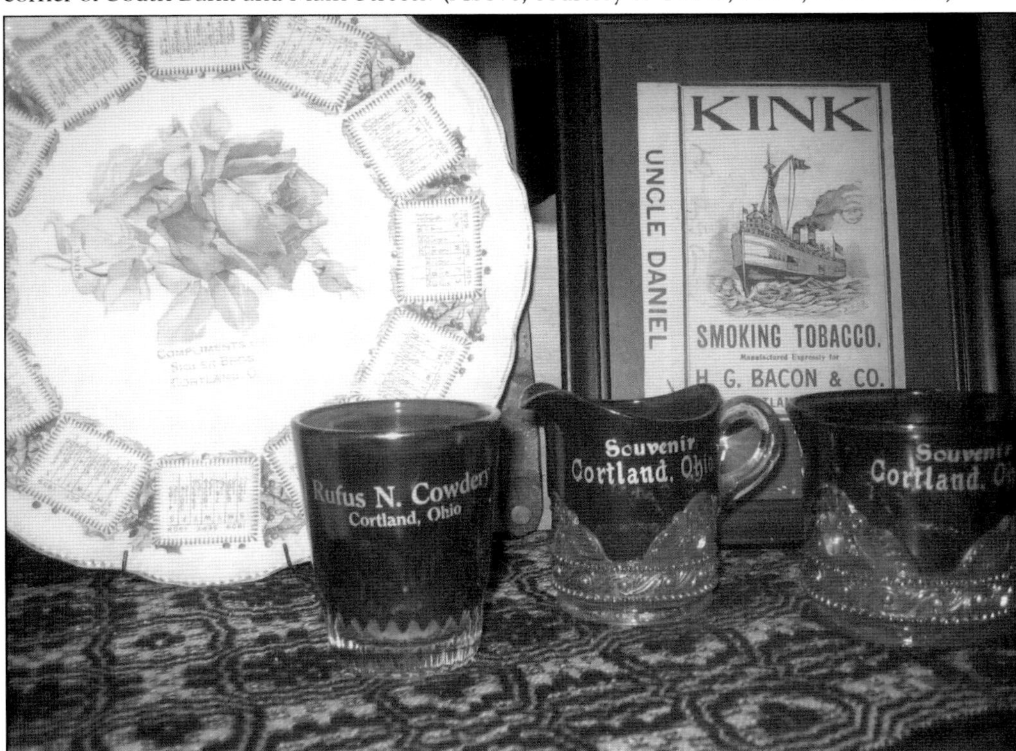

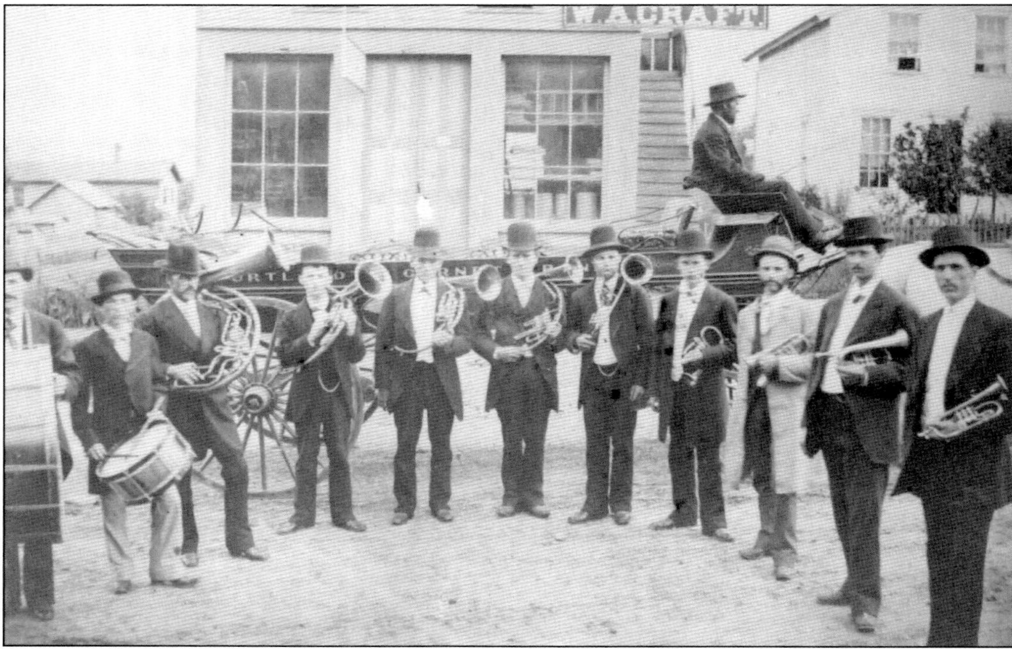

The 1876 cornet band played for parades, fundraisers, and celebrations. One story relates that the bandleader, Frank Coates, was accidentally thrown from the wagon while on the way to Kinsman to play in Decoration Day activities and the wheel passed over his band instrument, "demoralizing the sound." (Courtesy of Mary Case.)

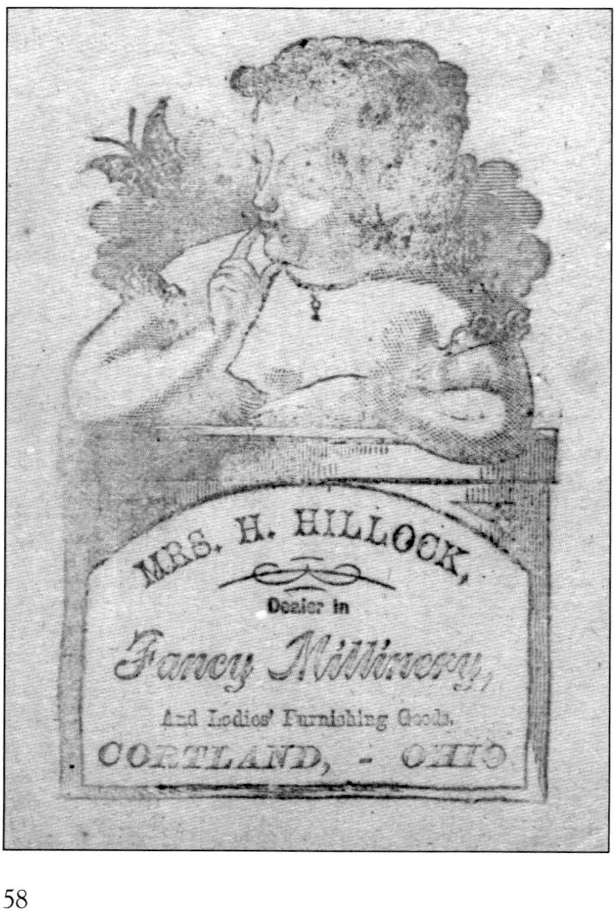

Hattie Hillock owned a high-end millinery shop on the north side of Main Street in the Gazette Building in 1873. She used a variety of feathers and ornamental items to fashion creative hats. Her husband, Thomas Hillock, was the mayor of Cortland in 1883 for four years. In 1888, a fire started in her shop, destroying six shops, including the post office. A few years later, the Hillocks moved to Iowa. (Courtesy of Mary Case.)

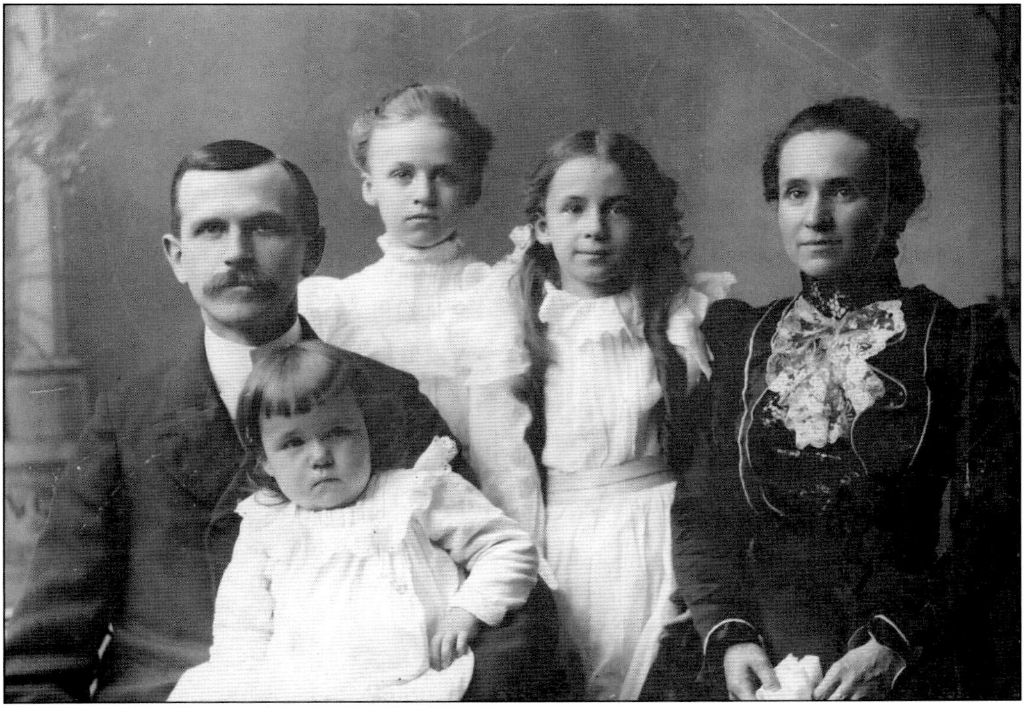

The E.A. Sigler (Austin) family built a home on Main Street opposite the intersection of Park Avenue and Main Street. In 1883, he became business partners with Calvin Clawson until Clawson moved to Warren. Then he partnered with A. Hathaway when they built the Sigler & Gilmore block on the southeast corner of South Bank and Main Streets. In 1892, Hathaway left the company, and Austin's brother Grant joined him; the brothers were partners for 47 years. Austin married Mary Mapes, and they had five children, three of whom are shown here: Adah, Alice, and Gladys. One died at birth, prior to the time of this photograph. A bag from the Clawson-Sigler time period is pictured below. (Above, courtesy of Carol Falkner; below, Mary Lou Reese.)

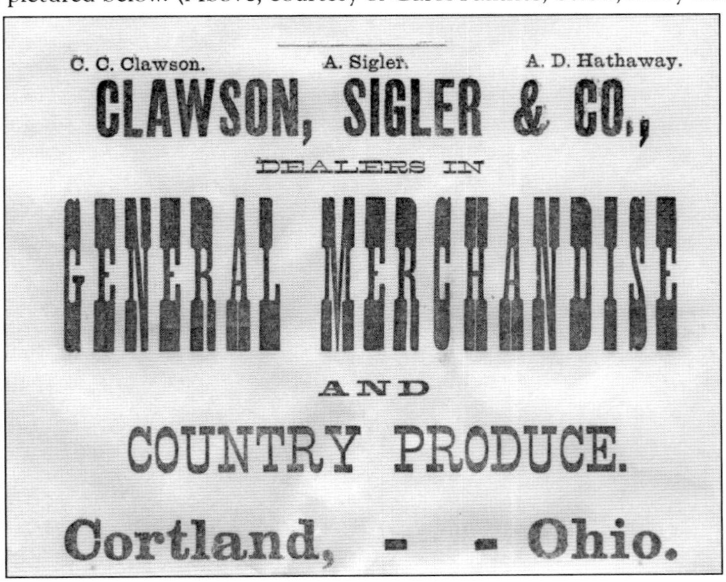

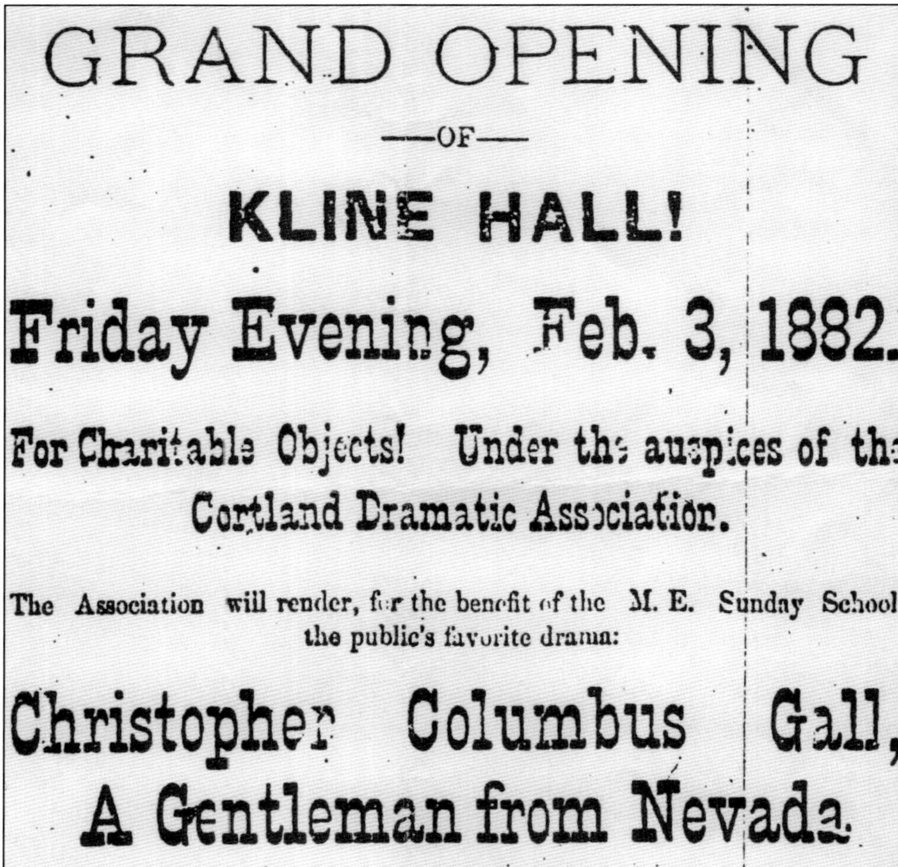

GRAND OPENING

—OF—

KLINE HALL!

Friday Evening, Feb. 3, 1882.

For Charitable Objects! Under the auspices of the Cortland Dramatic Association.

The Association will render, for the benefit of the M. E. Sunday School, the public's favorite drama:

Christopher Columbus Gall, A Gentleman from Nevada.

at Kline's new Hall, on Friday evening Feb. 3, 1882.

Let every citizen attend who is delighted with profitable and attractive amusements and at the same time aiding charitable objects.

The Entertainment will afford most appropriate and attractive Music. Selections made from the Classic and Modern Authors.

Our citizens and those living in surrounding towns will have a rare opportunity to witness a meritorious play, and at the same time enjoy the conveniences of one of the most commodious and convenient audience rooms on the Western Reserve.

Admission, ...	25 cents.
Children under 12 years, ...	15 "
Reserved Seats, ...	35 "

In the 1880s, art, music, and theatre flourished, as the town enjoyed a certain amount of prosperity. In February 1882, Kline's Hall was remodeled, fitted with a stage, and was ready for its grand opening. Seats were 25¢, while reserved seats were 35¢. The performance of the play *Christopher Columbus Gall: A Gentleman from Nevada* was presented to a full house. (Courtesy of CBHS.)

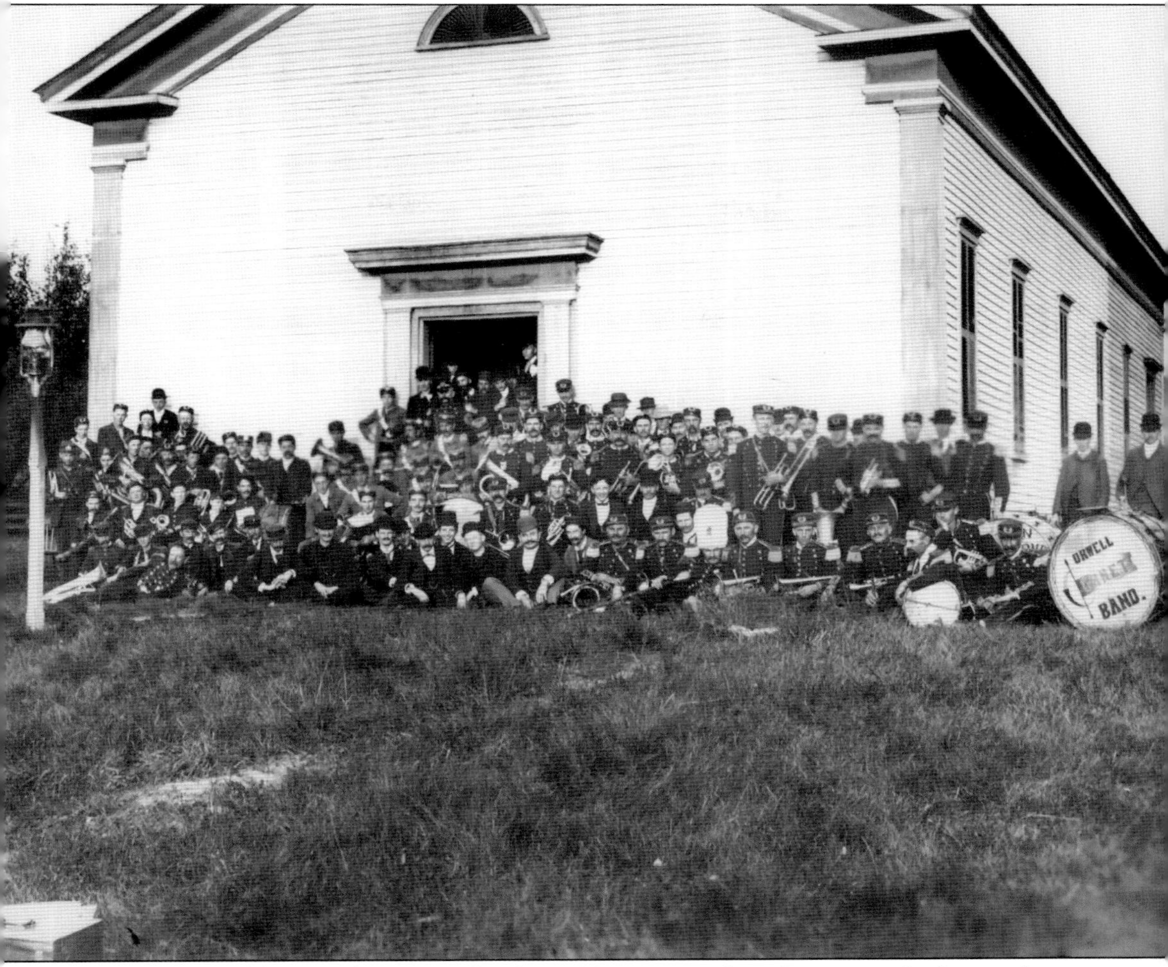

Soon, Kline's Hall became known as the Opera House even though an opera had never been performed there. There were graduations, dances, basketball games, plays, concerts, and many community events such as meetings of several bands, including Orwell's band seen here. This is the earliest known photograph of the Opera House in the historical society's collection. (Courtesy of CBHS from Chris Klingemeir.)

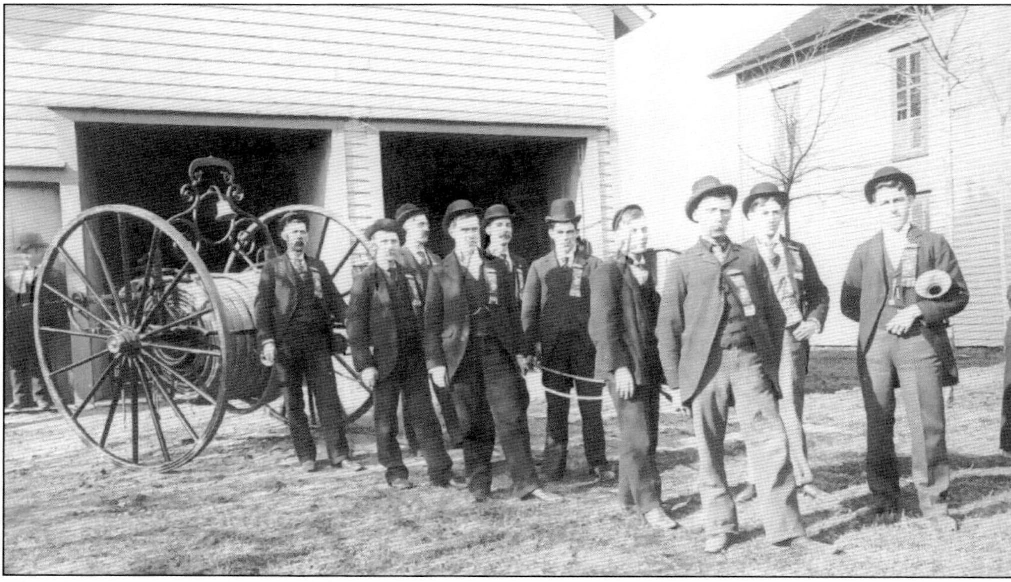

The Hose Cart Company of the Cortland Fire Department connected and handled the hoses during a fire and wound them up again when the job was done. The men on this job are, from left to right starting with the man on the far left behind the large wheel, Ira Herrick (a carriage maker by trade), Frank Johnson, Charles M. Post, George Marsh, Fred Carlisle, Burt Richards, William Meek, William Hadsell, Warner Post, Arlie Kennedy, and James A. Hardy, assistant fire chief and commander of the Hose Cart Company. (Courtesy of CBHS.)

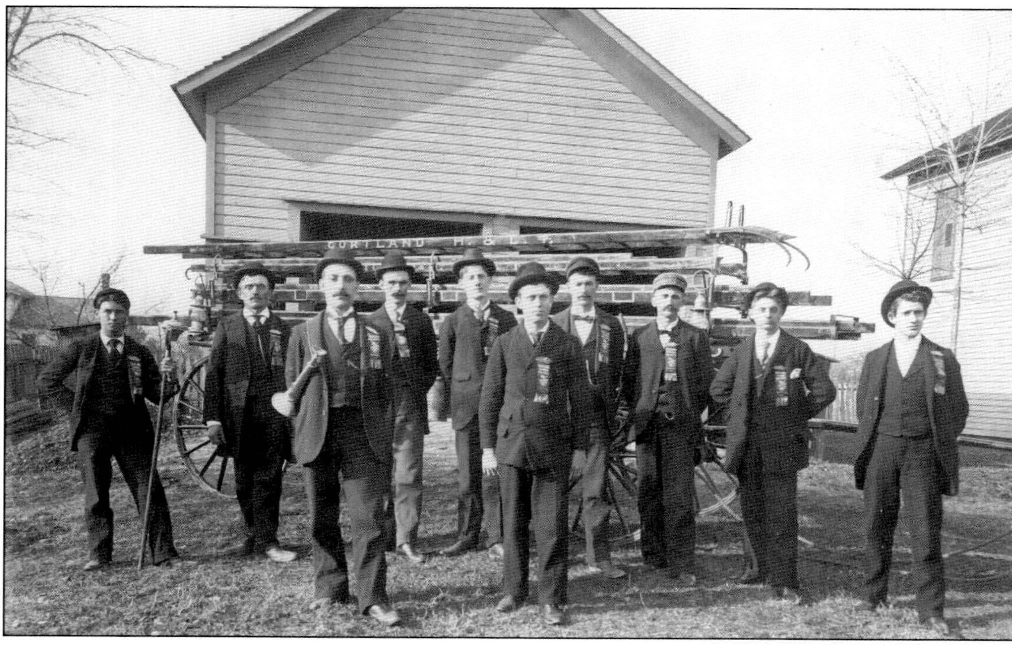

The Hook and Ladder crew members are, from left to right, George Morey, Dan Flickinger, Harry Koehler, Fred Post, George Hardy, Tom Hardy, Burke Oatley, Chris Henry, Burt Ramsdell, and John Meade. Both photographs date from the founding of the fire department in 1885. (Courtesy of CBHS.)

Since firefighters and their horses did not stay at the station between fires, the fire hall only stored equipment. When a call was received, the bell was rung and the first team of horses to arrive at the station earned $3. The location of the station on Lattin Street has not changed, but the current building was constructed in 1984. In 1885, the village hall was located next door. (Courtesy of CBHS.)

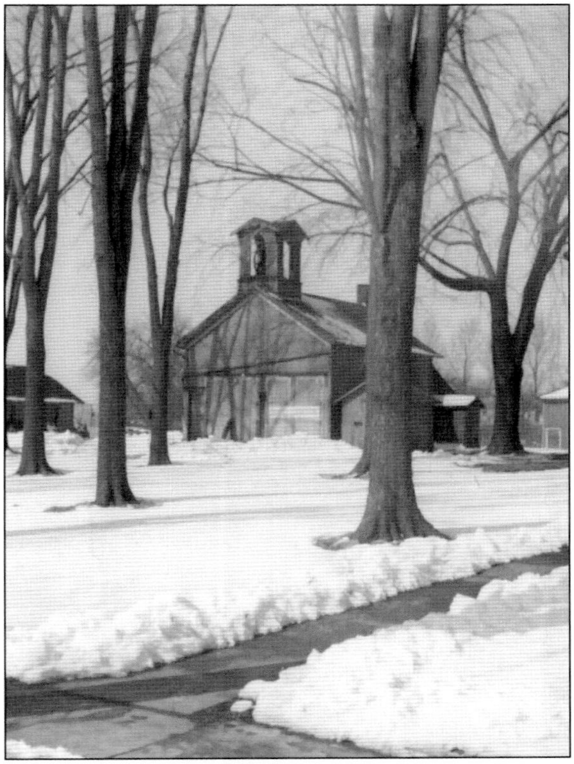

In 1886, the mayor was H.D. Holcomb, and the marshal was J.B. Hardy. A bell was ordered on May 22 of that year for the fire department, which weighed 418 pounds and cost $128.60. The bell rang out for many years until an electric horn, activated from the fire chief's house, was used. Firefighters had the old fire bell mounted, where it can be appreciated by today's volunteers. (Courtesy of CBHS.)

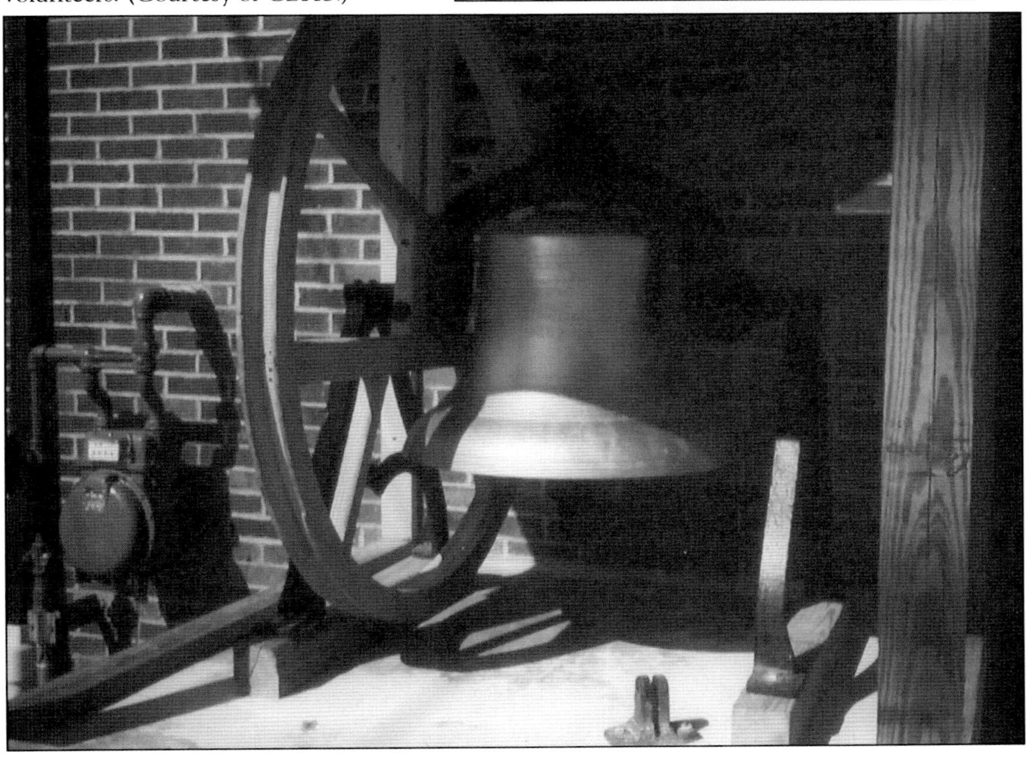

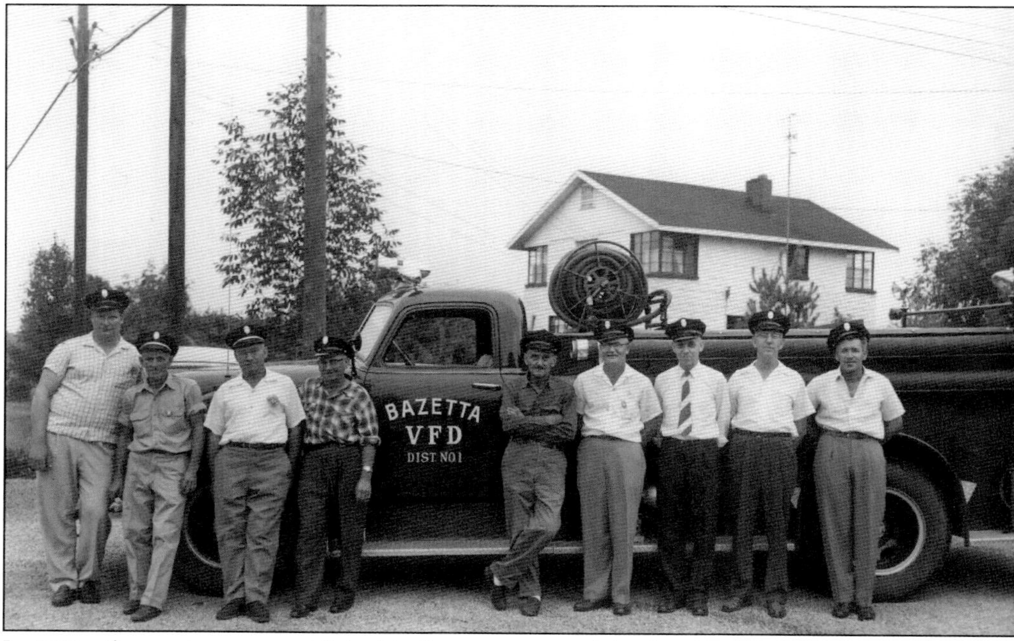

In 1961, a fire station was established in Bazetta as part of the Cortland-Bazetta Joint Fire District. The Fire Hall is located on Everett Hull Road near the fairgrounds. Nelson Reel Jr. was one of the early fire chiefs, as was Donald Murphy. In the 1980s, Cortland and Bazetta split into two separate districts. Bazetta also has a station on McCleary Jacoby Road. During the Trumbull County Fair, the fire station on Everett Hull is the site of pancake breakfasts. (Both, courtesy of Bazetta Fire Department.)

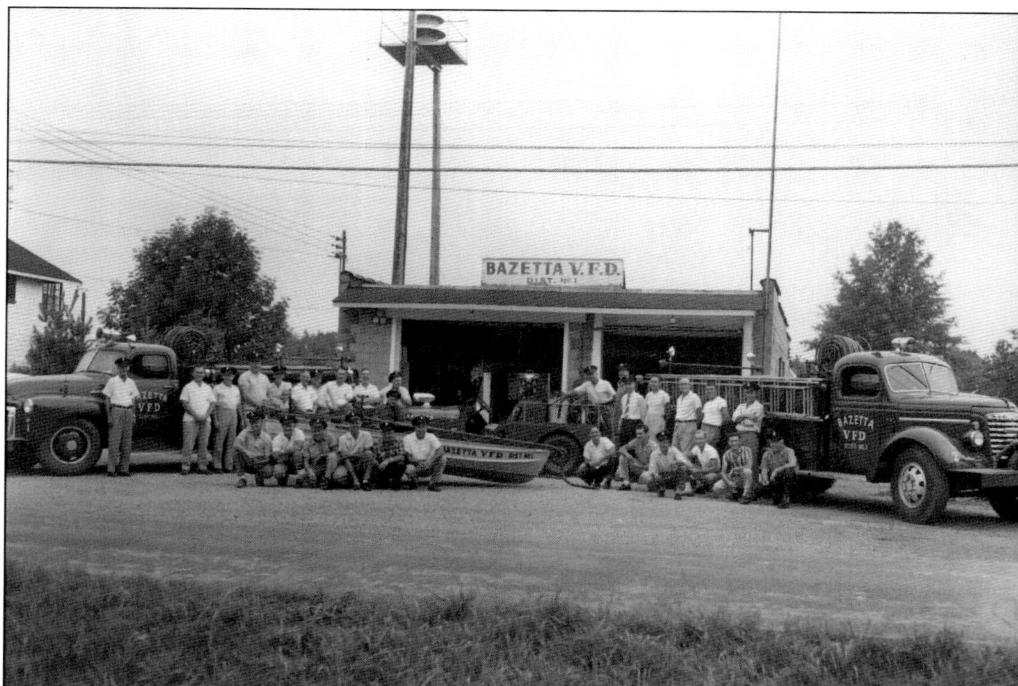

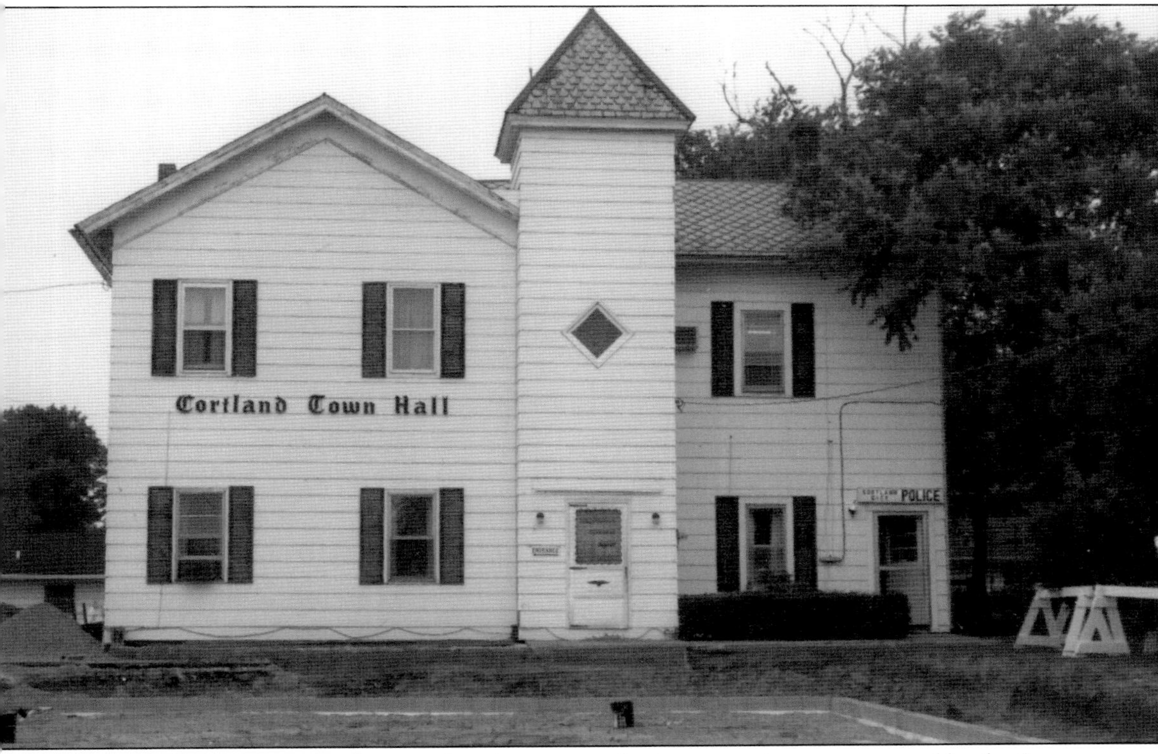

In 1873, as the town received notice that the petition for incorporation was accepted by the State of Ohio, a village hall was built. It was erected near the train depot, but as the downtown grew, so did complaints that the location was inconvenient. In 1887, the building was moved to Lattin Street, next door to the fire department, and landscaped into a park setting. Between 1963 and 1966, while Don Jones was mayor, the old town hall was remodeled inside and out; however, as the population continued to increase, more and more space was needed. Finally, in 1984, after Cortland had become a city in 1981, a new city hall was constructed at 400 North High Street. (Courtesy of Carol Harrison.)

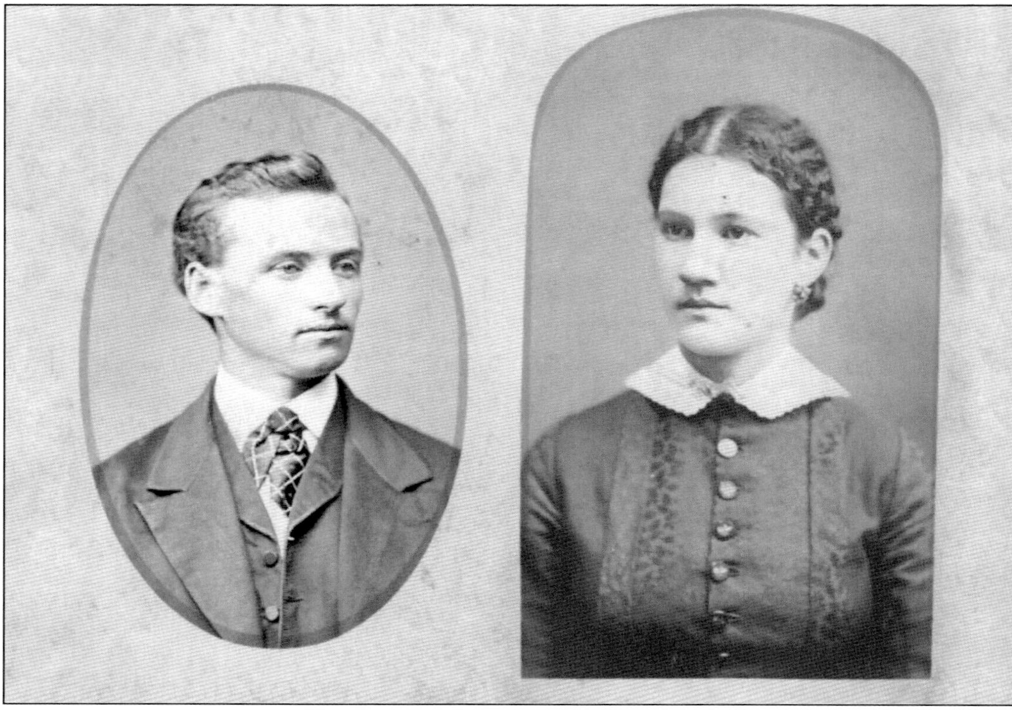

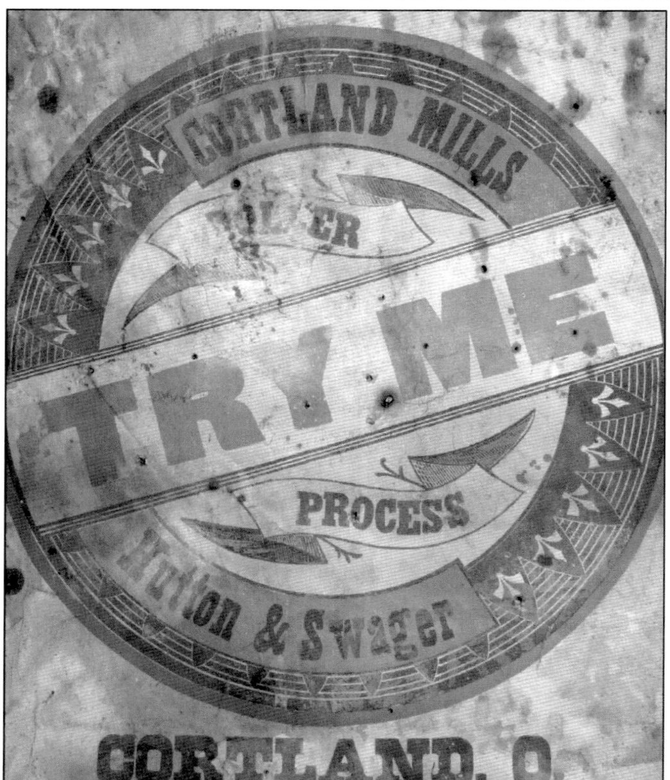

Lewis Hutton was originally from Pennsylvania and had served in the Civil War from 1861, at the age of 16, to 1866. He was wounded at Gettysburg but fought in at least 10 more battles before being discharged. He came to Cortland in 1871 and worked in the milling business for four years. He married Ella Post, daughter of M.C. Post. They moved to Michigan, then back to Trumbull County and finally back to Cortland. He operated the Kennedy mill that was renamed Hutton and Swager (the logo from a bag is seen at right) until 1891 when it burned. He was the last Civil War veteran in Cortland, where he also served as mayor and a stockholder for the bank and the telephone company. Lewis died in 1935 at age 90, and Ella died in 1915. (Both, courtesy of Florence Hutton.)

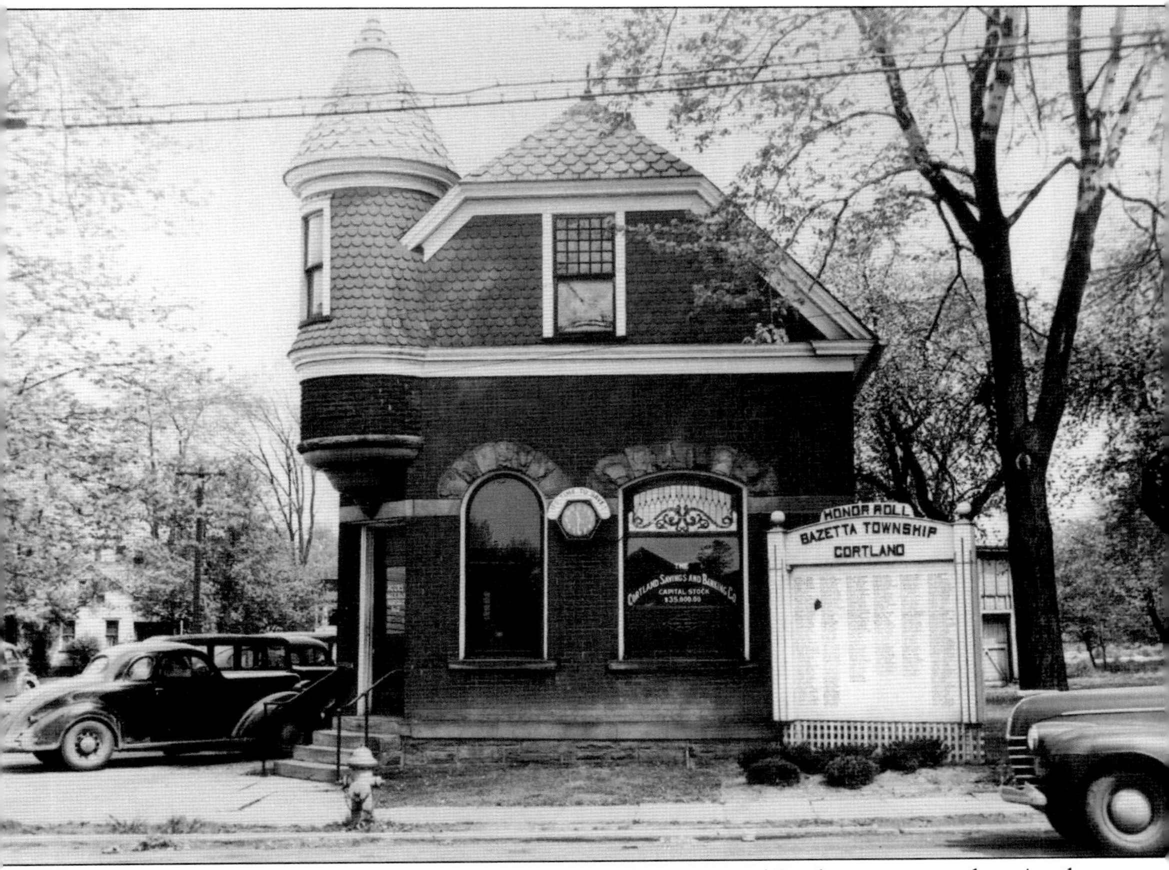

Originally called the First National Bank, the Cortland Savings and Banking originated on April 12, 1892. It was chartered on July 8 and built by Seth Hulse, and it opened its doors for business on September 26, 1892. In 1911, it became a state bank and was named Cortland Savings and Banking Company. The first officers were William Wartman, president; Nelson A. Cowdery, vice president; E.F. Briscoe, cashier; and C.R. Dodge, assistant cashier. William Davis, C.E. Fisher, Lewis Oatley, H.J. Gilmore, J.H. Faunce, and John J. Sullivan were directors. The building has been completely rebuilt, complete with drive-thru and ATM services, but it still is on the same corner of North Bank and Main Streets. (Courtesy of the Gessner family.)

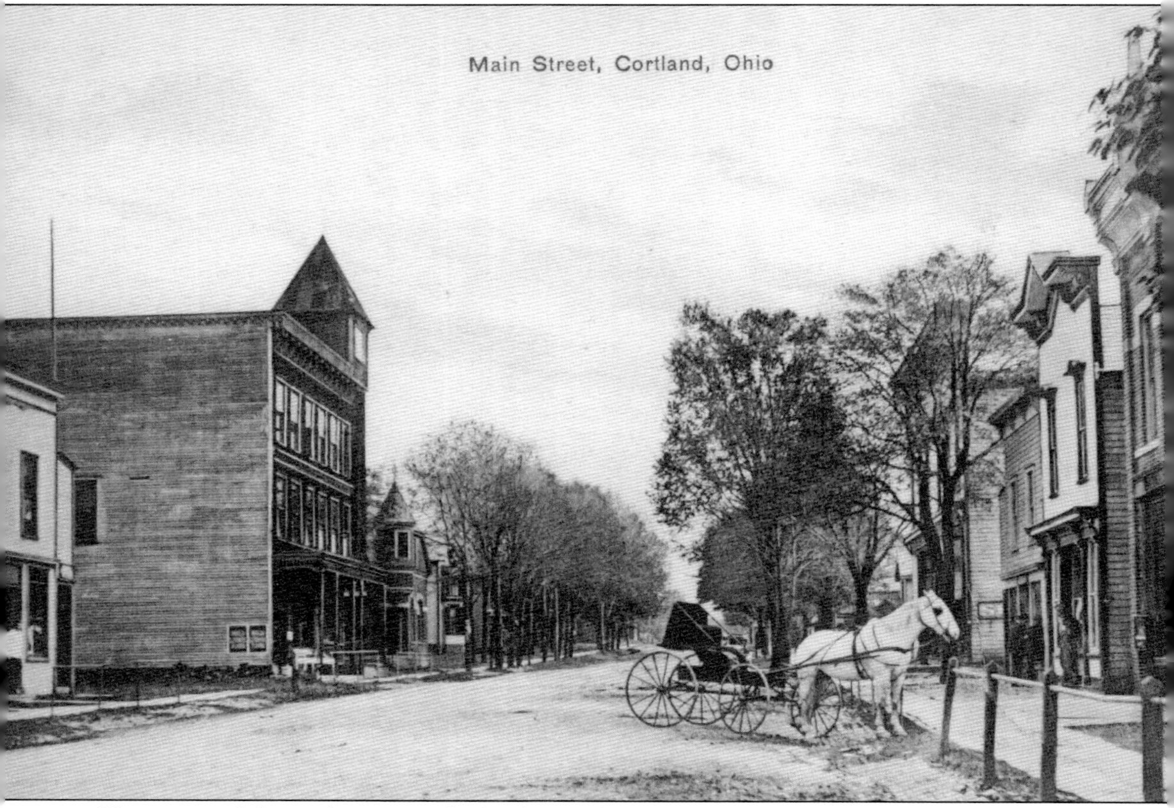

This postcard dates after 1892. The bank is visible on the north side of the street, and the Sigler and Gilmore building is visible on the south side of the street across from the bank. The large building on the same side as the bank is the Arner block. The ground floor was at different times a feed store, a grocery story, then the post office; the third floor on top of the building was a skating rink. Just east of the Arner block was Wildman's Barber Shop, with owner Charles Wildman standing beside the door. Across the street is the brick Cowdery's store, with people visible in that doorway. Other photographs indicate that the horse and buggy pictured here belonged to Rufus Cowdery. (Author's collection.)

Four

Richards Milling

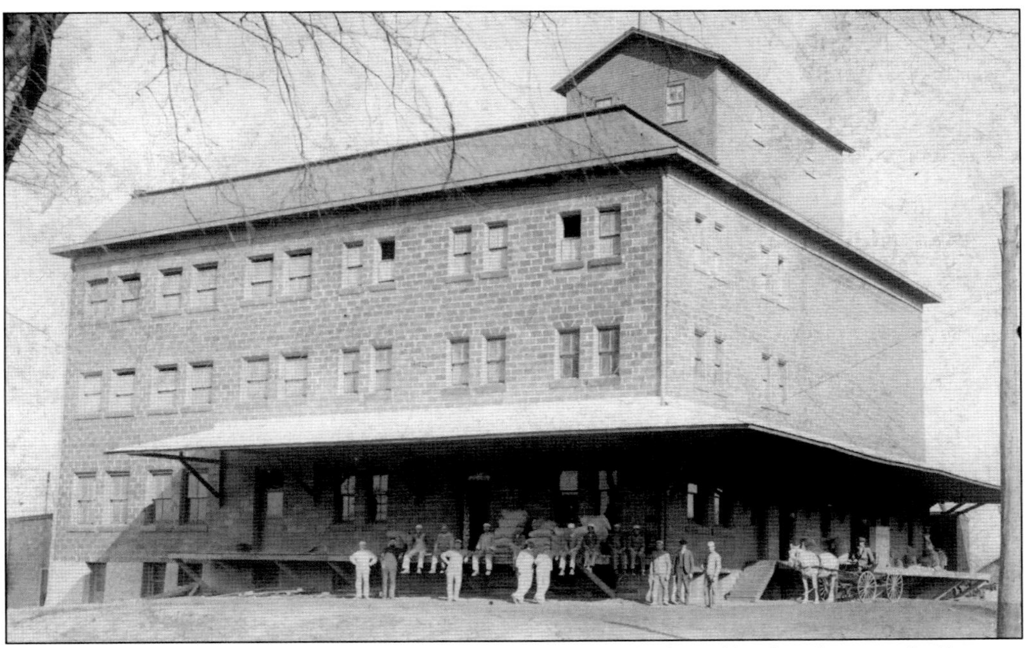

After a disastrous fire in May 1908, Richards Milling was rebuilt and back in business by January 1909. For the next 50 years, this mill, pictured here in 1912, dominated the landscape of Cortland both physically and economically. The owners and officers were community leaders who changed the town in many ways. (Courtesy of Dave Cover.)

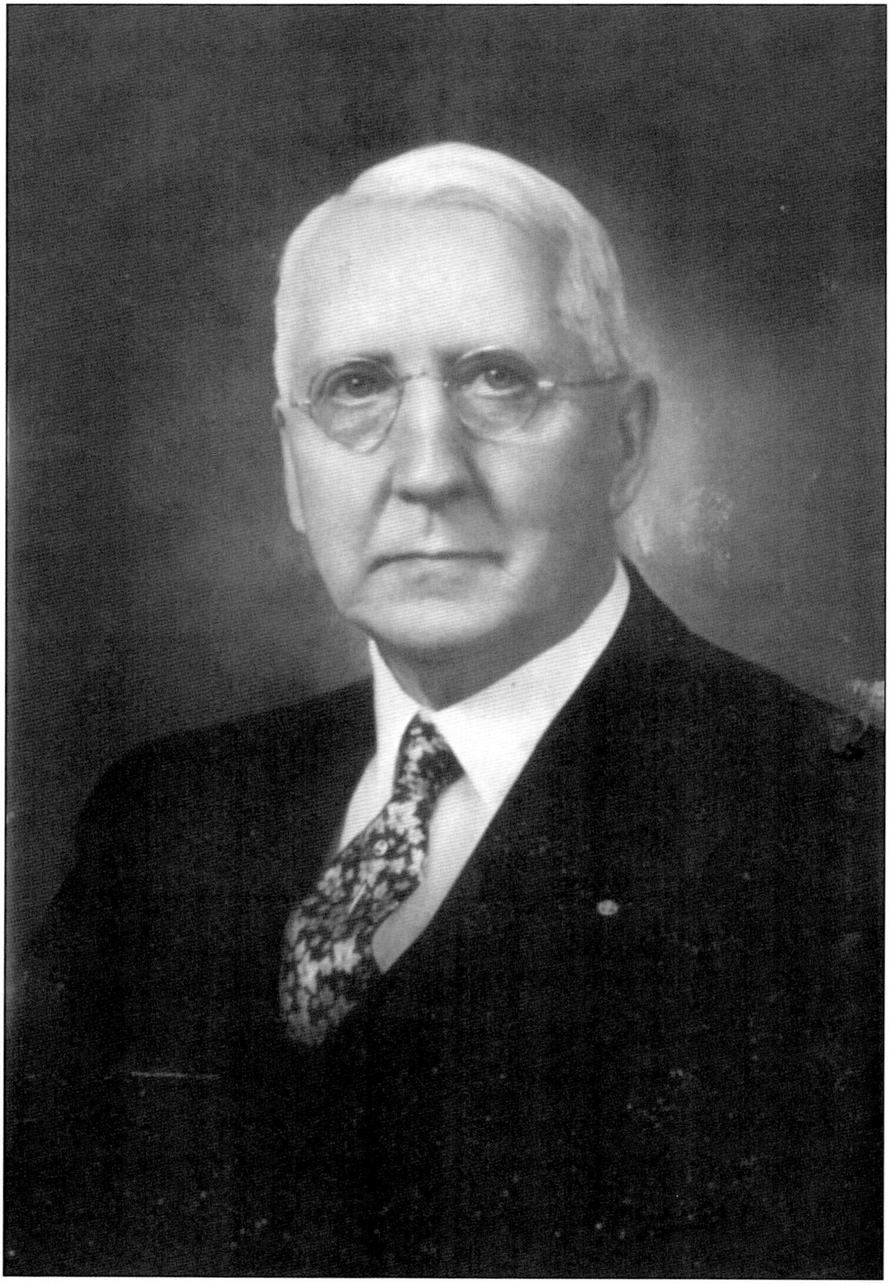

In 1882, Nelson M. Richards II was newly married to Ida Burrows and was a sewing machine salesman. In 1883, he saved up about $300 to go into the feed business. He rented the building shown on the next page, with the store downstairs while and he and Ida lived upstairs. There were three other feed stores in town, plus a flour and feed mill near the High Street and Main Street intersection; however, that mill ran by a water wheel, and when the weather was dry there often was not enough water to power the mill for more than a few hours. In 1885, Richards purchased an old steam threshing engine and a feed grinder and began to grind grain for farmers. (Courtesy of Walt Richards.)

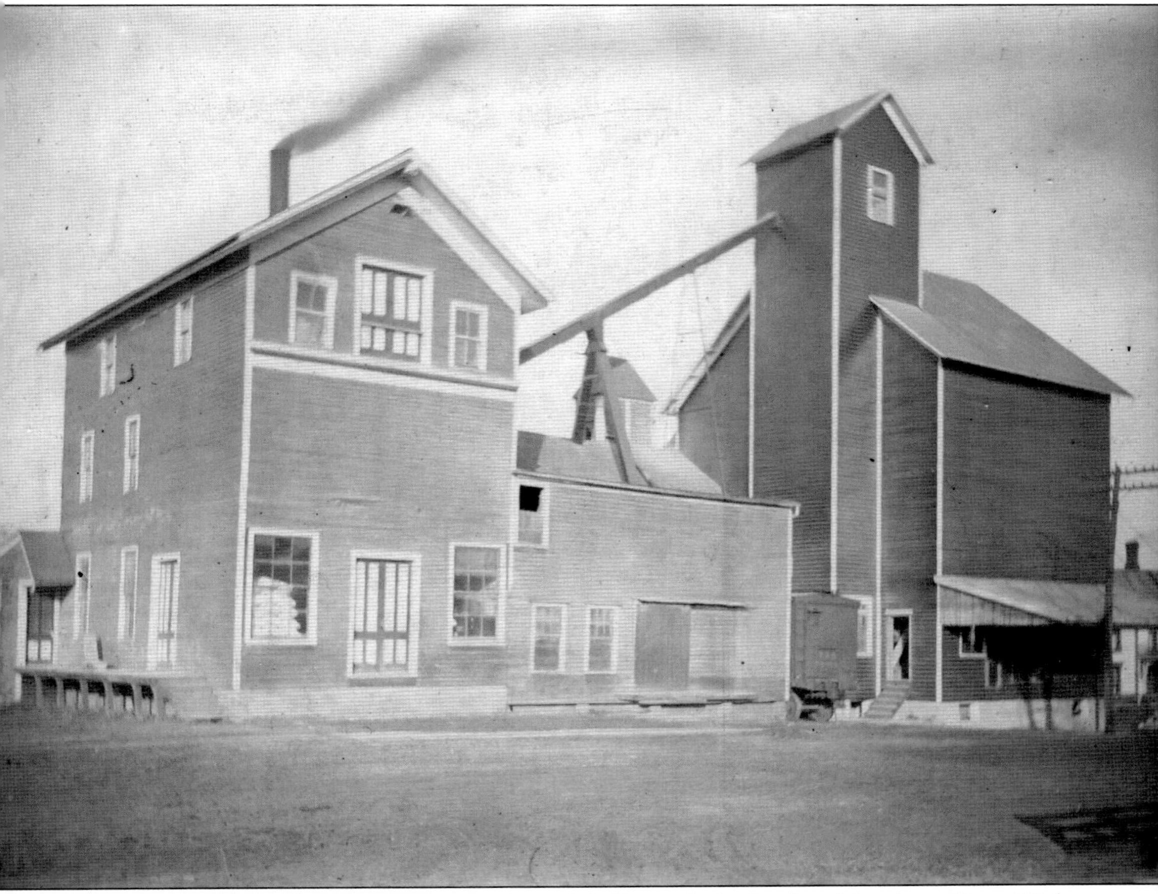

About 1892, Richards bought machinery that M.C. Kennedy had ordered for the mill on High Street, but he had not installed it before the mill burned in 1891. This new equipment would be installed in the building on the left in this image. It meant that the Richards family living in that space, which included three children, needed to move. They ended up settling in a house on Market Street. A railroad siding was installed in the building in 1900. The cheap cost of supplies arriving in bulk by rail helped the company stay in business and grow. A small grain elevator was erected on the railroad siding around 1904. (Courtesy of William Harned.)

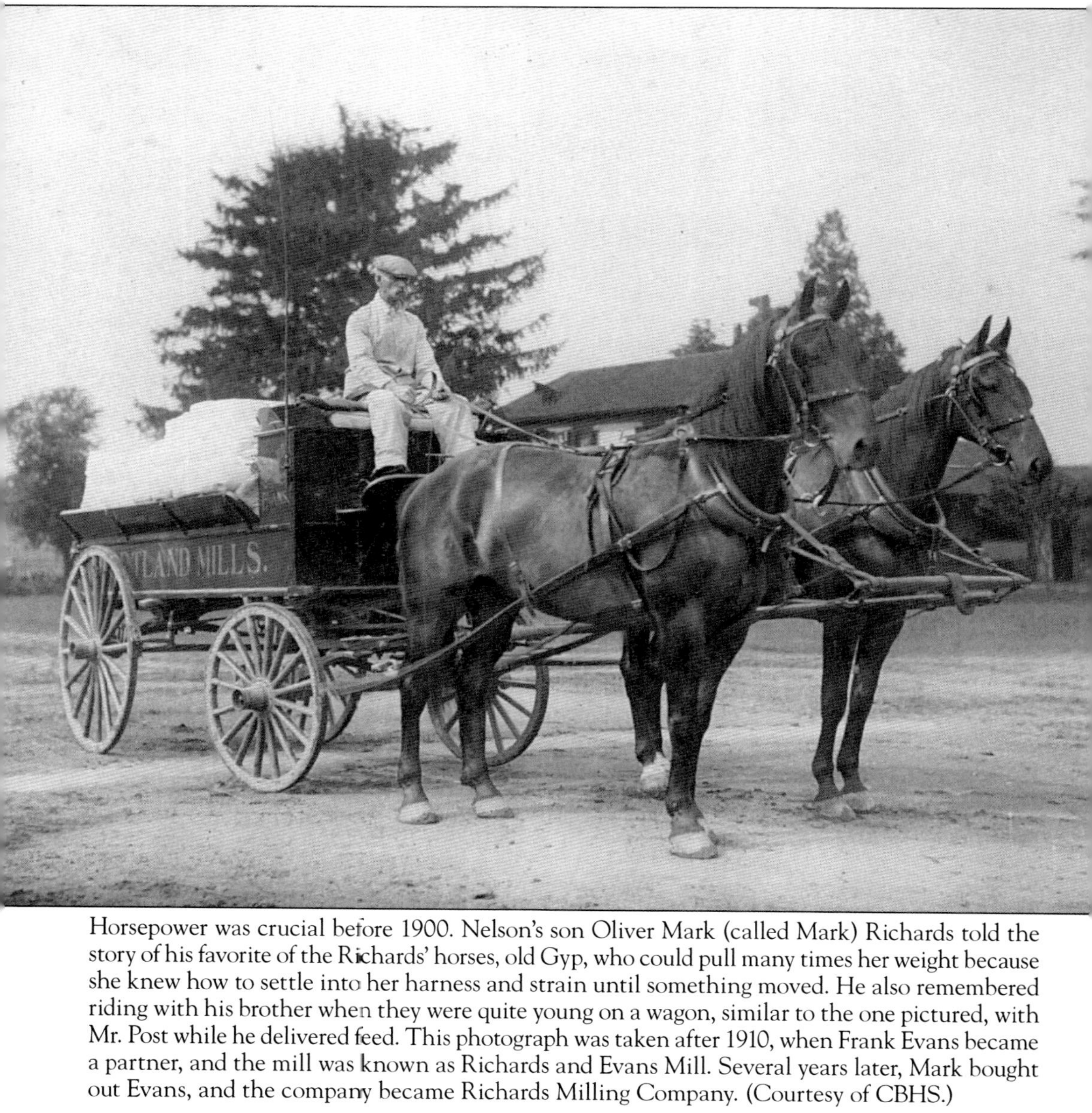

Horsepower was crucial before 1900. Nelson's son Oliver Mark (called Mark) Richards told the story of his favorite of the Richards' horses, old Gyp, who could pull many times her weight because she knew how to settle into her harness and strain until something moved. He also remembered riding with his brother when they were quite young on a wagon, similar to the one pictured, with Mr. Post while he delivered feed. This photograph was taken after 1910, when Frank Evans became a partner, and the mill was known as Richards and Evans Mill. Several years later, Mark bought out Evans, and the company became Richards Milling Company. (Courtesy of CBHS.)

The mill was a success, but in May 1908 it caught fire and burned to the ground. New, modern milling equipment was bought. To house the mill, Mark Richards built a huge tile-covered building. The concrete was mixed in large mortar boxes and wheeled to the forms in wheelbarrows. Timbers for joists and cribbing were cut by handsaws. The hole for the basement was scooped out with two-handled scoops pulled by horses. Workers labored for 10 hours a day. (Courtesy of CBHS.)

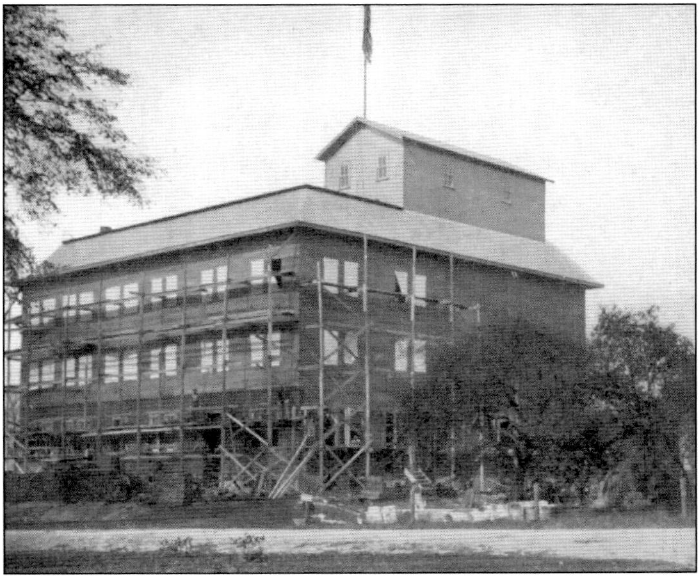

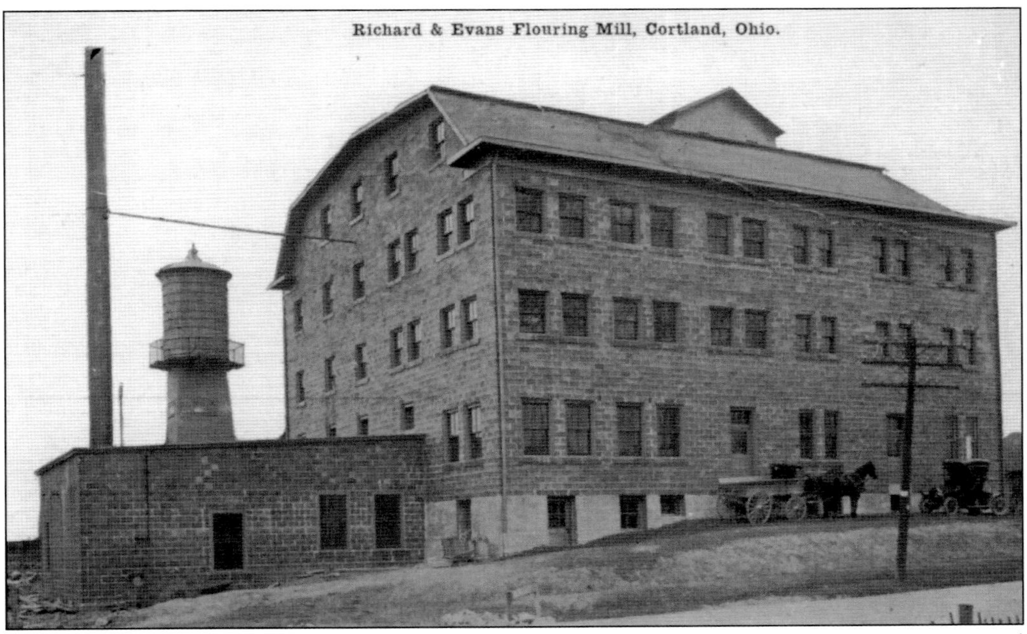

The new mill had a larger capacity than could be used by local farmers, so they began to travel to cities about 50 to 60 miles from Cortland to sell their products to bakeries and stores, and the mill became a commercial mill. This was a successful enterprise until World War II, when people started buying bread in stores and bakeries instead of baking it themselves, and the larger bread makers used western wheat with higher gluten. The opening of the Panama Canal lowered shipping rates for western farmers getting their wheat to eastern US markets. There were some lean years. (Courtesy of Walt Richards.)

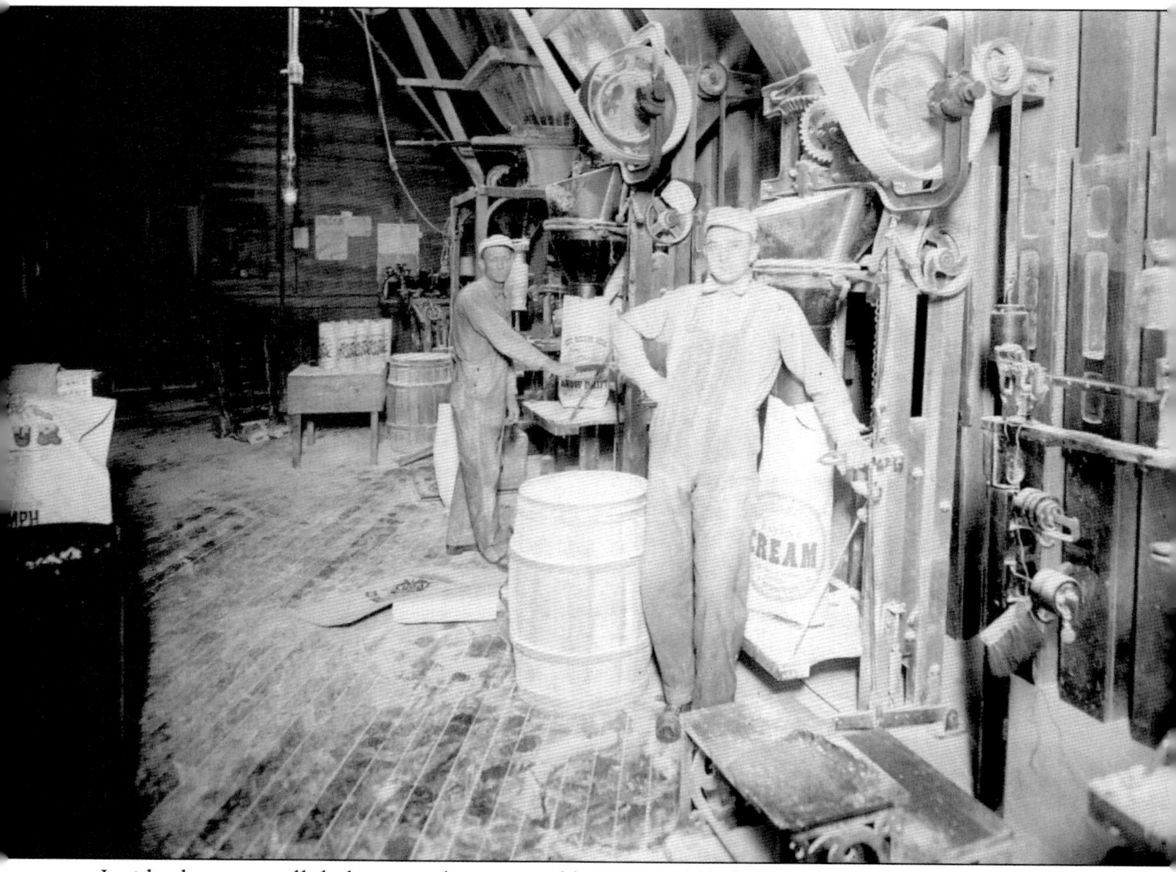

Inside the new mill, belts moved grain, and bags were filled and then stitched. Gaylord Kean is pictured here working at the mill. Almost everyone in town at one time or another worked for the mill. Equipment was installed to mix feed first by hand before the business bought automatic mixing and bagging machinery and endless belts running to cars for loading. The feed business grew. In 1914, the company was generating more electricity than it could use, so it began selling electricity to Cortland. From 1914 to 1926, townspeople had electricity until midnight before being turned off until morning. After 1926, electricity was sold to the company that would become Ohio Edison. (Courtesy of Louise Hadley.)

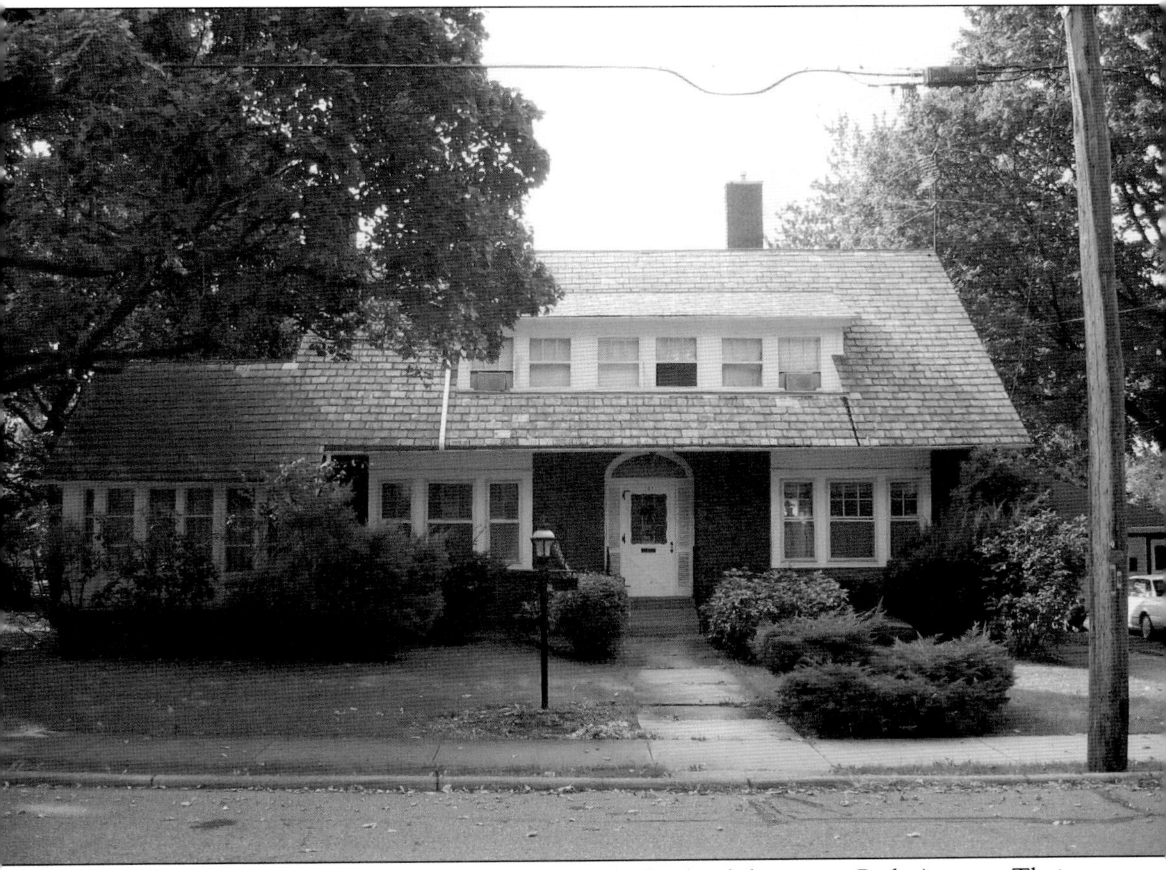

In 1920, Nelson M. Richards and his wife, Ida, built this brick house on Park Avenue. Their children were adults at the time. Daughter Lola had married Rev. Garfield Morgan and lived in Massachusetts. Son Walter died tragically when he accidentally drowned while attending Cornell University. Son Mark, secretary-treasurer of the company, married Gertrude Hocking in 1913 and lived on Market Street with their five children. When Nelson Richards II died in 1938, this brick house was remodeled as the office for the mill. The community lost someone who had energy, foresight, and talent who had a great impact on the town. His son Mark became president of the firm when times were changing for flour and feed mills. The area was evolving from agrarian to industrial, and fewer and fewer families had their own livestock. (Courtesy of William Hallett.)

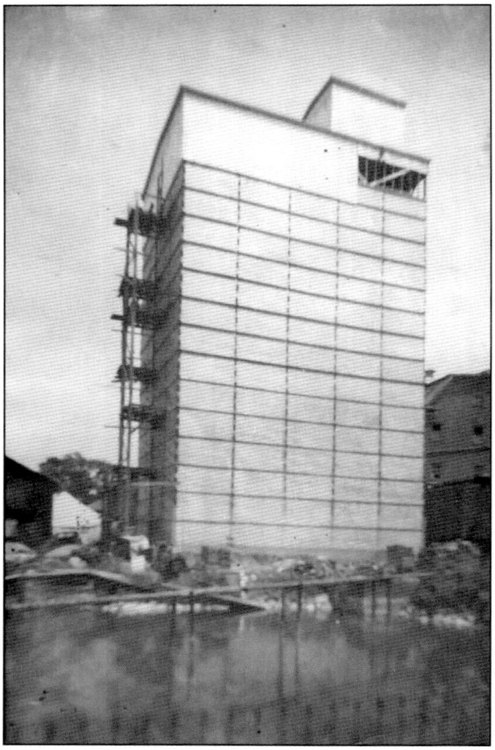

Just before World War II, the company built a large grain and bulk feed elevator. This enabled them to handle a greatly expanded business, and shipments went to seven states. The grain elevator was built by laying two-by-six-inch planks flat on top of each other and nailing them together. There were 20 compartments for each type of ingredient in a feed mixture. From the top of the elevator, one could see the causeway on Mosquito Lake at Mecca. In 2011, when the elevator became the last of the mill to be torn down, it took a few days to dig through those planks to topple the structure. The compartments can be seen in the photograph below. (At left, courtesy of Flo Hutton; below, Duane Jesse.)

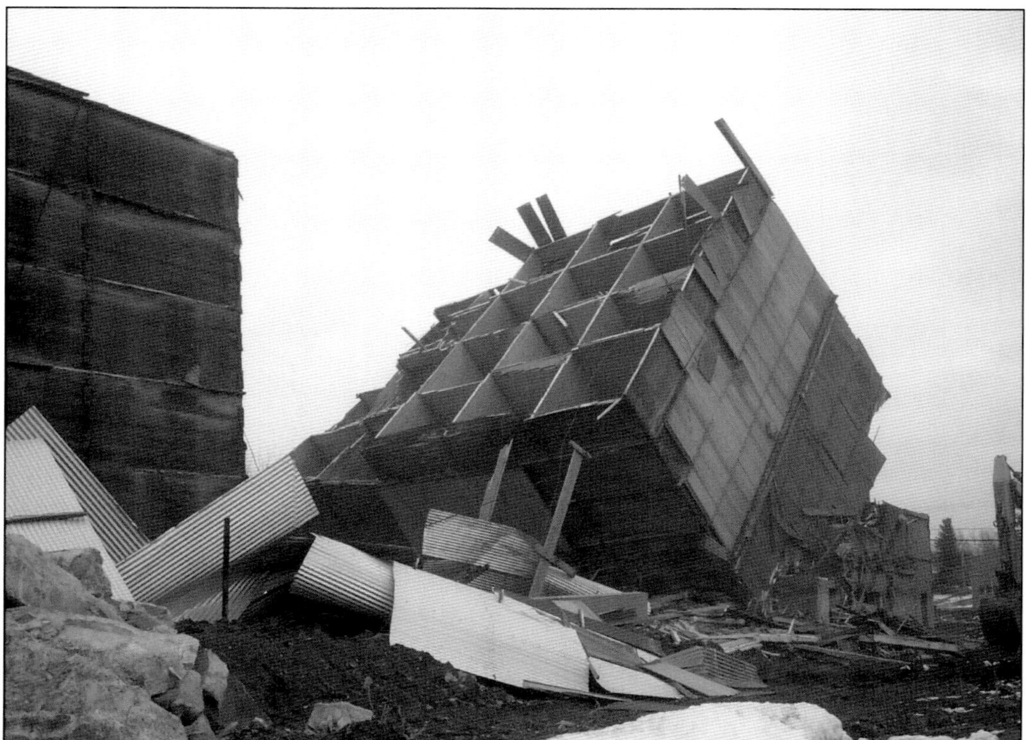

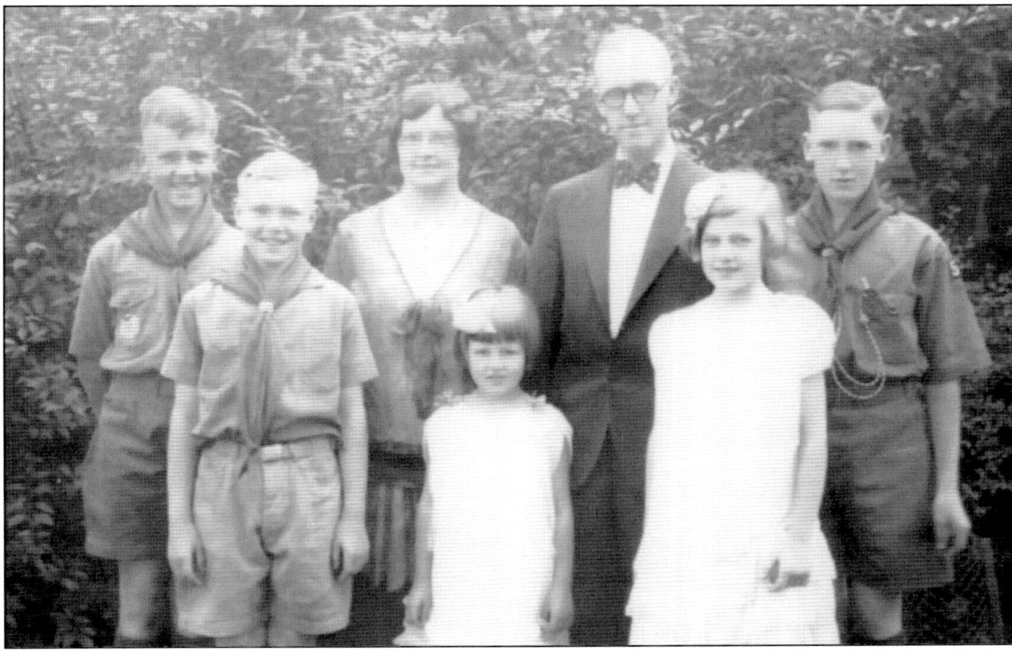

Mark and Gertrude Richards and their children appear here in 1929. From left to right are children Nelson, Richard, Ruth, Barbara, and Walter. The boys were active in the Boy Scouts, while the whole family participated in 4-H for the Trumbull County Fair. Mark was the mayor just before electricity was to be sold to the village, but he resigned to avoid conflict. He was also the president of the school board when Cortland High School was built in 1923. The photograph below is the original family homestead on Market Street where Mark grew up. (Above, courtesy of Walt Richards; below, William Hallett.)

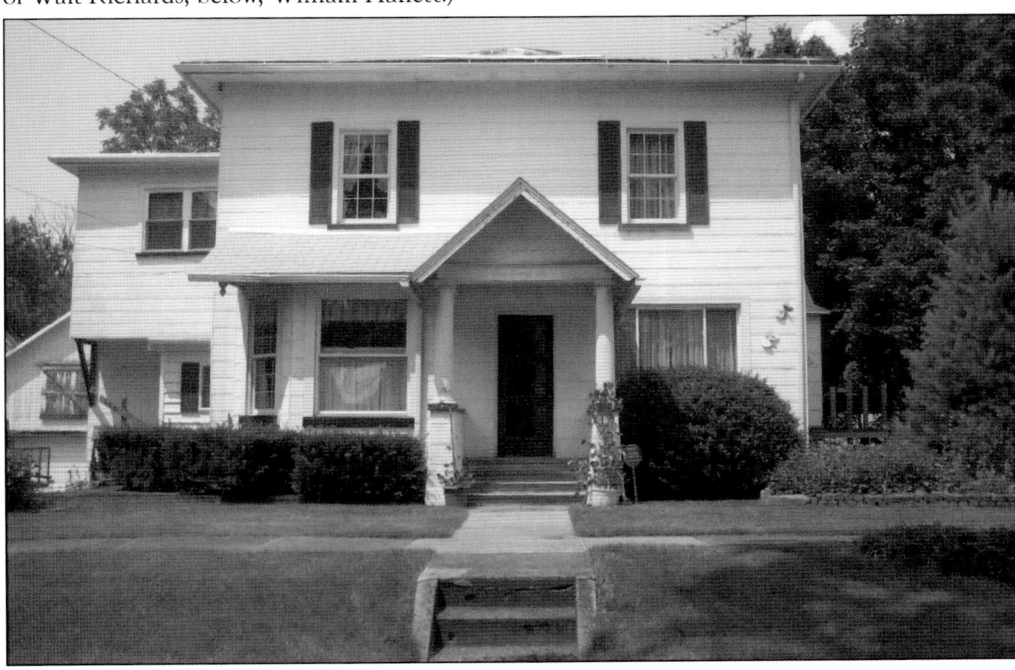

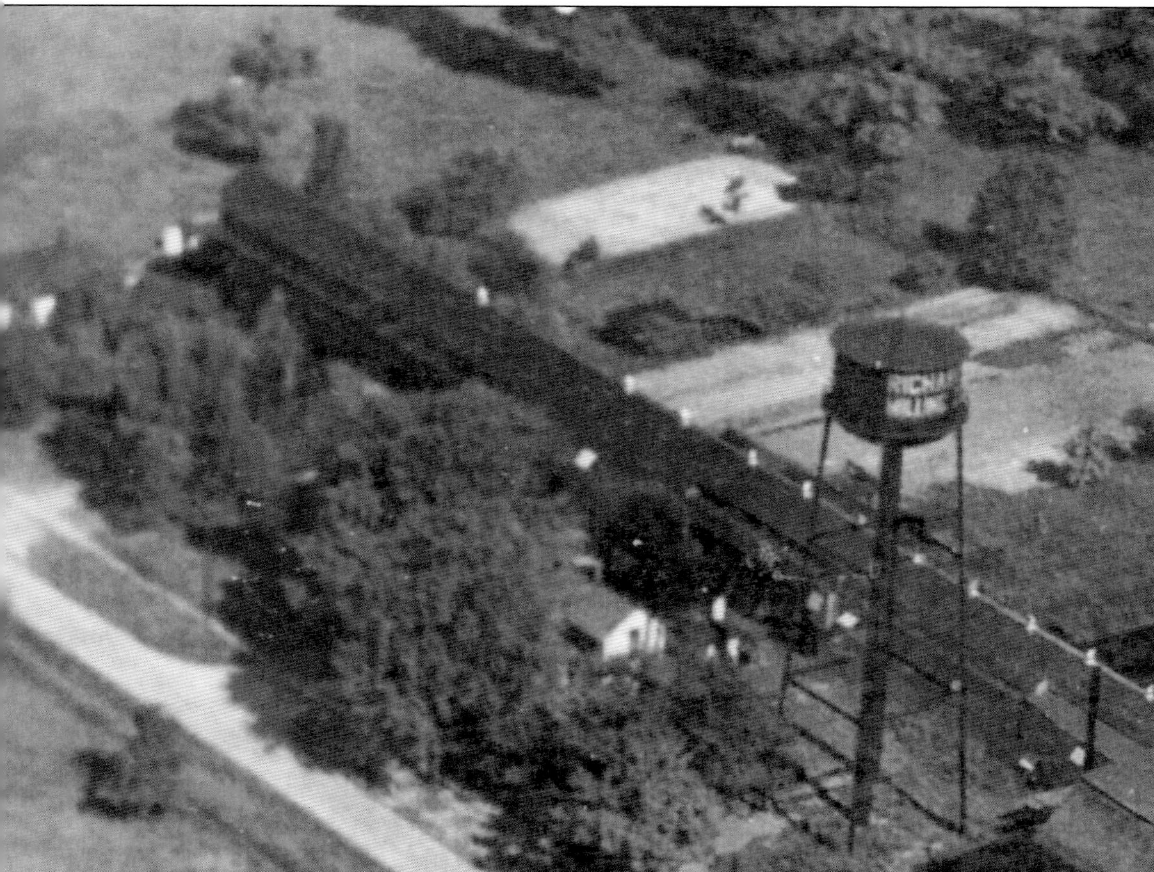

This 1950s aerial photograph shows the Richards milling complex. At this time, Mark Richard's son Walter was the president of the company, and business was not good. The mill closed in 1962 after 80 years in business, a victim of changing times. West Main Street is the diagonal road on

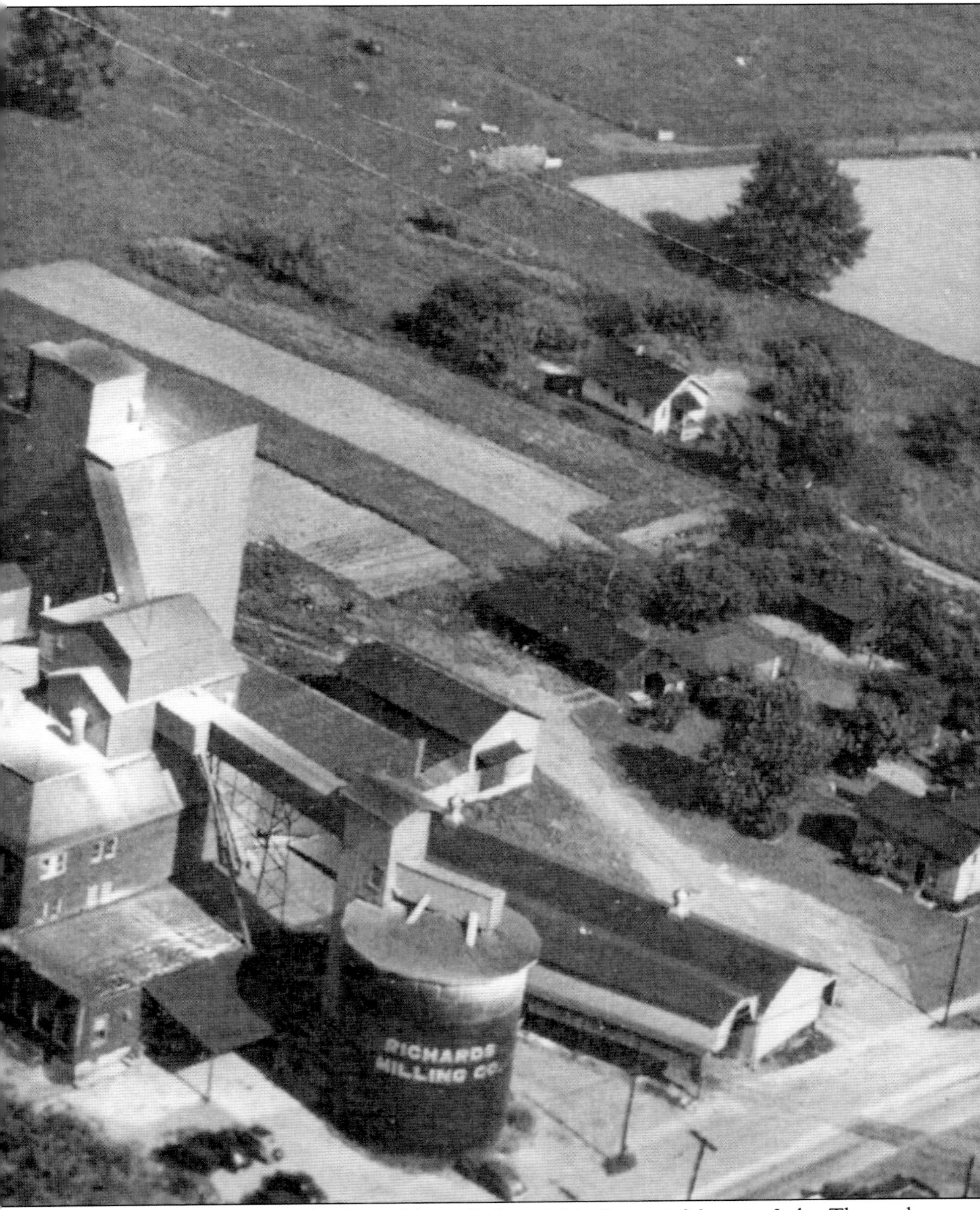

the left side of the photograph. West of the mill, down Main Street, is Mosquito Lake. The road in the lower right corner is Mecca Street. Ainsley's gas station was on the northeast corner of this intersection. (Courtesy of Walt Richards.)

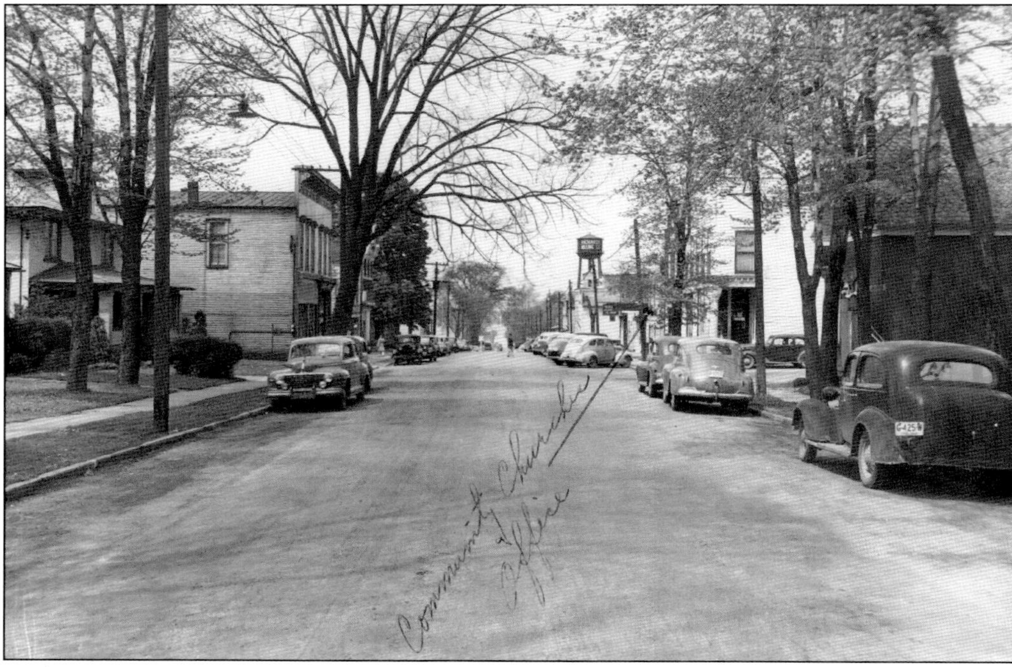

Looking east on West Main Street, downtown Cortland appears here in 1946. The first building on the right is the Cortland bank, while the first building on the left is McCurley's Hospital. At the end of the street, the tower of Richards Milling is visible. In the picture below is the same view of West Main Street but in the 1920s. Model Ts line the street. (Both, courtesy of the United Methodist Church.)

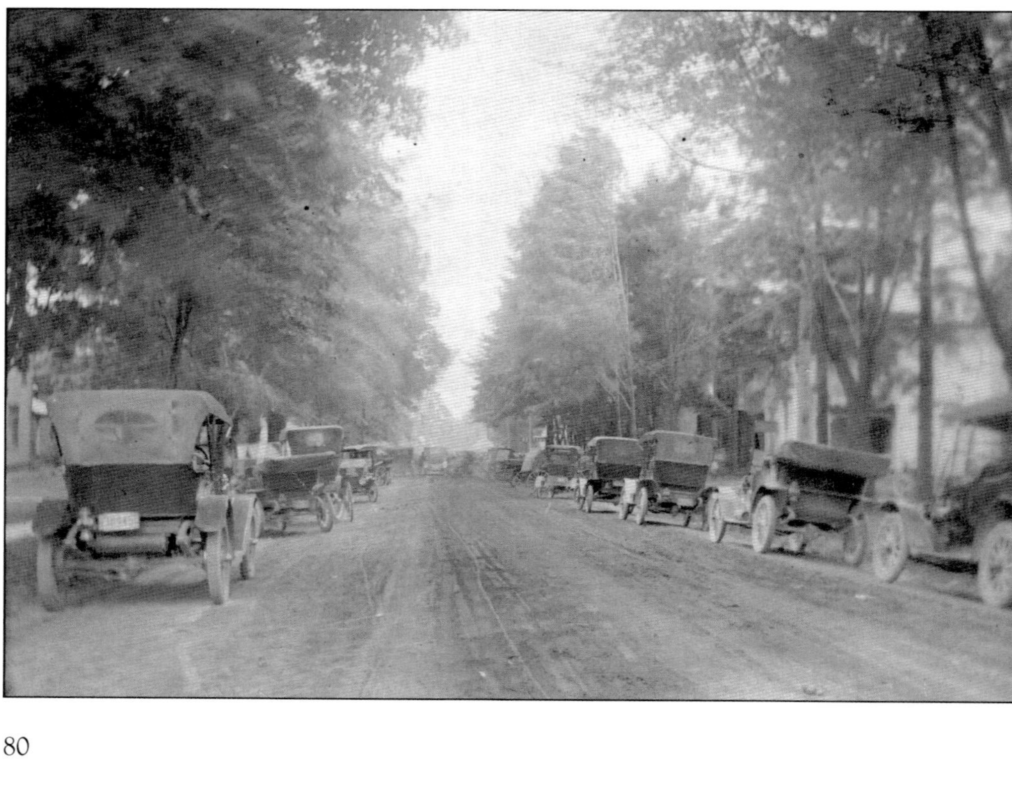

Five

New Century, Many Changes

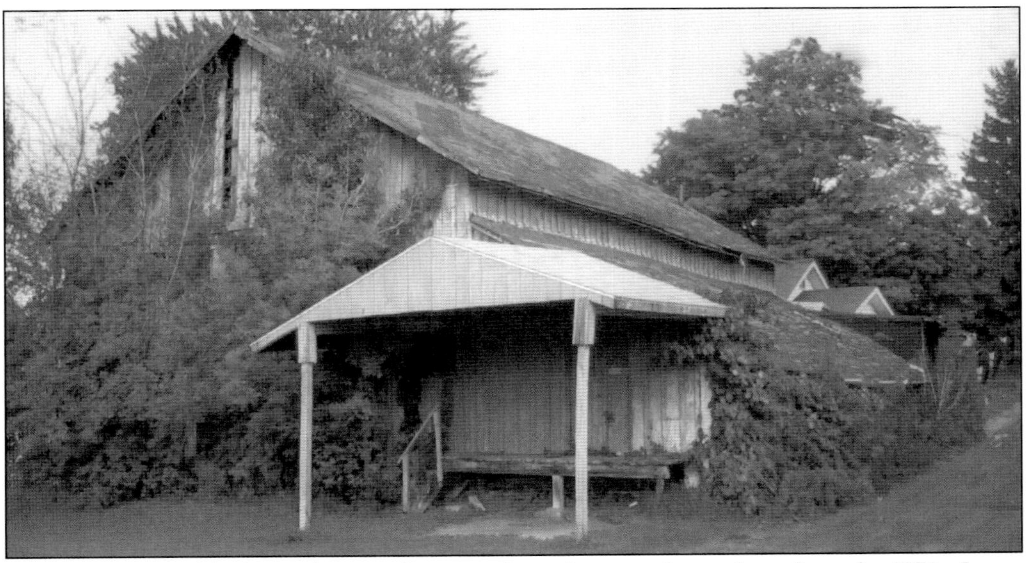

This old livery stable, located across the street from the train depot, dates from the 1870s. It was near the original site of the town hall before that building was moved to Lattin Street. Two hotels were within 100 feet of this 19th-century "rent-a-horse" business. It survived into the 1900s, when automobiles became the transportation of choice; it then became a storage barn for Shaffer Feed after it opened a feed store across the tracks. Slowly, the condition deteriorated, and the building was torn down around 2010. While standing, it was one of the last ties to the horse-and-buggy days. Dairies, such as Reick-McJunkin (or Strait-McJunkin), Brookside, and Biggin's, also faded from the community's landscape. The following pages highlight just a few of the businesses that began in the 20th century and lasted for many years, some into the 21st century. (Courtesy of CBHS.)

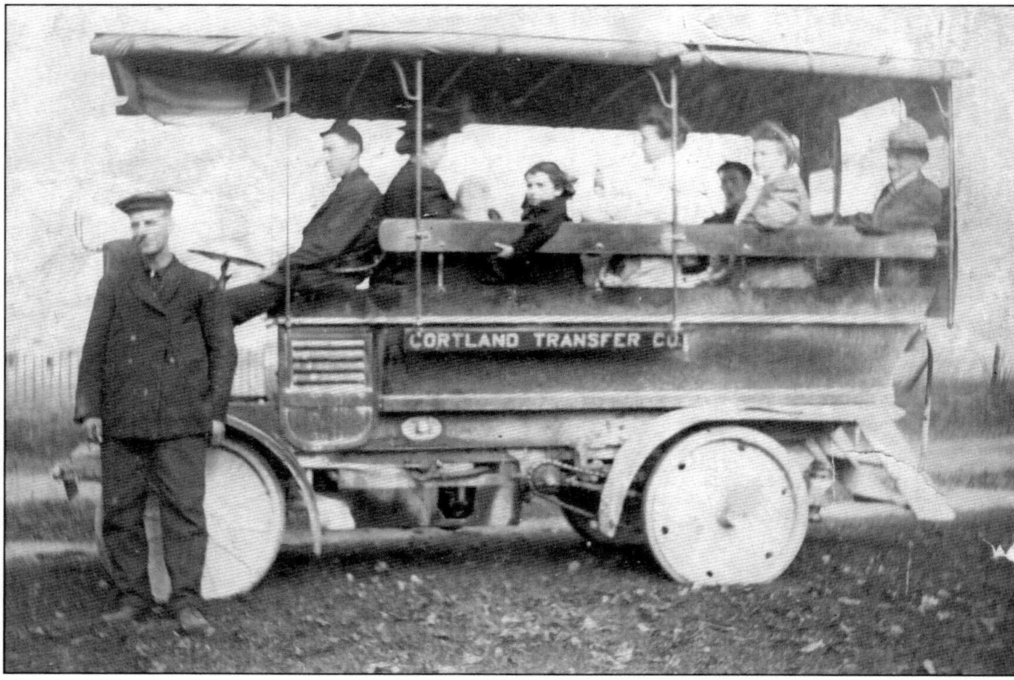

As the 20th century dawned, the first order of business seems to have been transportation. People were used to riding the train into Warren, but there were complaints about service. In 1908, the Cortland Transfer Company was formed and made four trips daily into Warren. The service was a huge success, and soon larger and more comfortable transfer automobiles were on the road. (Courtesy of CBHS)

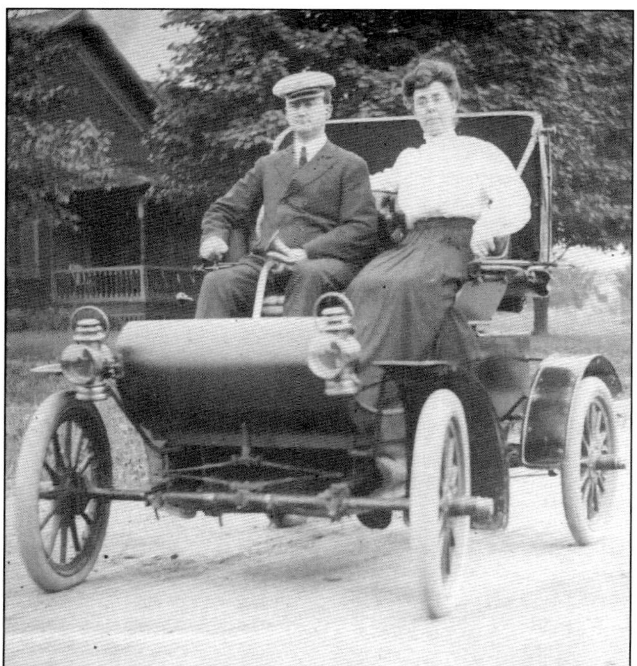

In 1912, there were 30 automobiles in Cortland. Pictured is one of the first in town that was owned by Harry S. and Alice Bacon Post. Harry was born in 1864, and his wife, a daughter of Henry and Kate Grim Bacon, was born in 1863. Harry was a grocer, taking over his father-in-law's store in the early 1900s. (Courtesy of Alvin Mizner.)

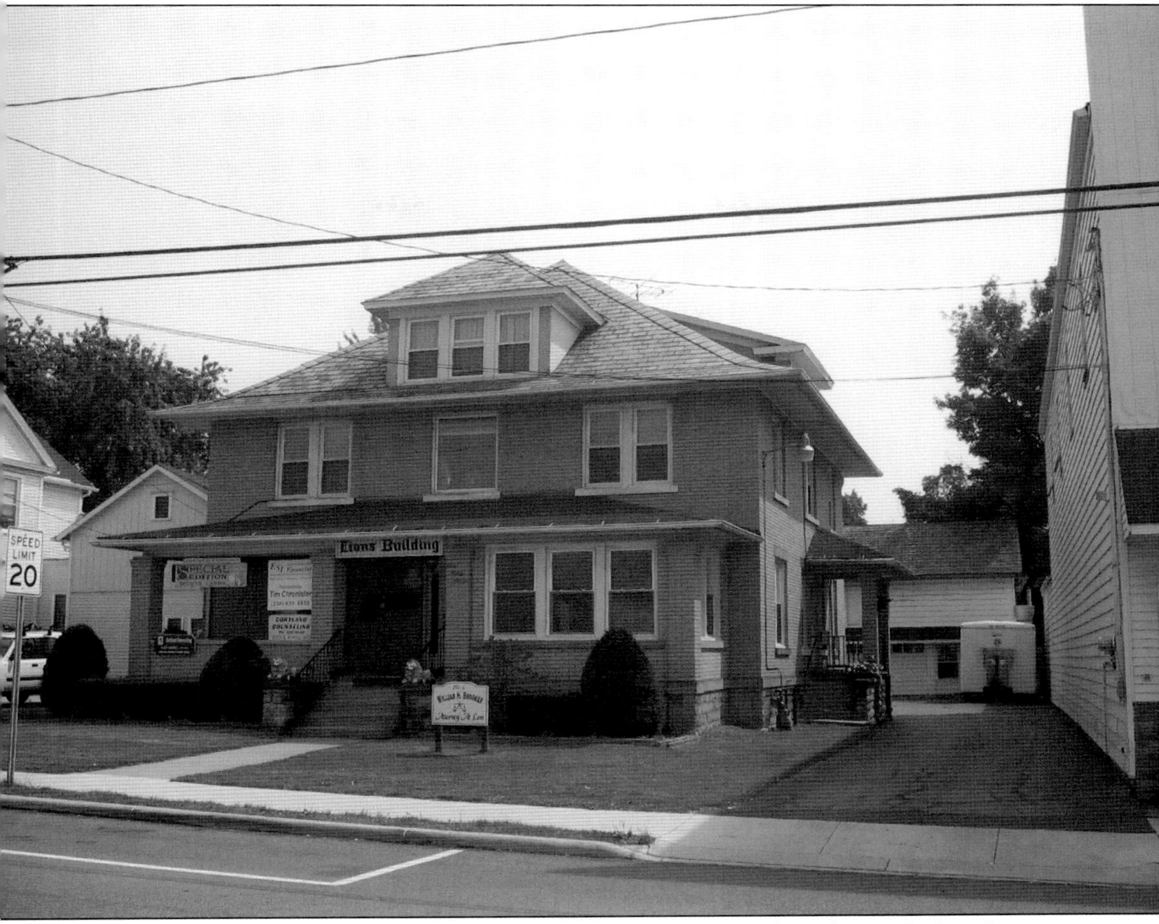

McCurley's Hospital was built in 1913 as a home for Dr. B.G. McCurley, who studied medicine in Chicago and returned in 1899 to open a practice in his hometown. As the home was constructed, McCurley planned on converting part of it into a hospital, which was completed in 1916. It was a state-of-the-art model for the times, with 10 beds, an operating room, and a sterilizing room, as well as x-ray and oxygen equipment. The doctor raised vegetables to supply food for his patients. Two nurses were on duty at all times, and more were called in when needed. During the flu epidemic of 1919, the hospital was constantly full. Even as the doctor and his family moved out to provide more room for the ill, there still were not any open beds. Dr. McCurley operated the hospital until 1938 and served as physician for the community for 51 years. He died in 1951 at the age of 75. (Courtesy of William Hallett.)

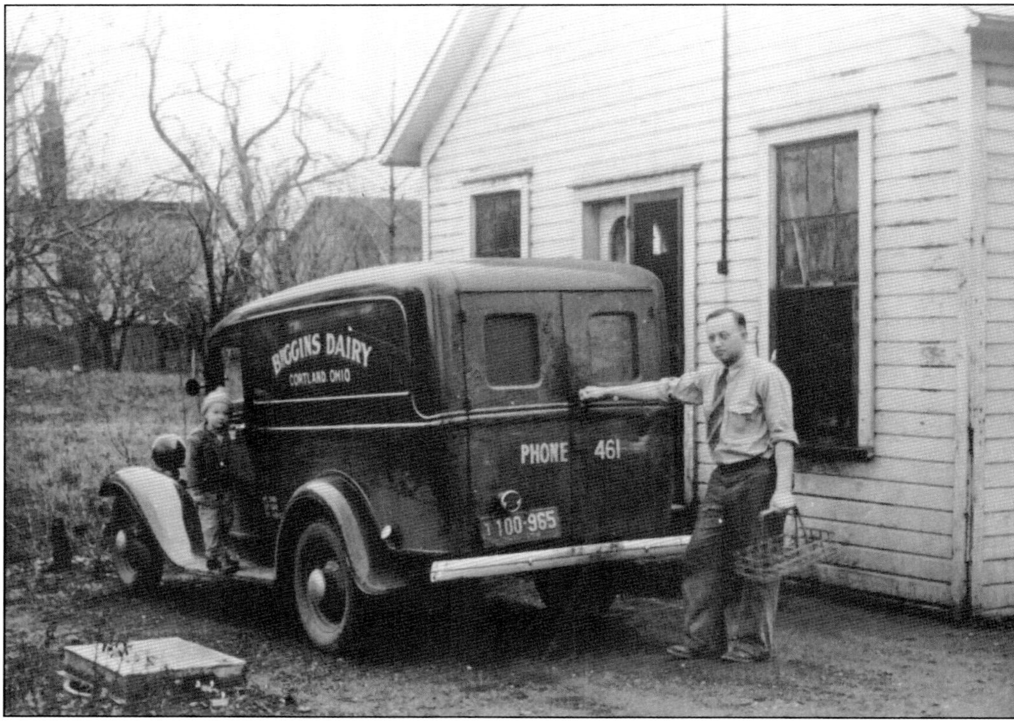

Lake Vista Retirement Community on Mecca Street was once the Biggin's Dairy farm, owned by Orlo Biggin, with a farmhouse located where the clubhouse is now. The photograph above is of the milk house that was in front of the farmhouse; Don Biggin and son Gordon pose for the camera. Orlo Biggin was Don's father. Many people in town remember going to his shop on Erie Street for ice cream. The advertisement below was frequently found on the programs of events and in the yearbooks of schools in the community. (Above, courtesy of CBHS; below, Don Biggin.)

Compliments of

Biggin's Ice Cream Company

Cortland, Ohio

Phone (Cortland) A-492

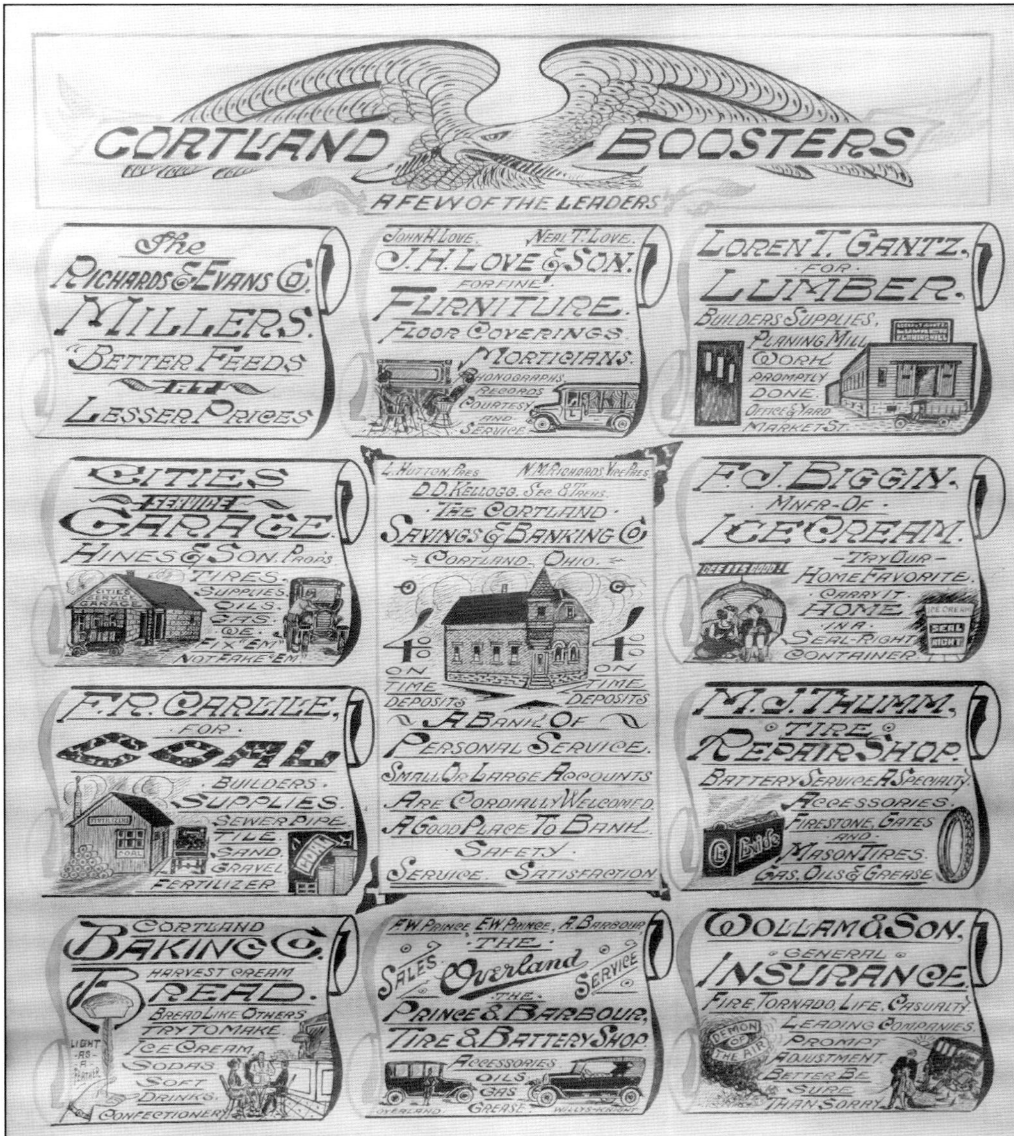

Insurance providers were not new in Cortland. W.A. Craft was a Phoenix insurance agent in the 1870s. In the 1910s, three insurance agencies appeared and have thrived for close to 100 years: Wollam, Greenwood, and Bowers. This hand-drawn, pen-and-ink poster of Cortland Boosters dates from the 1920s and comes from Wollam & Son general insurance (lower right corner.) It features many of the businesses in Cortland at that time and is a unique piece of local history. (Courtesy of Wollam Insurance Company.)

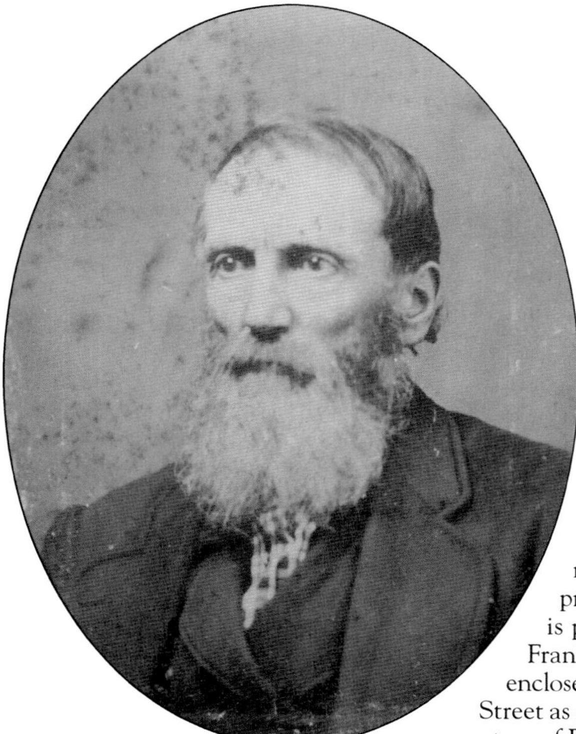

Bowers Insurance Group began under the name C.J. Bowers Insurance in 1913 and primarily insured farms. Charles J. Bowers is pictured at left. Bowers's wife and son J. Frank Bowers continued the business using the enclosed front porch of this house on North High Street as an office after Bowers died in 1934. (Both, courtesy of Bowers Insurance Group.)

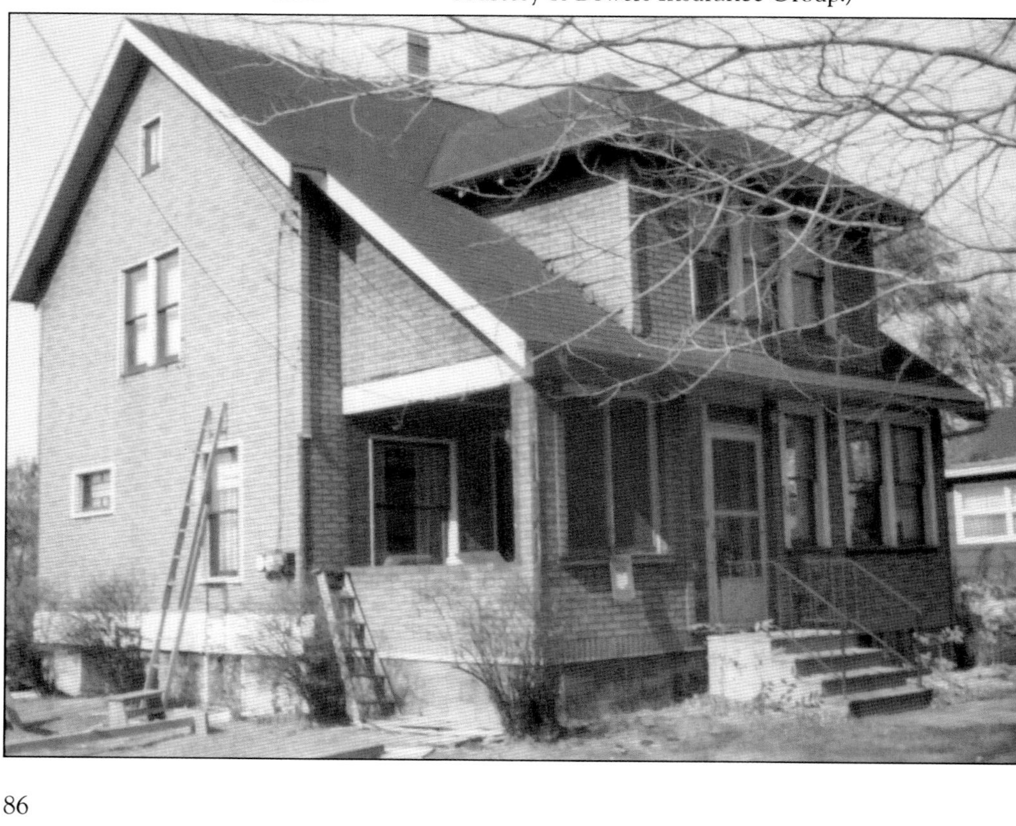

In 1940, J. Frank Bowers's son Paul C. Bowers, shown at right, joined the agency part-time to add automobile insurance to the group. In 1962, Paul became president of the company and expanded services to include life and health insurance. A new office building was constructed south of the family home, with additions in 1978 and later. This is the 1978 building, with agency members (from left to right) P. Bennett Bowers, Paul Bowers, Richard Rose, and Elmer Kassay Jr. posing for the opening. (Both, courtesy of Bowers Insurance Group.)

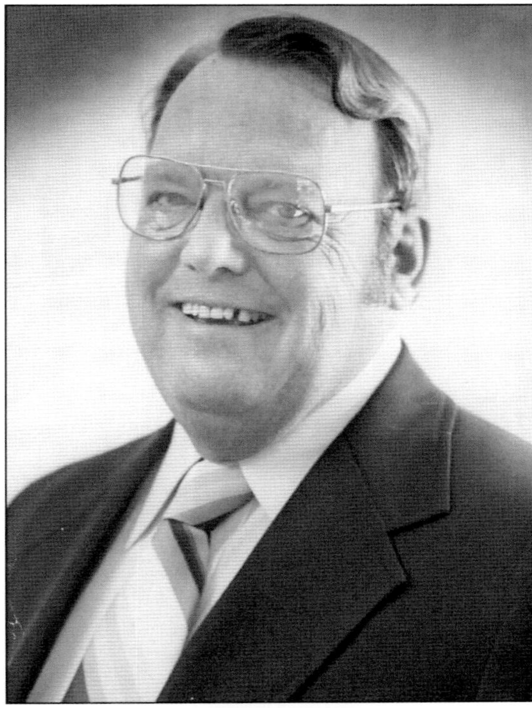

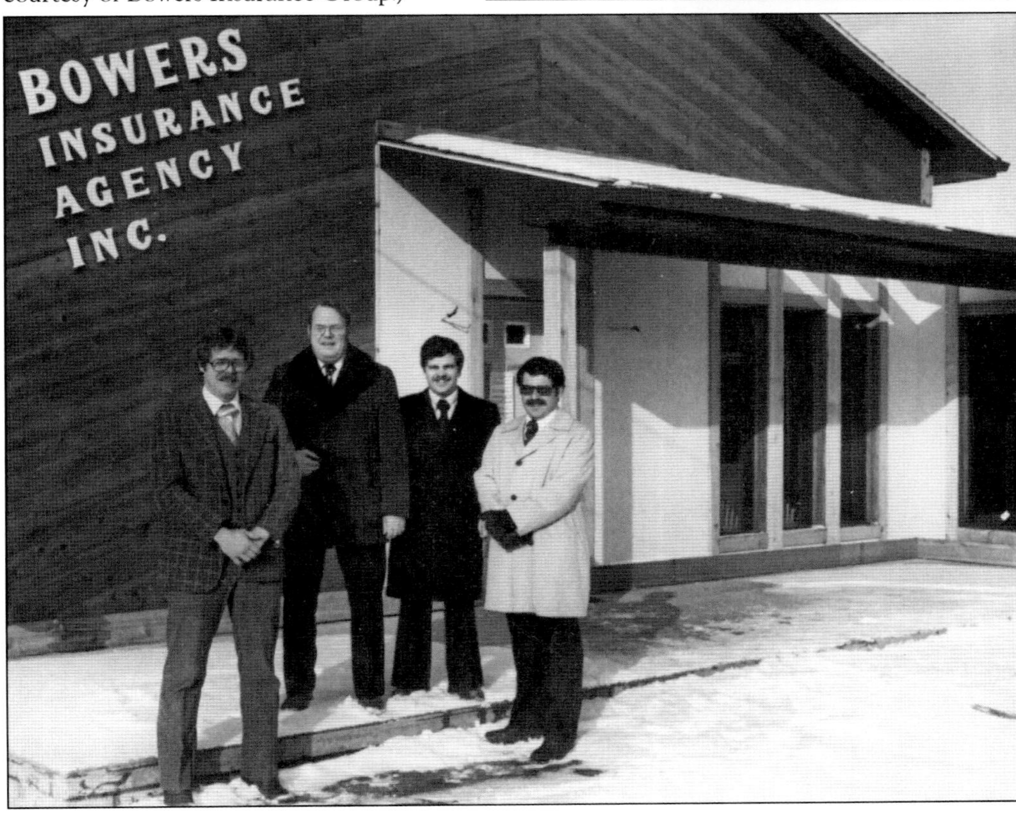

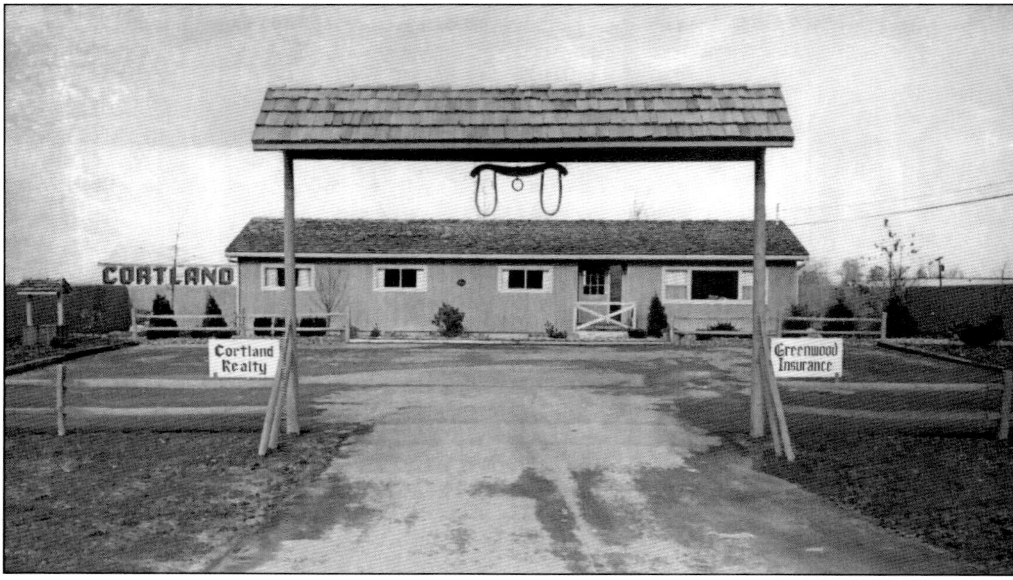

Greenwood Insurance was launched in 1959 by Robert Greenwood Sr. Robert had been in business together with his father, Wayne Greenwood, and brother Bud in their automobile dealership, but he took the opportunity to purchase an insurance business. Since then, five of his six children have grown up to become insurance agents, either with the family business or agencies of their own. (Courtesy of Robert Greenwood Jr.)

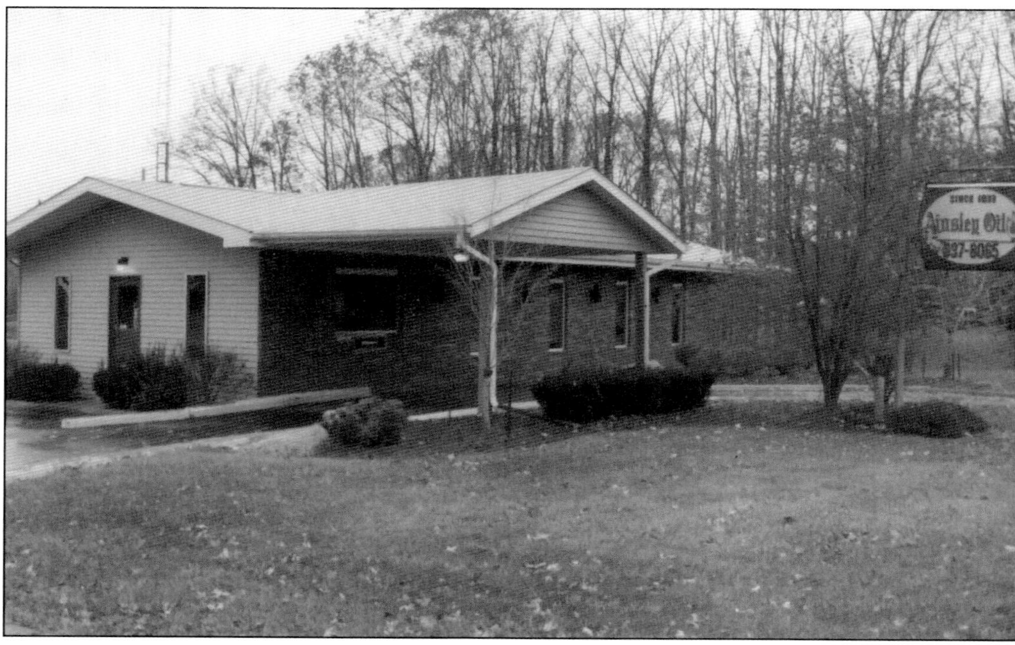

Ainsley Oil Company began in 1933 and was the first of several oil-, gas-, and fuel-related local companies to be owned by members of the Ainsley family. The company is located at 440 South Mecca Street and offers gasoline, diesel fuel, motor oil, grease, cartridges, pails, drums, and kerosene. The gas station on the corner of West Main and Mecca Streets was one of the first in town. (Courtesy of Robert Greenwood Jr.)

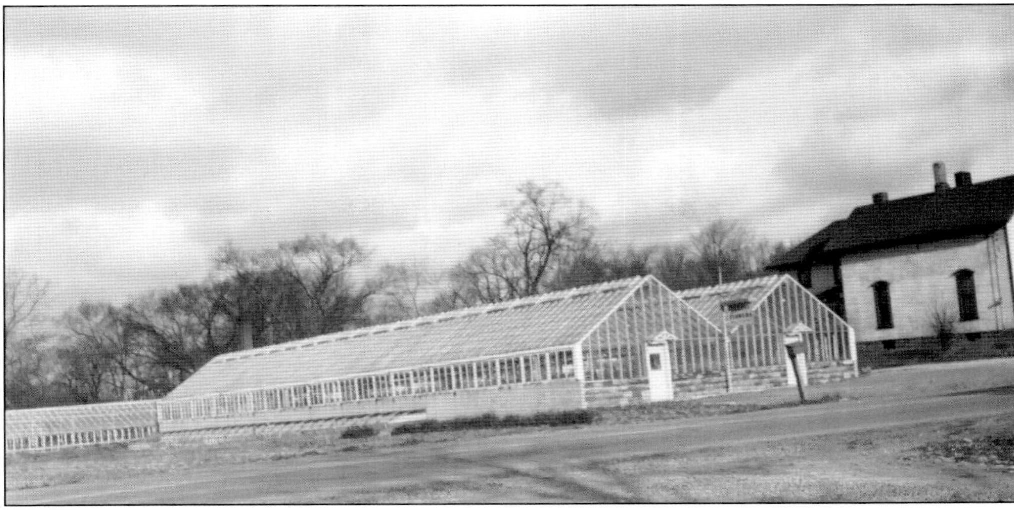

About 1929, Lewis Stanley Hutton and his wife, Helen Bettiker Hutton, went into the greenhouse business and later added a florist shop, a combination that thrived and became one of the town's most attractive businesses for over 70 years. In 1962, five years after Lewis's death, Helen sold the business to Richard and June Blank, who continued the business under the Hutton name, with just a slight change to Huttons' Florist and Gift Shop, and later broadened the scope of the store by adding furniture and decorative items. (Both, courtesy of Florence Hutton.)

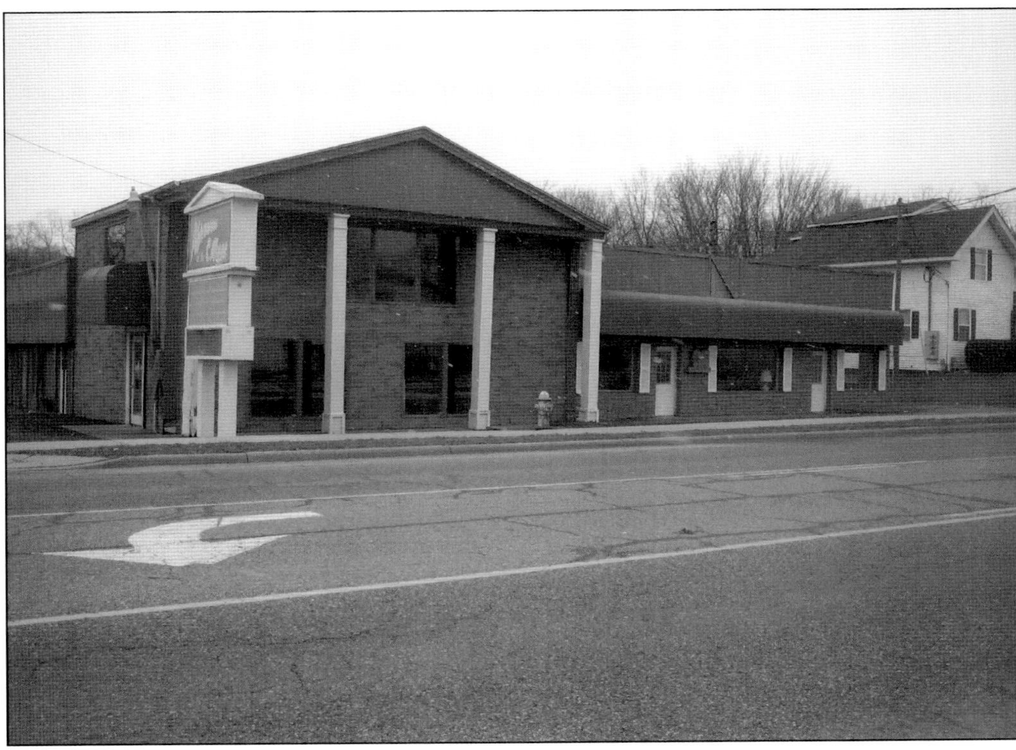

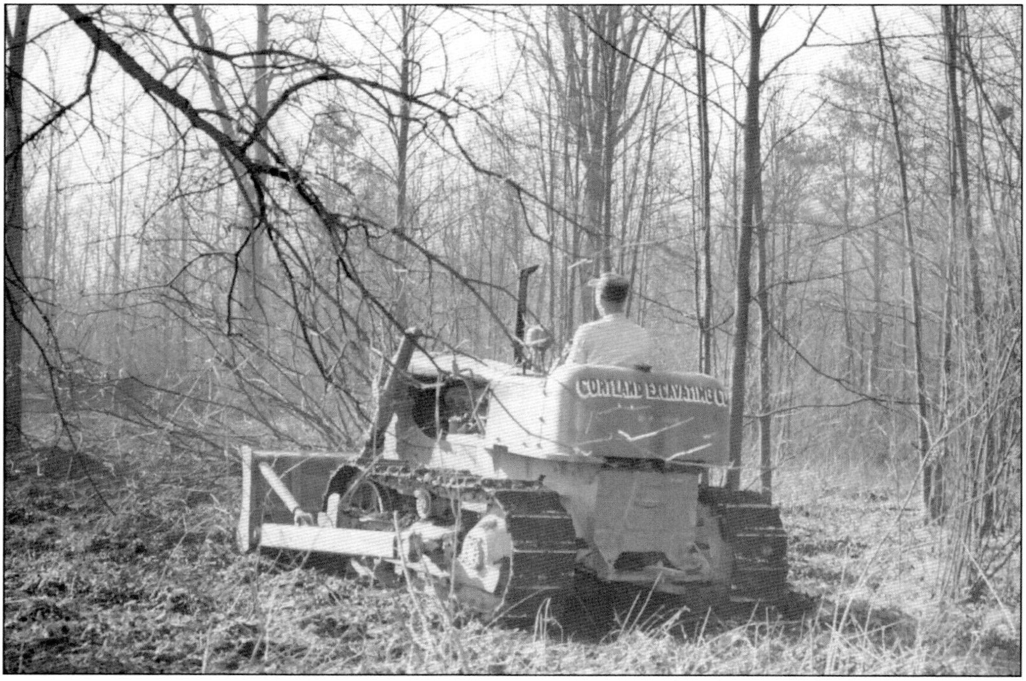

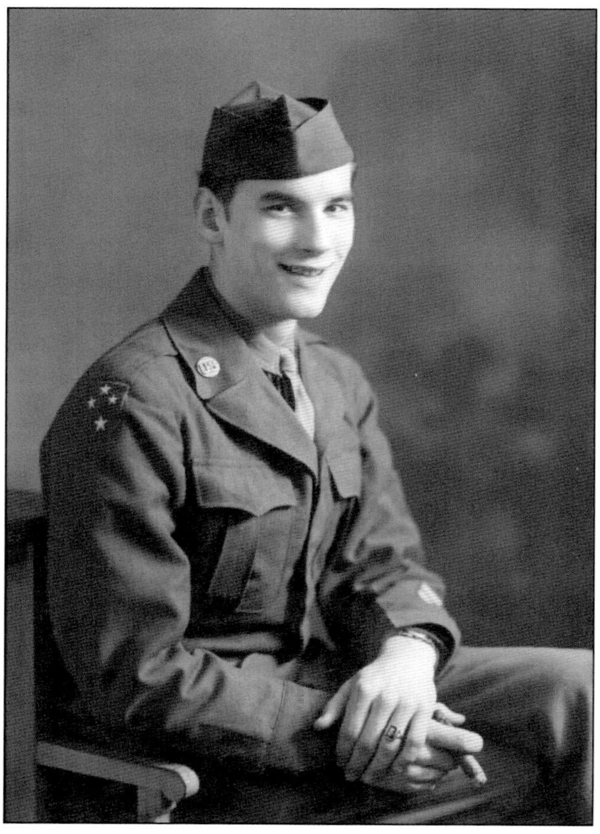

Cortland Excavating and Paving (above) was started by Verne Hutton in 1951. Verne, son of Lewis S. and Helen Bettiker Hutton, was born in 1926. He grew up helping in the family greenhouse business. In 1944, he graduated from Cortland High School and joined the US Army. The patch on his right shoulder (at right) is similar to the one worn by Gen. Colin Powell, signifying the American unit. After the war, he was a member of the fire department and served on the city's planning and zoning commission. He married Florence Pahon, and they had two sons, Rick and Tim. After his death in 1994, Florence and son Rick continued to operate the business. (Both, courtesy of Florence Hutton.)

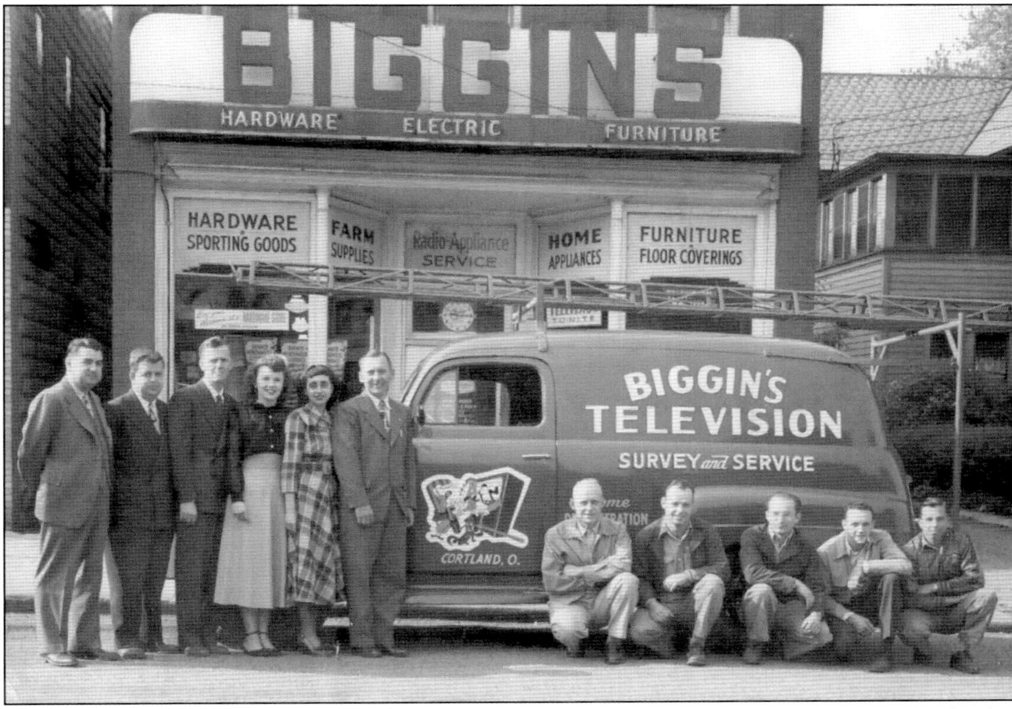

The Biggin family started out in the dairy business, but then family members opened other businesses in town, starting with a hardware store (above) on the south side of Main Street in the late 1940s. As television was embraced, family members branched out into electronics and soon had a large service department across the street (below.) Furniture was added, and the buildings expanded on the north side of the street, with a warehouse built where the old Oatley Hotel had been. Linville's Clothing, purchased from the Brubakers in 1964, was owned by Richard and Betty Biggin Linville. The clothing store is now Daybreak Music store in 2012. (Both, courtesy of CBHS and Peg Mellott.)

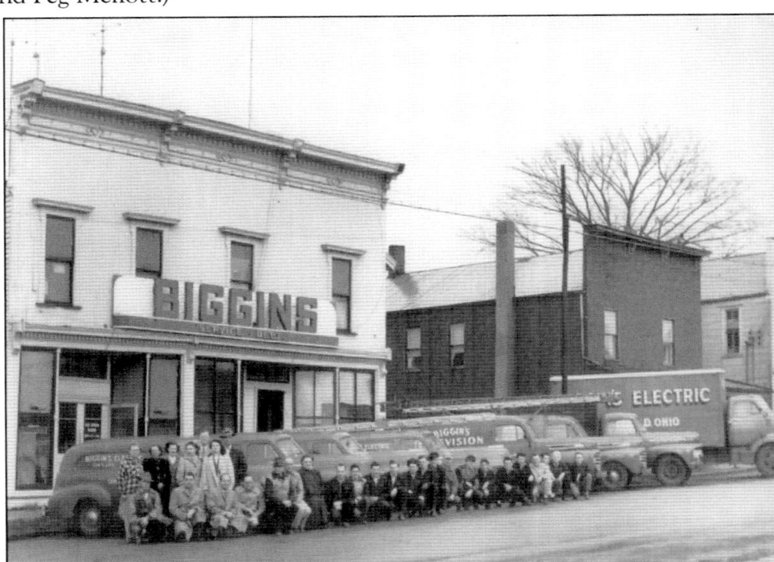

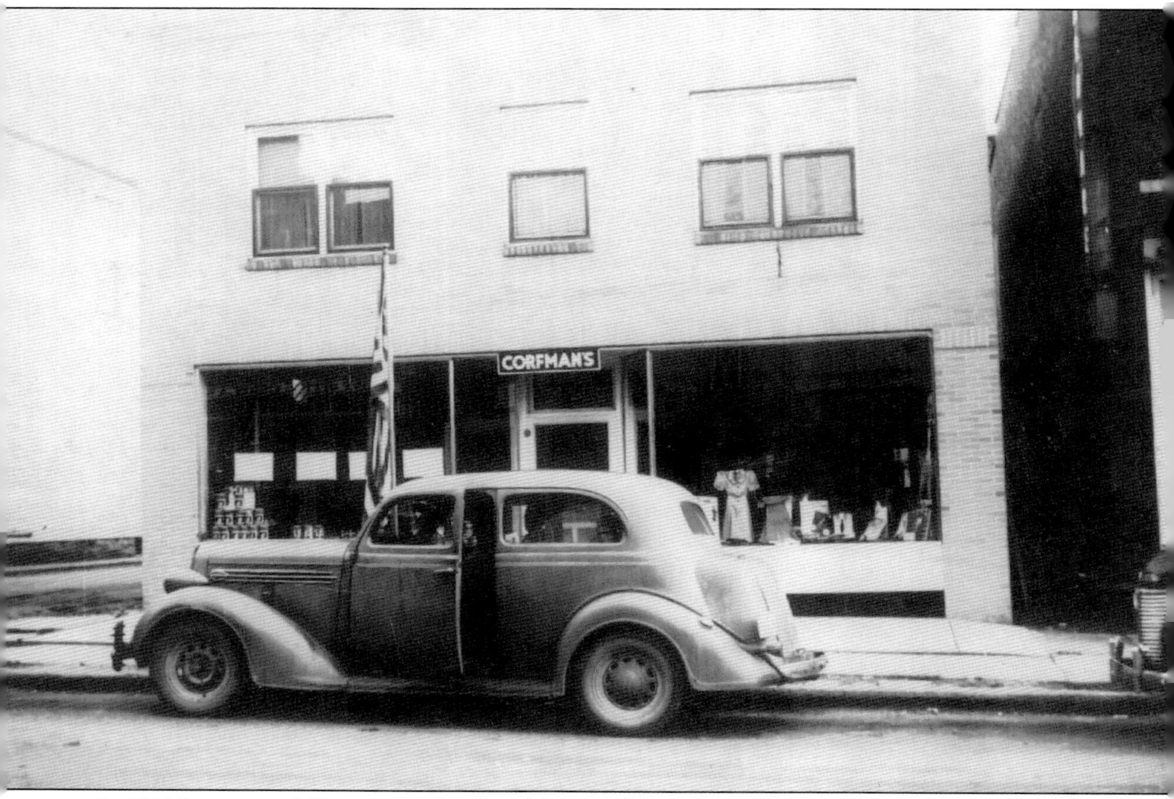

In 1914, Martin and Eleanor Corfman and their children arrived in town after purchasing a general store on the north side of Main Street. They lived in the Cortland Hotel until they could fix up an apartment over the store. In 1923, son Sherman, who had just married, bought his father's half interest in the store, and the parents moved away. After the big fire in 1939, when much of the south side of the street burned down, he bought the property on the southwest corner of North Bank and West Main Streets and built a new building, pictured here. The couple lived in one of the two apartments above the store until they built a home on Park Avenue. In 1962, they sold the store to Wilbur Biggin, who also owned the building next door. (Courtesy of W.J. Hallett.)

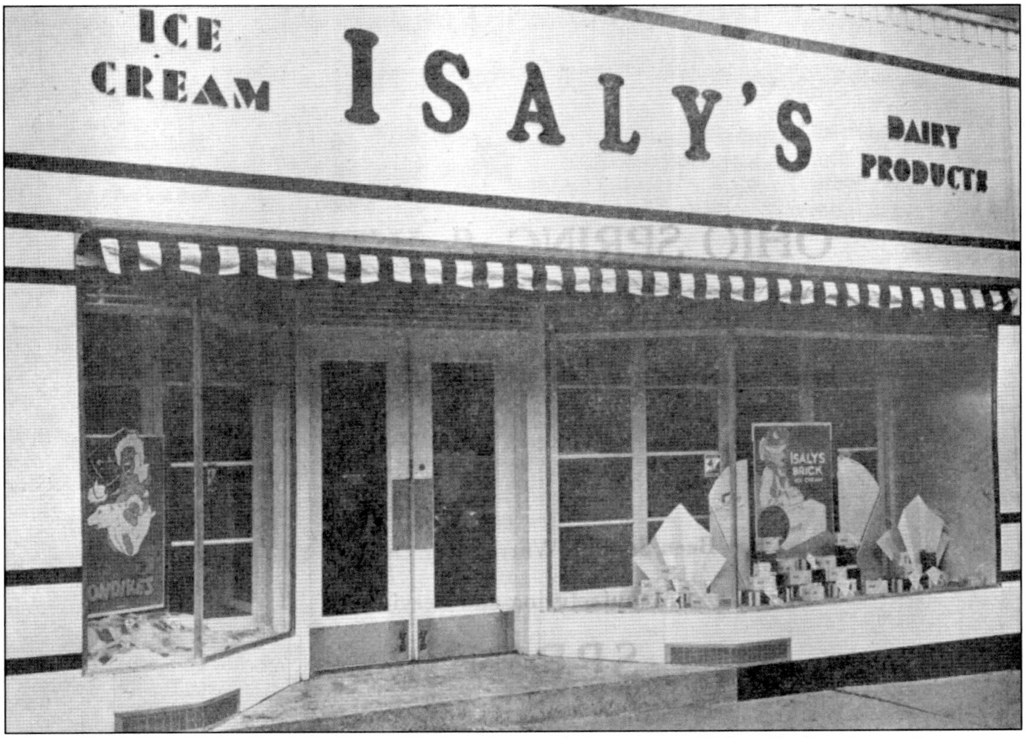

Isaly's became part of the downtown landscape in the 1930s, with Jim Finley Sr. as the owner. Older photographs show that it was next to where Gessner and Platt's law offices are located on Main Street, but the business later constructed a cement block building about three doors west. Skyscraper cones were a favorite offering at the store. The items shown in the photograph below were collected by Jim Finley's son Jim and daughter-in-law Nancy. (Both, courtesy of James Finley Jr.)

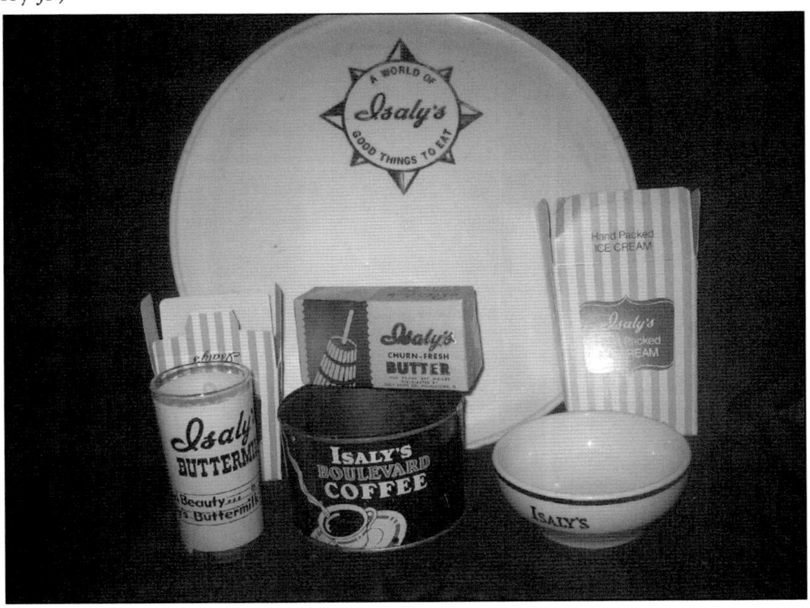

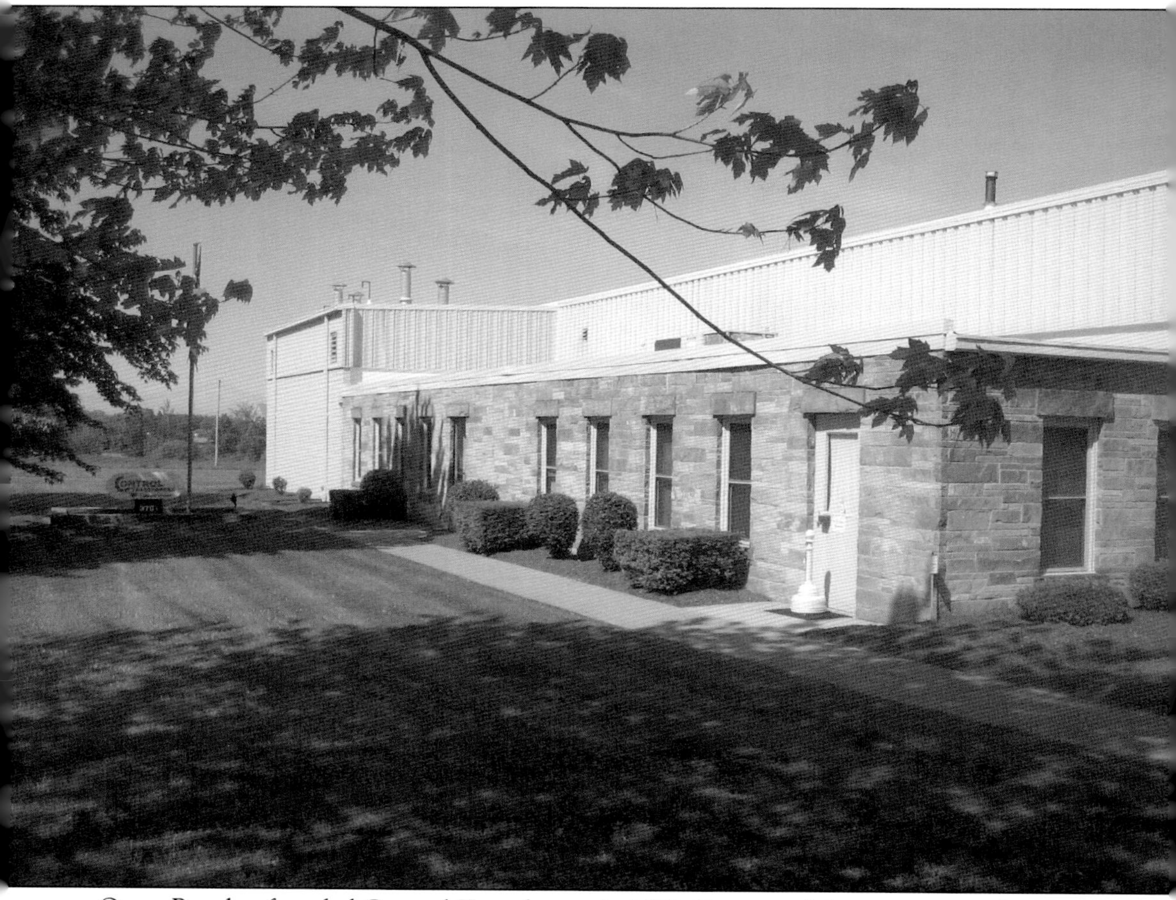

Oscar Bowden founded Control Transformer in 1953. He started the company in his garage, supplying transformers to Reliance Electric Corporation in Euclid, Ohio. Over the next six decades, the company grew from that one-man operation to the facility seen today. CTI is incorporated under Park Ohio Holdings and is a $1 billion operation based out of Cleveland, Ohio. (Author's collection.)

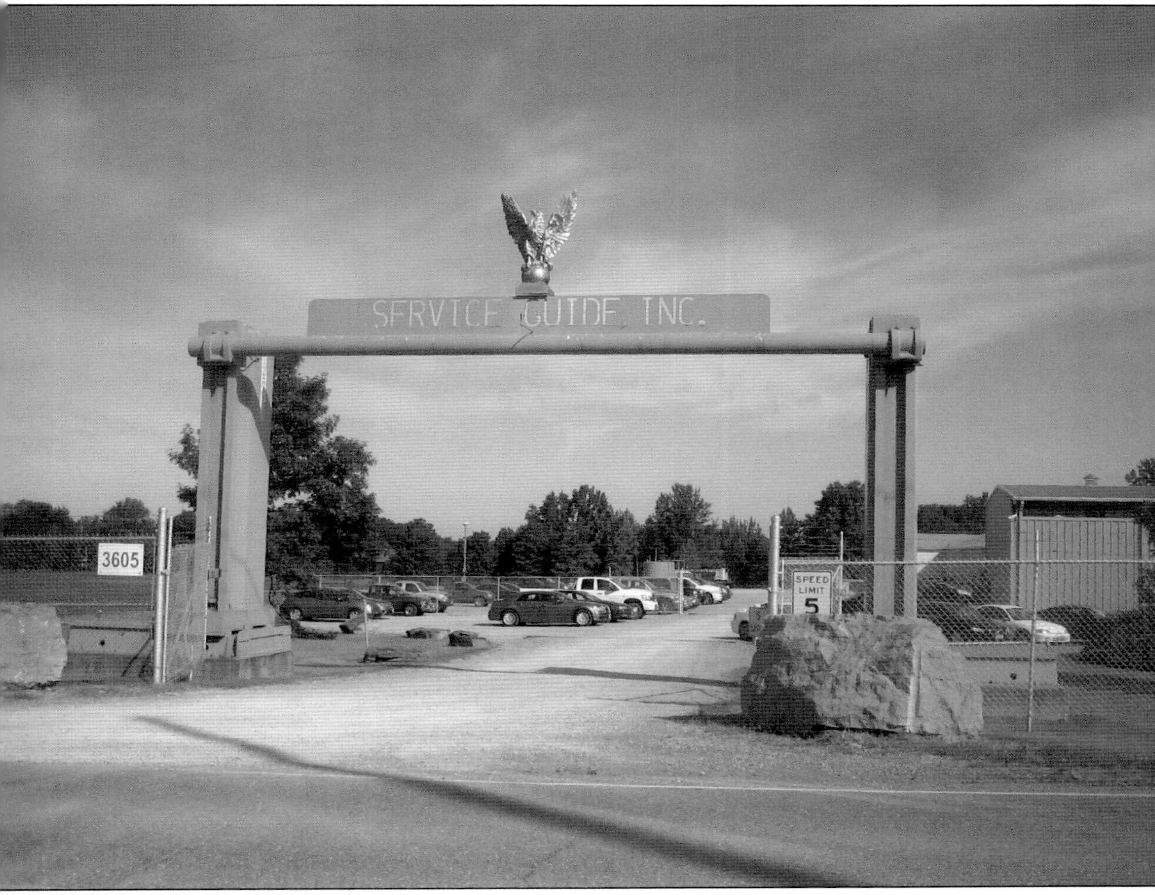

Service Guide was incorporated by Grant A. Oakes II in 1964, but the company's roots go back to 1929 when the Oakes family incorporated Oakes Foundry. Oakes bought the foundry from his grandmother after his grandfather, father, and uncle passed away. The fourth generation of the Oakes family still owns it. Service Guide, Inc. is a leading industrial repair business for steel mills, aluminum plants, paper mills, and mining operations all over North America. Grant A. Oakes II was born in 1938, graduated from Lakeview High School in 1956, and donated in many ways to the community; he was a major contributor to Imagination Station, cancer drives, and the annual fireworks display in Cortland. He died in 2010. (Author's collection.)

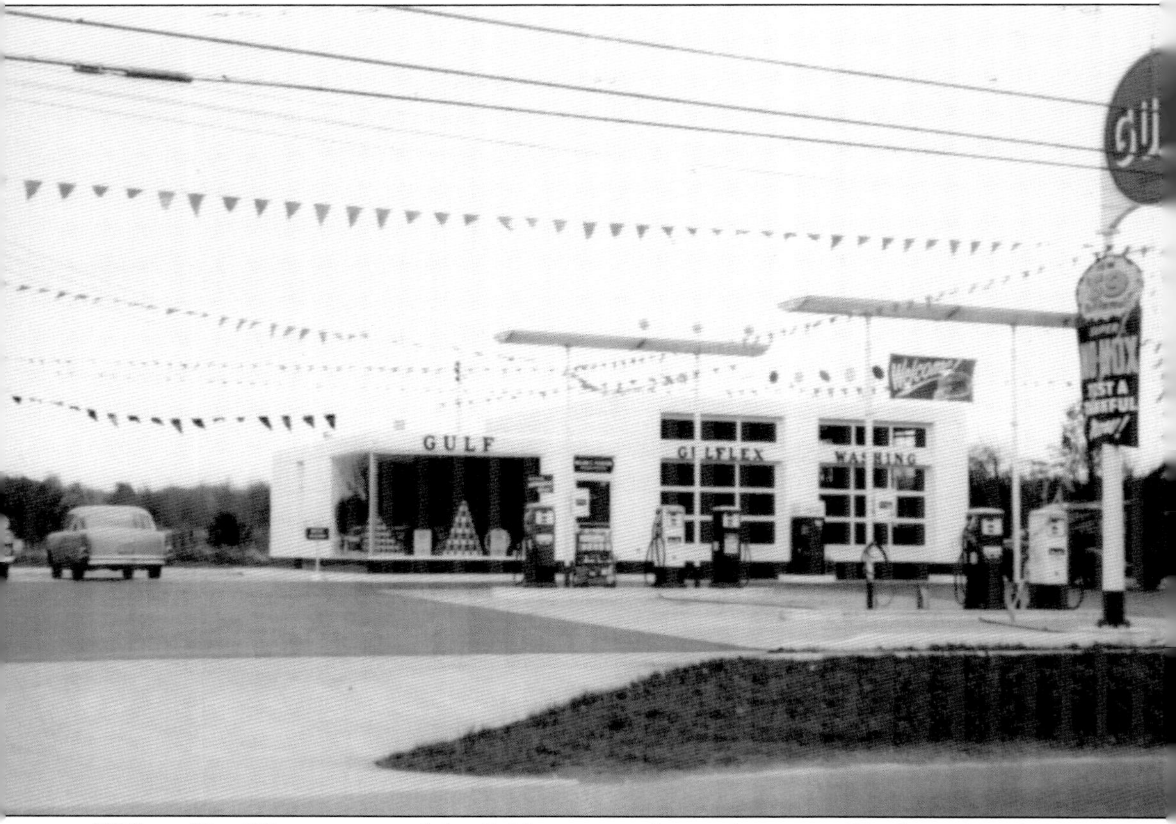

William "Pete" Peterson owned the Gulf station on the south corner of Fowler and High Streets from 1958 to 1961 before Brent Westbay took it over, who then sold it to the Johnson family. Over the years, the station had other owners until it was torn down and dentist Gregory Davenport built his office there. (Courtesy of William Hallett and Carol Peterson.)

Lou Wollam did not take cows in trade for wheels, but his predecessor, Dick Knight, did. When automobiles were first sold in Cortland, the first dealership offered Fords. Dick Knight began selling Chevrolets, and he amassed quite a herd of cattle and thus sponsored children in 4-H. When he decided to retire, Wollam, who owned a gas station on the corner of High and Main Streets, bought the business in 1964. Members of the Wollam family have been in business in Cortland since the 1880s, starting with a grocery store, gas stations, insurance, tractors, mowers, and automobiles. (Both, courtesy of Lou Wollam Chevrolet.)

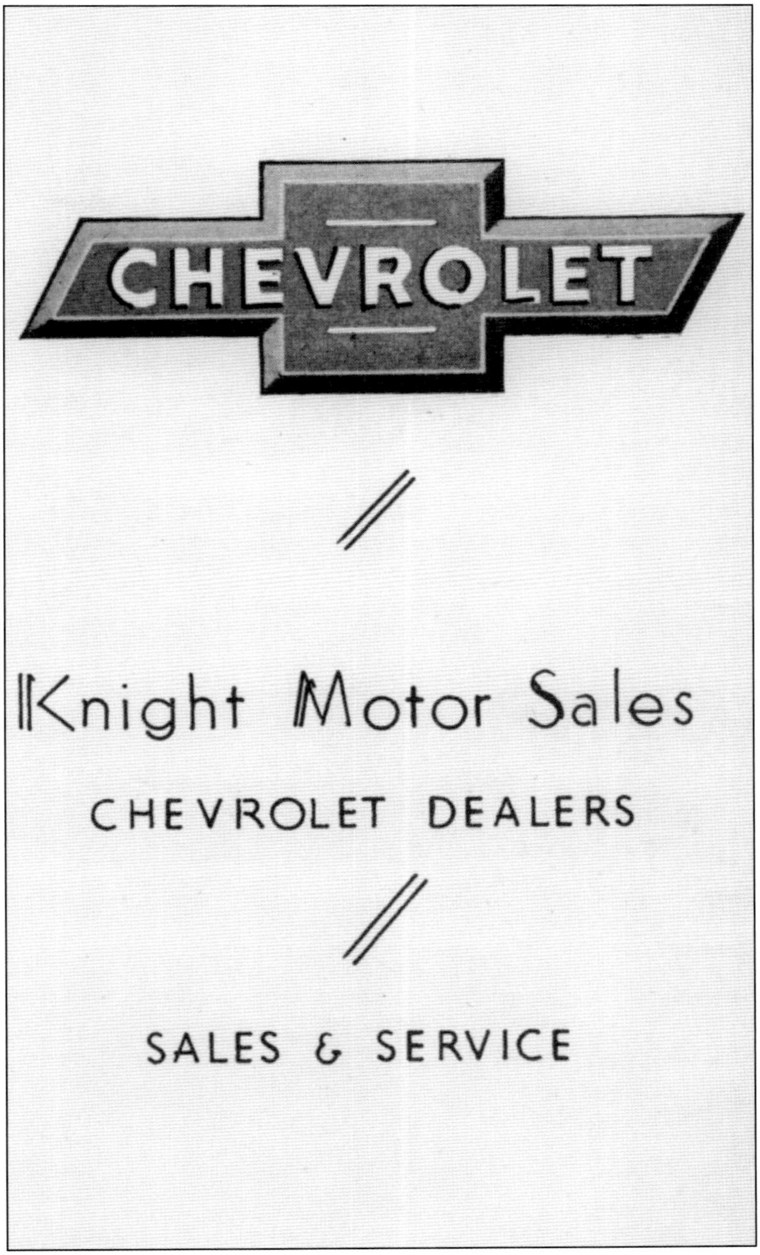

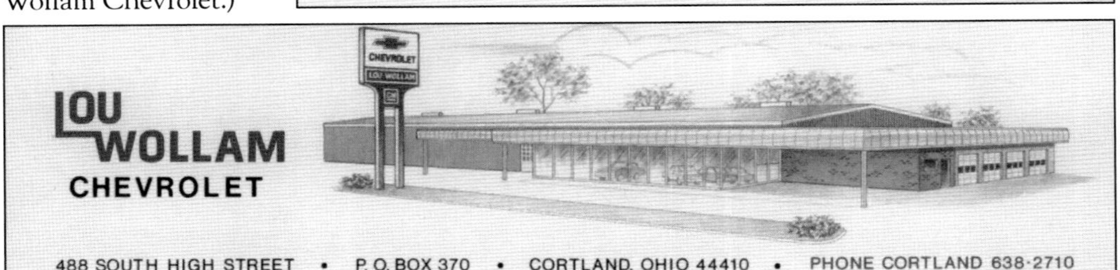

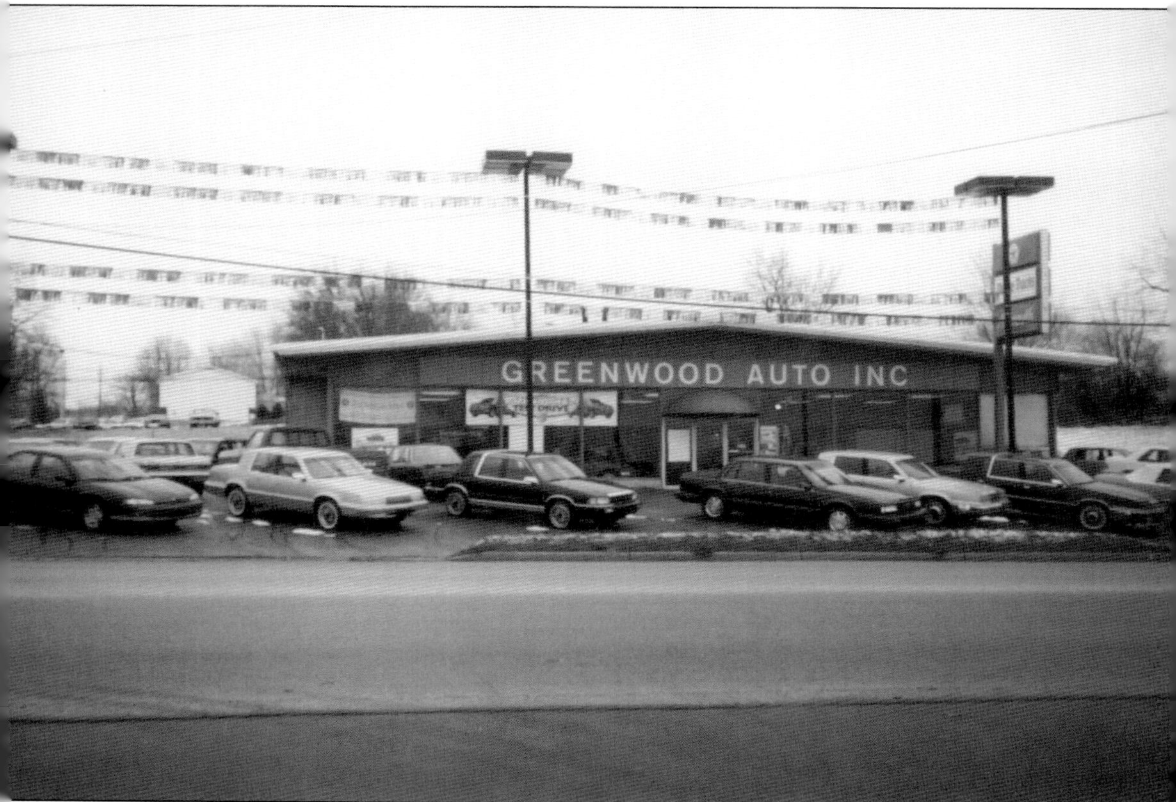

The Greenwood family has been selling cars at the corner of Routes 5 and 46 in Cortland since 1953. Bud and Wayne Greenwood Sr. started with a Rambler dealership next door to their current building, now occupied by Rite Aid. Eventually, Greenwood became a Dodge dealer and in the 1990s began offering Chrysler, Dodge, Plymouth, Jeep, and Eagle with his grandson Terry Greenwood. Since that time, the brands have consolidated to Chrysler, Dodge, Ram, and Jeep. Fourth-generation Greenwoods Chris and Patrick are also in the business. (Courtesy of Greenwood Auto.)

Six

Mosquito Lake

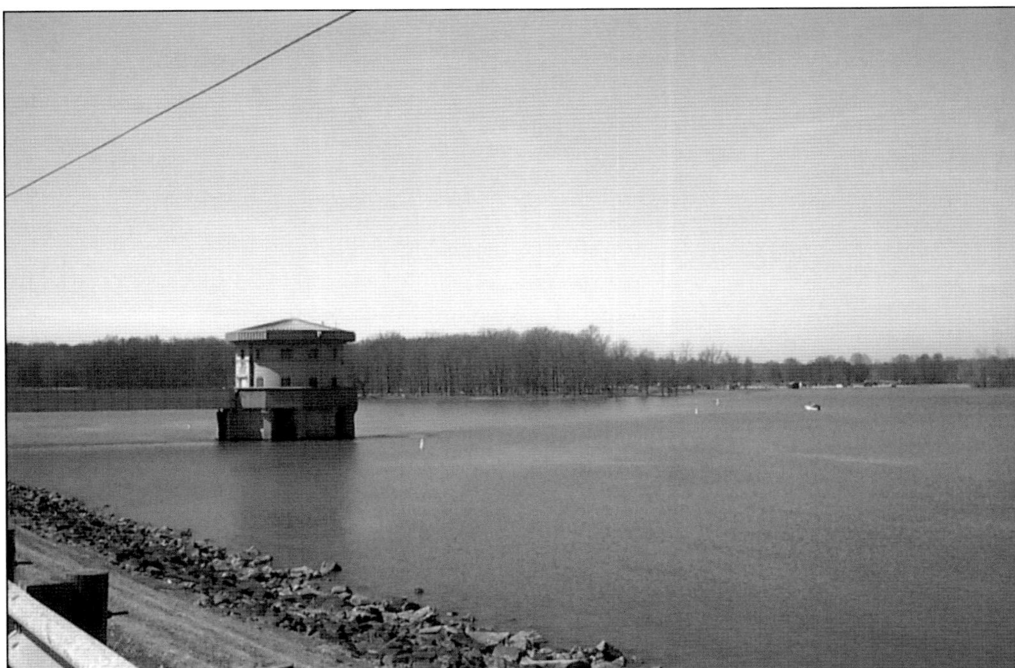

More than 200 years ago, surveyors named the creek that bisects the county from north to south Mosquito Creek, and the name was appropriate. From Colebrook in Ashtabula County to Niles in Trumbull County where it meets the Mahoning River, the area was a thick forest. Because the creek often overflowed its banks in the spring, settlers preferred lands some distance from the creek banks. However, fishing was always good, as was catching frogs, picking berries or nuts, and finding game if one could tolerate the mosquitoes. The lake that was created in 1944 from this creek is the second largest in the state. Its main purpose is flood protection for the Mahoning River Valley. It also stores water in dry times and releases it downstream to improve water quality. (Courtesy of the Durst family.)

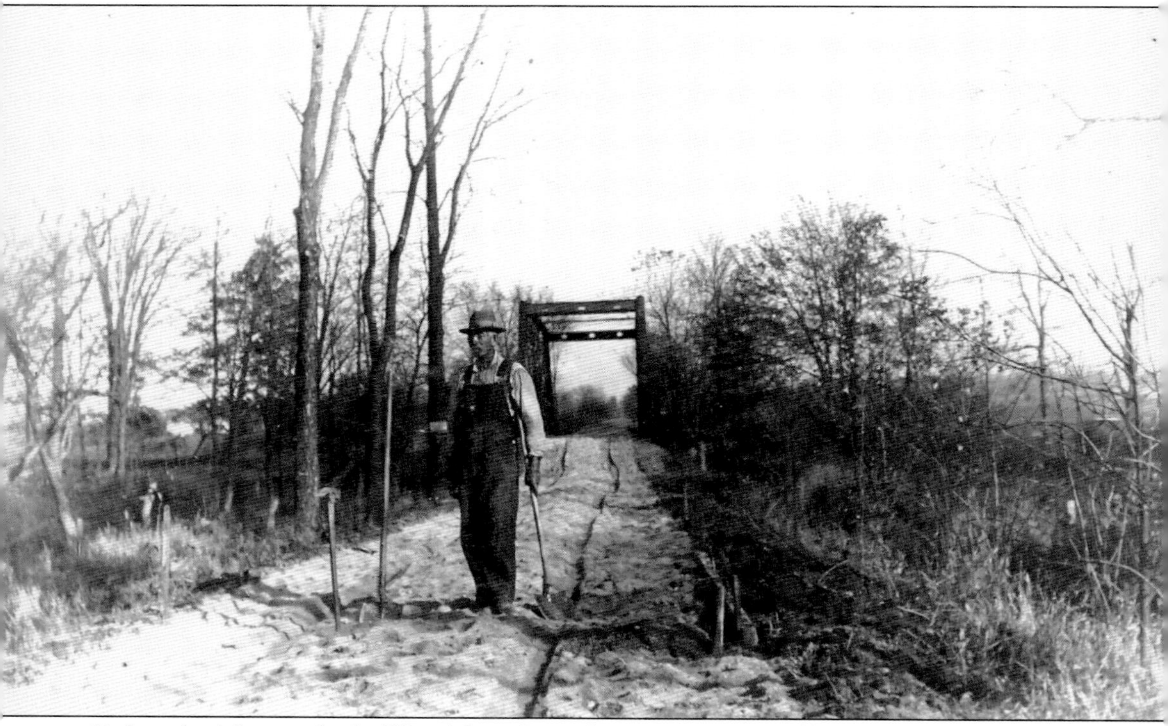

Before the lake was built, West Main Street became Everett Hull Road across a bridge. The crossroads called Klondike was there, with a post office for West Bazetta, a church after 1848, and a mill that ground cereal grain. Notice the ruts from the buggies that traveled a sometimes-muddy road to the bridge. When the lake was created, this bridge sat in the middle of the lake until winter, when ice pushed against the abutments and the bridge fell into the water. Eventually, most of the metal was removed, but some of it remains. (Courtesy of CBHS.)

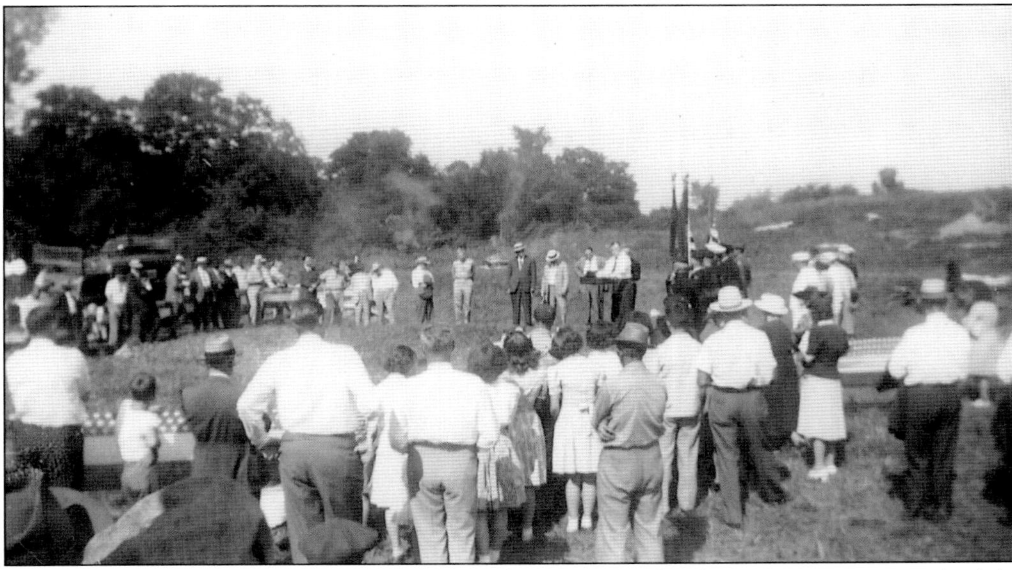

Ground-breaking ceremonies were held on July 24, 1943. The decision to construct the lake meant that many people who had homes and farms from the middle of Bazetta, Mecca, and Greene Townships had to move. There are still many people who remember that it felt like an invasion of the area when the US government took needed land by eminent domain. (Courtesy of the Durst family.)

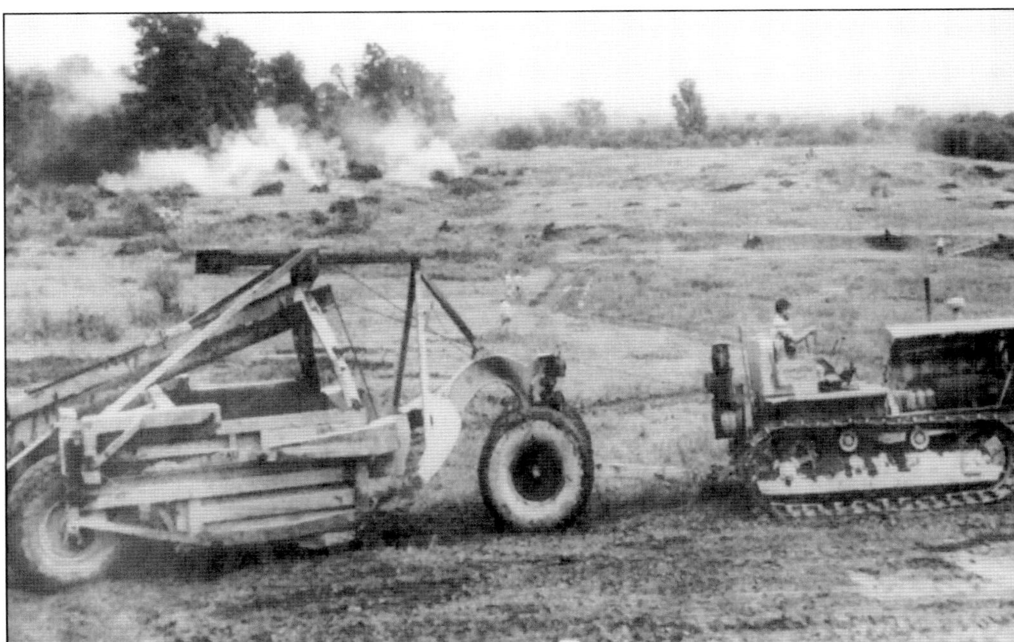

Just five days after the ground-breaking ceremony, the construction of the dam began; it was finished within 90 days. The area near where the dam and tower were planned was the only part excavated. There was some large machinery like that pictured for digging, but much of the logging work was done using horses. (Courtesy of US Army Corps of Engineers.)

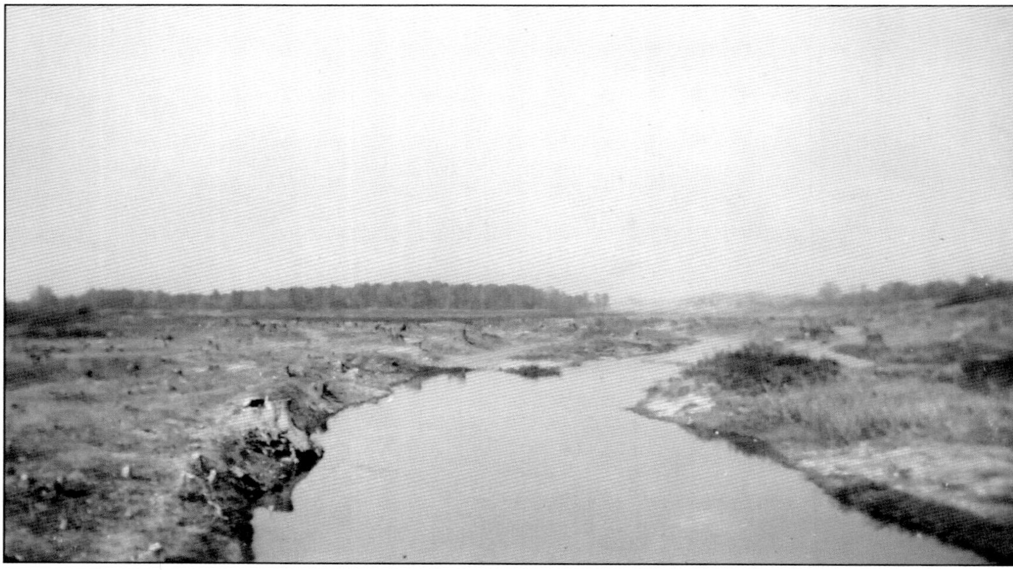

The photograph shows what the creek looked like after the trees were cut, while the image below shows parts laid out to be used for building the lock and the dam. The dam is located nine miles upstream from its junction with the Mahoning River at Niles, Ohio. (Above, courtesy of the Durst family; below, US Army Corps of Engineers.)

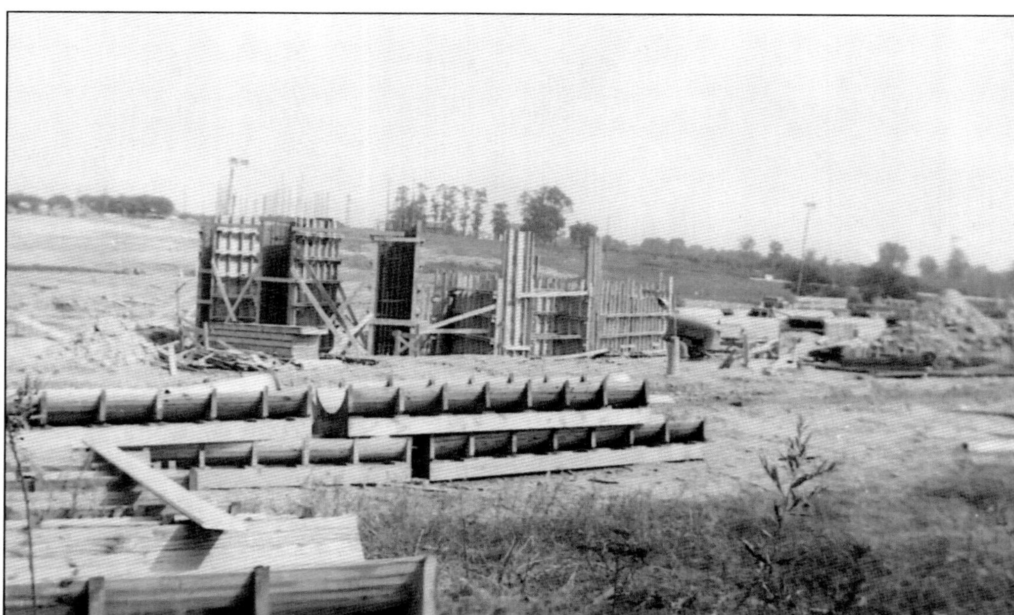

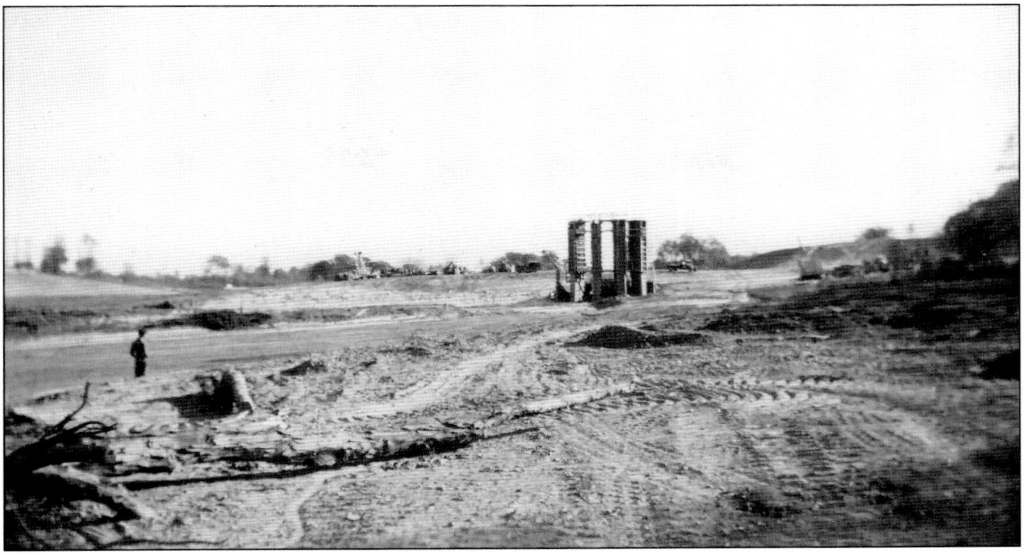

The photograph above shows the tower as it was being built on dry land. There were sluice gates, valves for the gate, and valves for the water supply, and they were all put together to adjust and monitor the water height. The lake has a natural spillway located in the Grand River Divide. If the water level gets too high (about 904 feet above sea level), the outflow of the lake is reversed and drains into the Grand River to Lake Erie. The photograph below shows the stilling basin being installed. Today, the tower conducts tours for interested groups. (Both, courtesy of the US Army Corps of Engineers.)

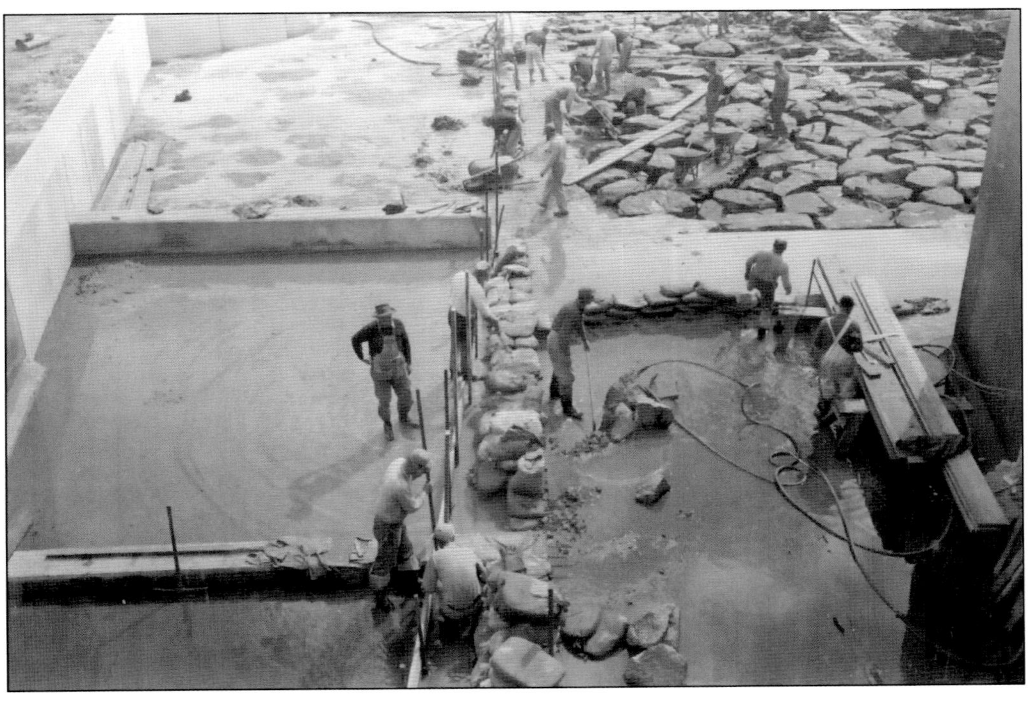

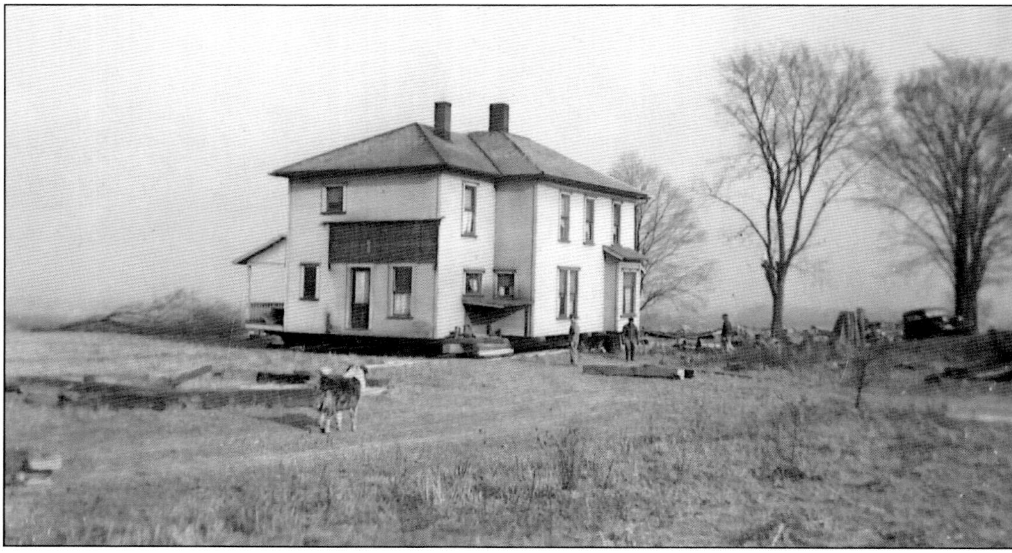

The family of Harlan Durst chose to move their house rather than build another. Above, the family dog watches as beams are placed under the house; the barn was torn down. The house was moved about a mile west on State Route 305, a little past Bazetta Road. From their windows, family members could watch as the lake was constructed. Harlan is pictured below standing on a log as the lake filled up. (Both, courtesy of the Durst family.)

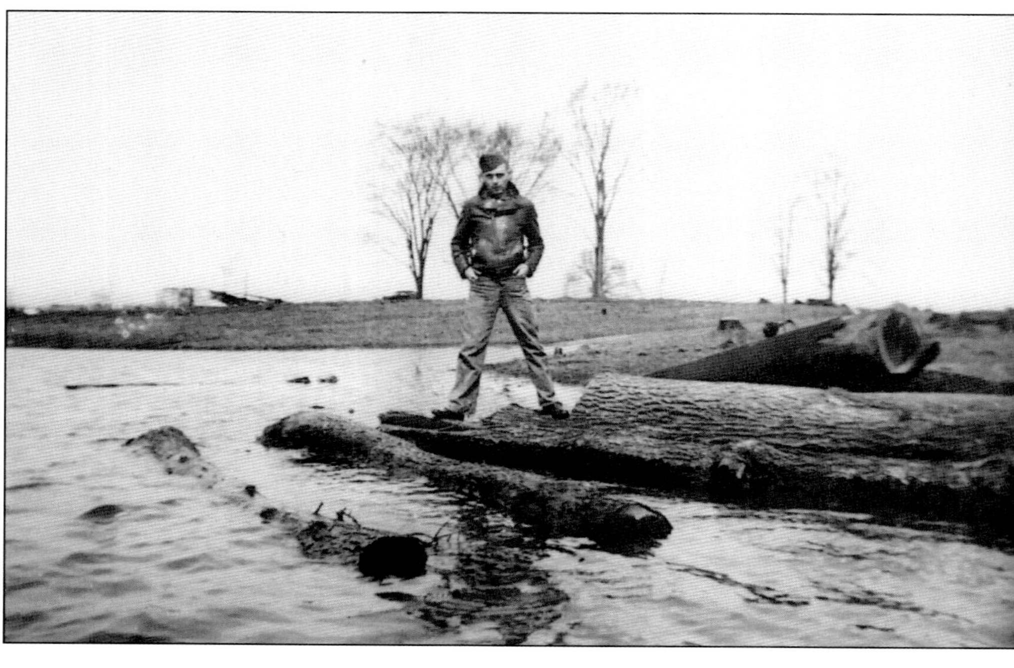

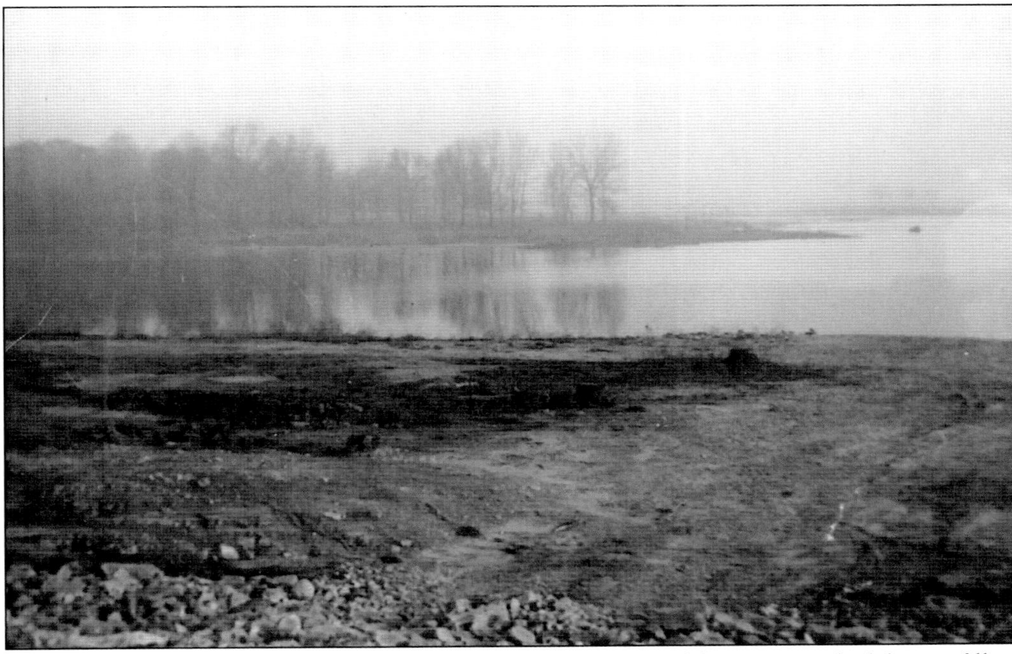

This photograph was taken near the south end of the lake, west of the tower, as the lake was filling up. Today, it is a part of the lake that is visible when driving on State Route 305 and is a favorite spot for fishermen. Nearby picnic tables and nature trails make it a pleasant spot. (Courtesy of the Durst family.)

The dam, seen here, is a rolled earth fill embankment. It is 47 feet above the streambed, 5,650 feet long, and 430 feet wide at the base. The water discharged is controlled in the tower. The Mosquito Creek Reservoir was completed in 1944. (Courtesy of the US Army Corps of Engineers.)

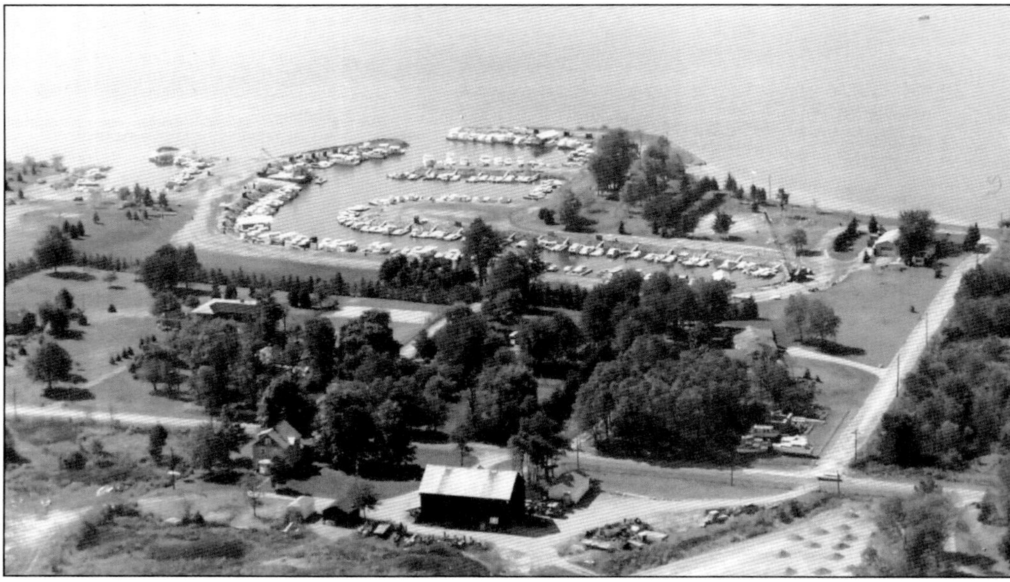

It did not take people long to start enjoying the lake. The lake and most of its surrounding lands are leased by the Army Corps of Engineers to the Ohio Department of Natural Resources as Mosquito State Park. The northern end of the lake is leased to the Ohio Division of Wildlife for fish management. As expected, the entire area is a haven for birds and fish. A yacht club, shown here, was started on the east side of the lake in Bazetta in the 1960s due to the efforts of Grant A. Oakes II. Yachts can be seen on the water all summer long. (Courtesy of CBHS and Mary Oakes.)

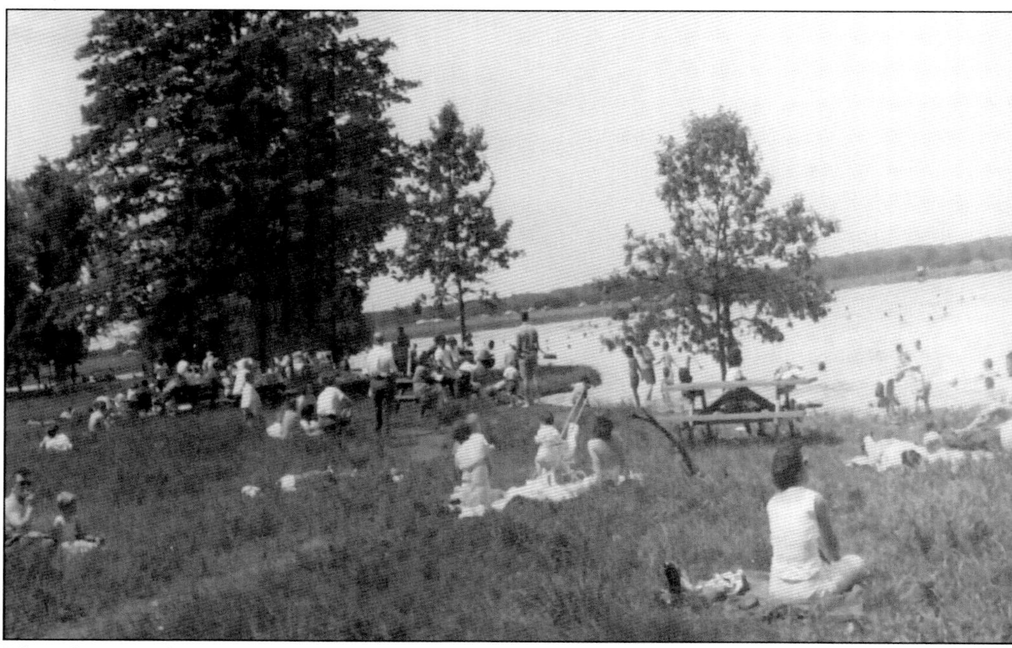

This photograph from the late 1940s shows people at the picnic and swimming area of Mosquito State Park. The tower on State Route 305 would be in the background on the right side of the photograph. (Courtesy of the US Army Corps of Engineers.)

Seven

Fires and Wrecks

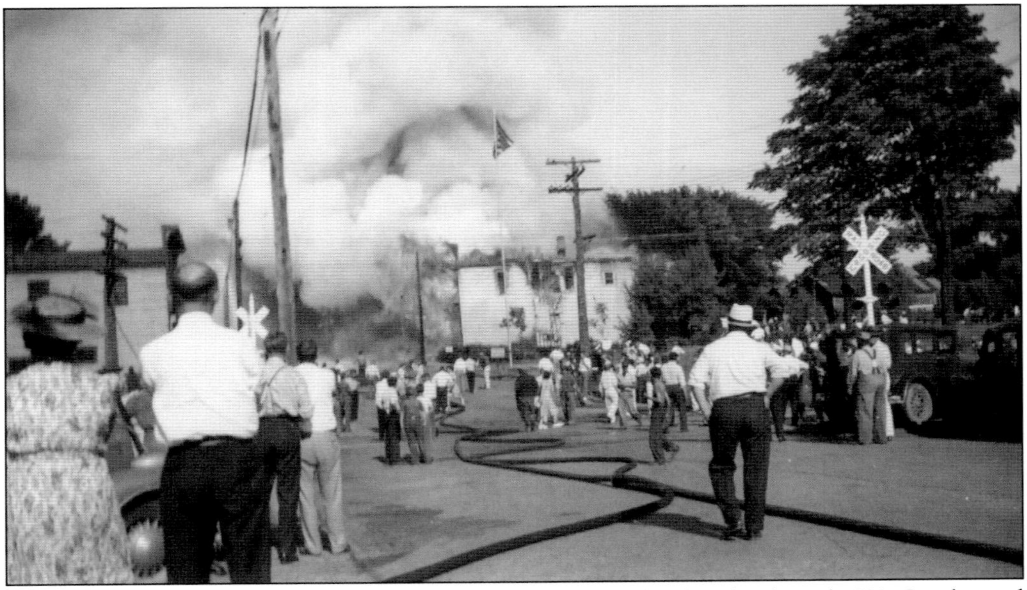

One of the most vivid memories shared by people in Cortland is the fire of 1939. Smoke and flames could be seen for miles as the fire consumed three buildings and a residence on the south side of Main Street. Telephone operators on duty sounded the alarm, and one operator leaned out the window to give the first fireman arriving at the station the key to the fire truck. The fire was still smoldering the next day. (Courtesy of the Gessner family.)

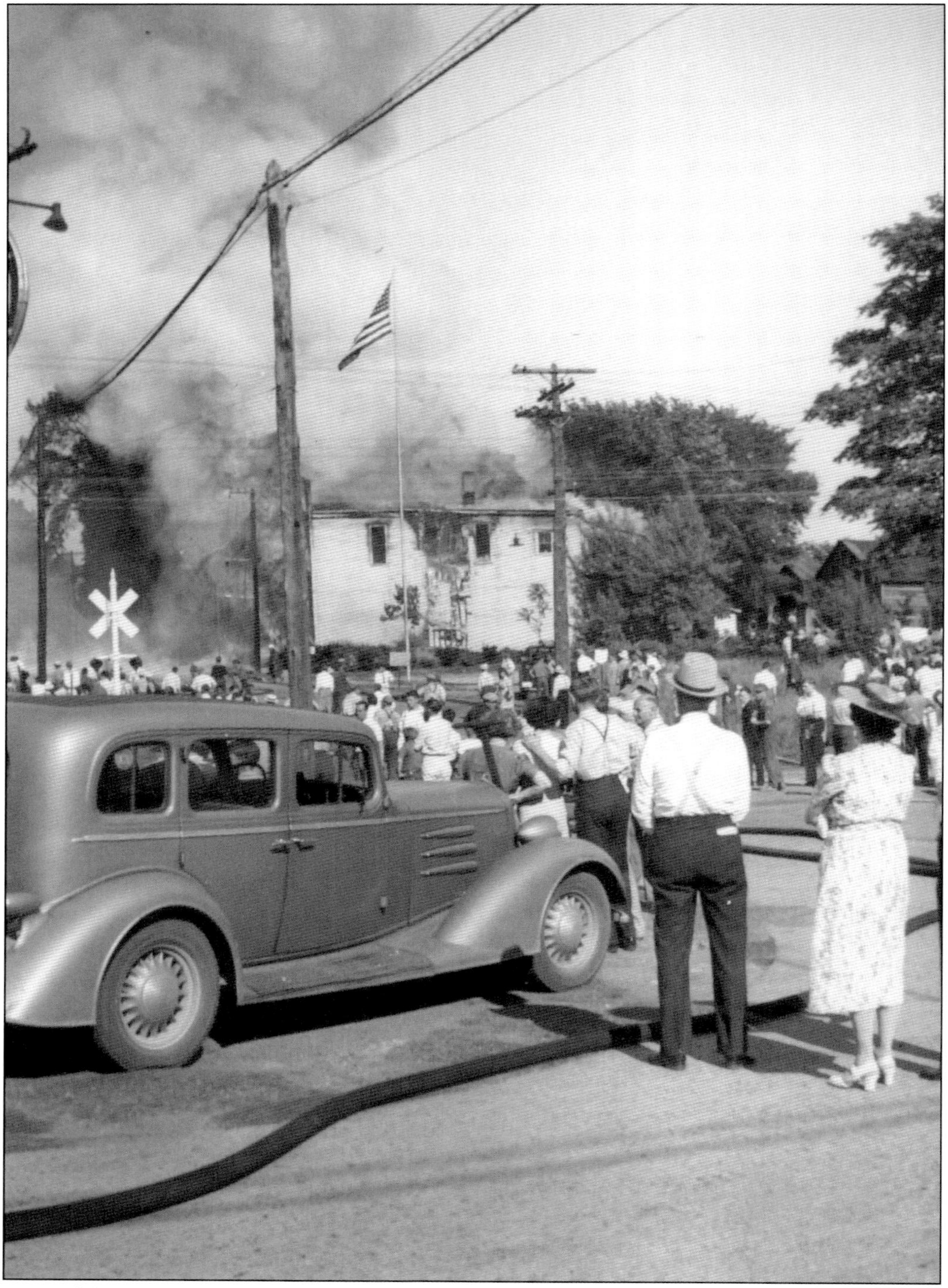

Most of the town turned out to either watch or help put out the fire. Here, onlookers standing on the west side of the railroad tracks, near Richards Mill, watch as the fire billows. When the cisterns were pumped dry, hoses, which can be seen here, were run from the mill's pond, and the fire was finally controlled. (Courtesy of the Gessner family.)

This truck brought down a bridge and overturned a little south of the intersection of Mecca and West Main Streets in 1927. Townspeople turned out to help the driver and later rebuilt the bridge. (Courtesy of the Gessner family.)

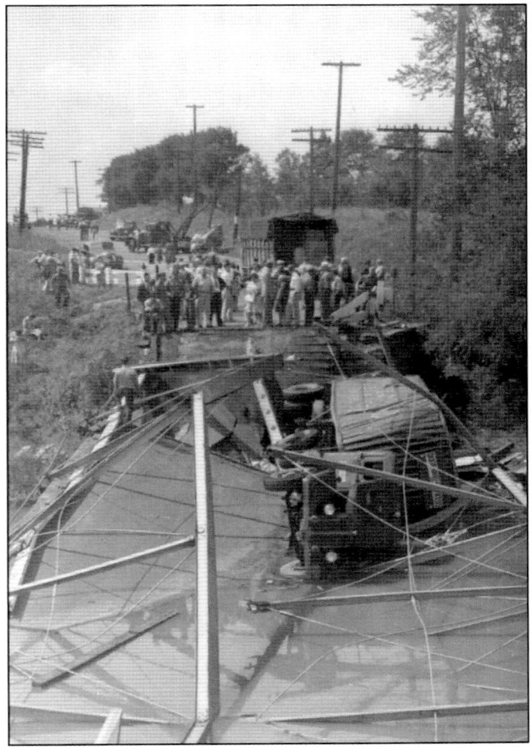

In 1929, this engine derailed near the train depot at the intersection of Pearl and Erie Streets. The lumberyard building can bee seen in the background, along with the twisted track. Note the old automobile of the investigators. (Courtesy of the Gessner family.)

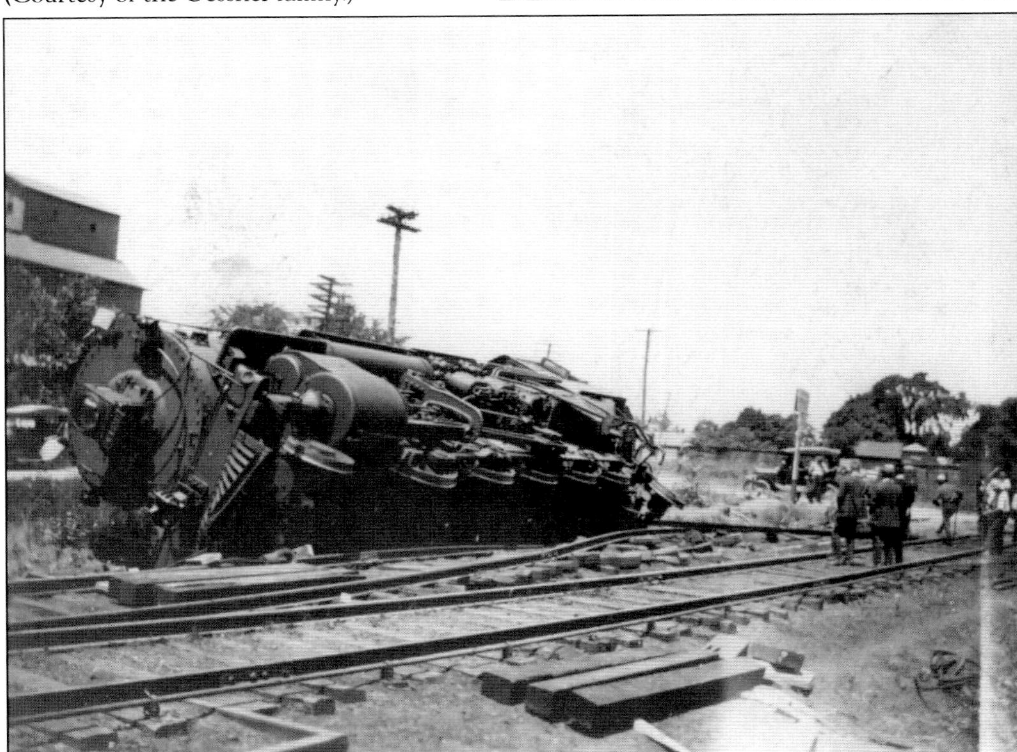

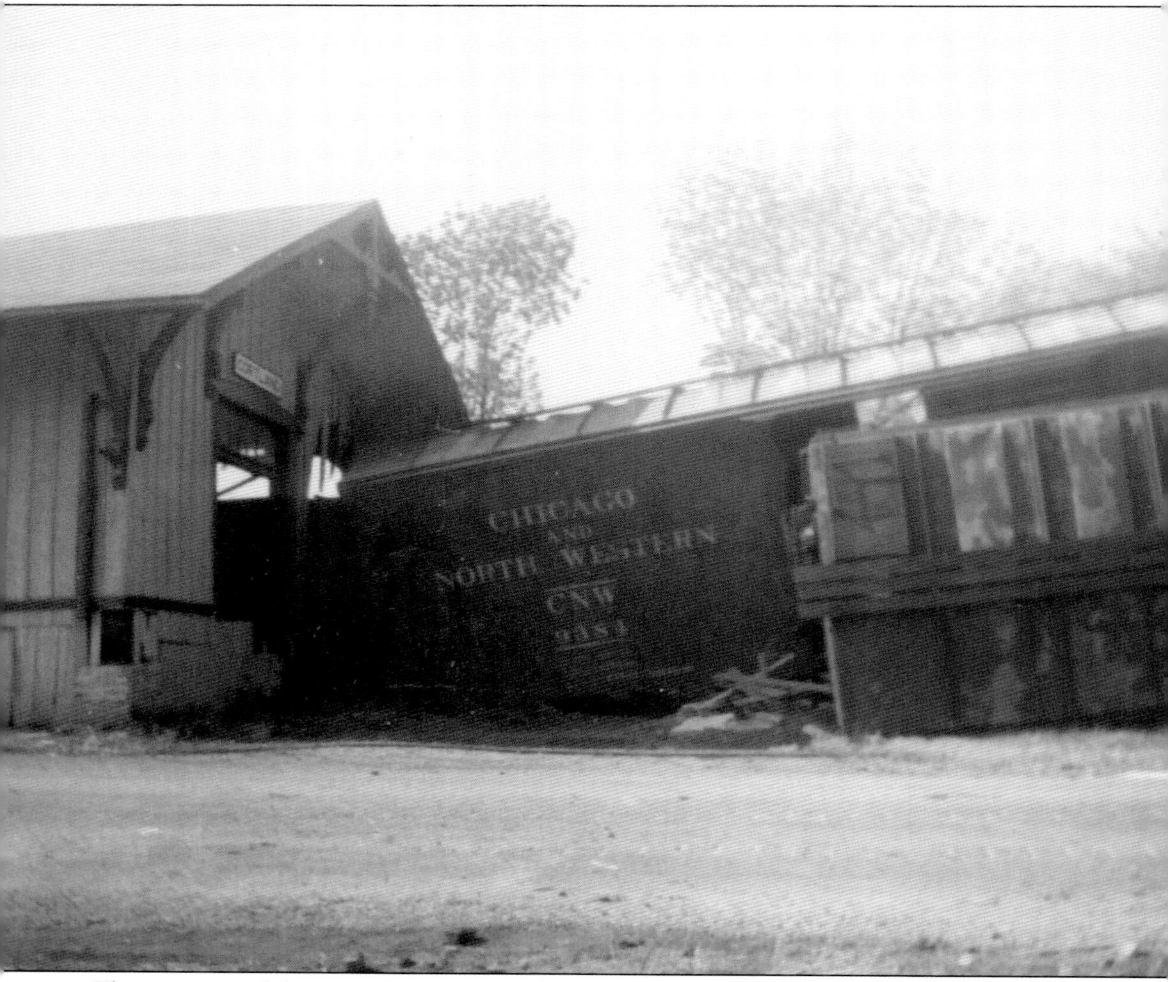

This train wreck happened in 1961. The Wagner family lived on Erie Street between Market and Lattin Streets, and the main part of the derailment was near the Market Street crossing. For some time, the Wagner family had a front-row seat of the cleanup of the accident. Carolyn Wagner Sparhawk remembers that the wreck "about shook us out of bed." Jim Finley, who came upon the scene shortly after it happened, observed, "I could see the cars had derailed along Erie Street. . . . There was also a pair of very hot steel wheels from one of the derailed cars. We couldn't get too close but I could feel the heat. As I recall, that's what caused the wreck. I also remember some coiled steel rolls that were partially unrolled in the grass along the tracks just north of the depot before the Market Street crossing." (Courtesy of James Finley.)

Eight

Government, Post Offices, and Libraries

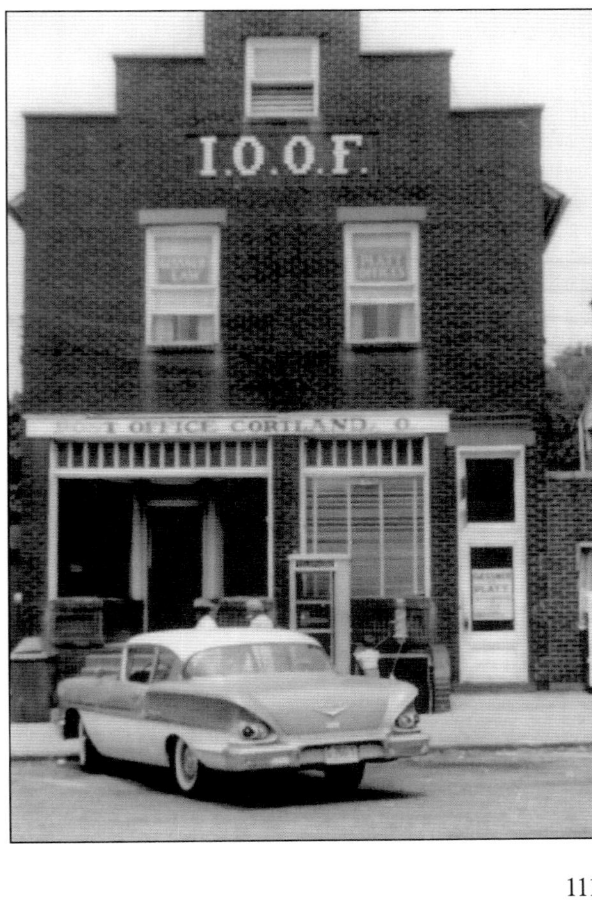

Many different buildings housed the post office over the years. This one was constructed in 1923 on Main Street; the post office moved there in 1924. Because of fires, the village passed an ordinance requiring all new buildings to be of brick. Upstairs, the International Order of Odd Fellows (IOOF) had lodge rooms that later would be Gessner & Platt's law offices. Later, it became the Palmer Building. The distinct facade identifies this building despite the modern siding. The post office moved a few more times since it was hosed there. In 1991, the newest, largest building joined the city on South High Street as the most modern, up-to-date facility. (Courtesy of the Gessner family.)

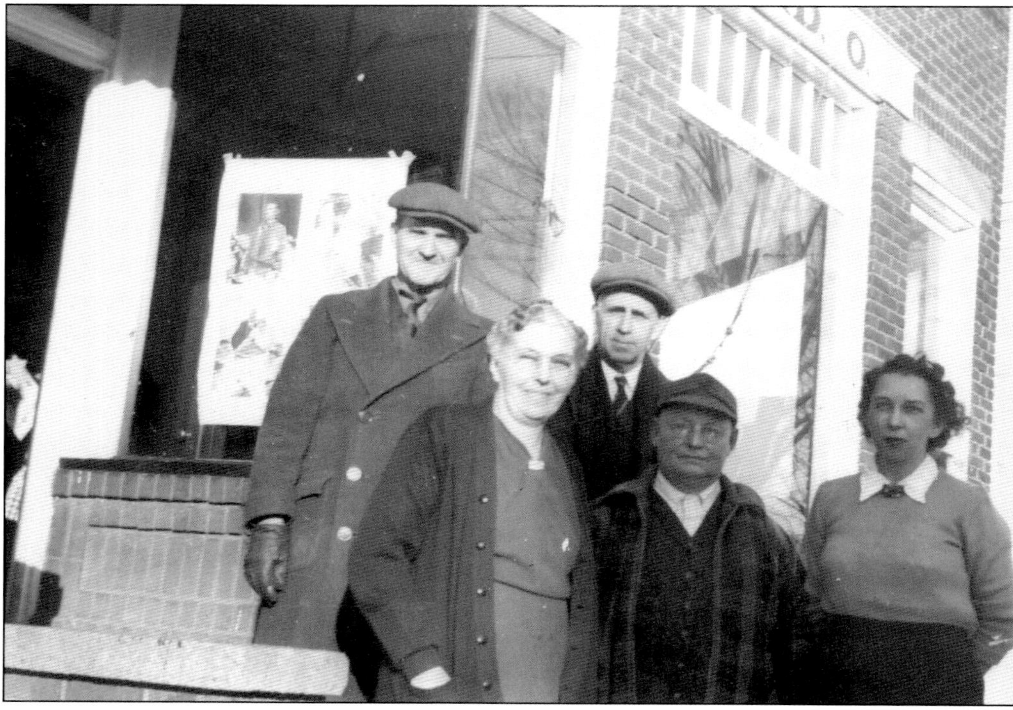

Posing on the steps of the post office pictured on the previous page are postal workers. From left to right are (first row) Dorothy Dilworth, Bruce Stinson, and Georgia Hines Cowdery; (second row) Charles Irwin and Charles Grant. Behind them is a patriotic poster of Abraham Lincoln. (Courtesy of Mary Case and Donna Durst.)

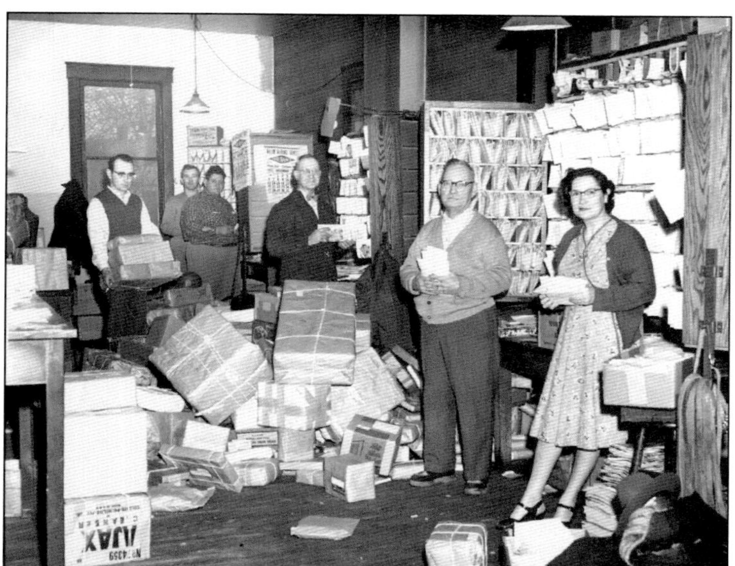

Christmas is a very busy time for post offices. These postal workers, from left to right, were swamped in 1953: Harlan Durst, Bob Davis, Howard Hector, Charles Irwin, and Bruce and Faye Stinson. It is uncertain where this particular post office was located; it may have been in the Arner block, across the street, on the same side as the Cortland Bank. (Courtesy of William Hallett.)

During the term of A. Harned, mayor of Cortland from 1953 to 1963, a board of public affairs was created along with six council member positions. From left to right are Roy Palmer, A. Harned, and a county commissioner as they inspected the sewer department site. A new 270-foot sewer line was laid in 1963 from Park Drive to Fourth Avenue. (Courtesy of William Harned.)

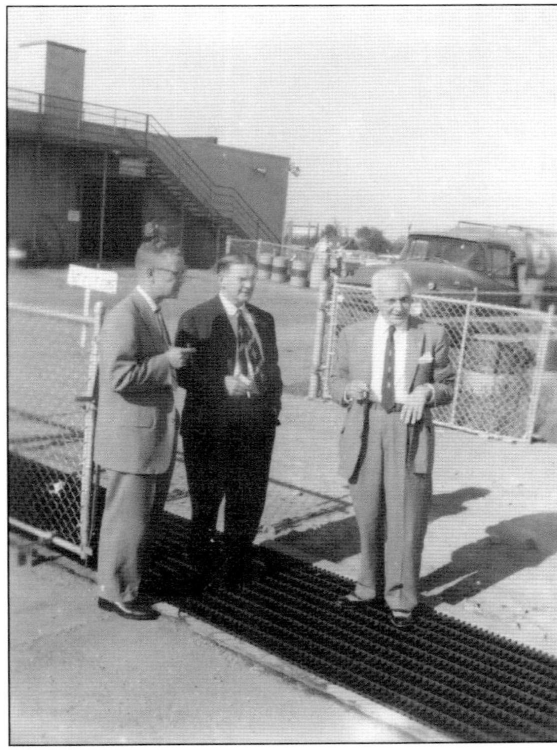

Donald Jones became the next mayor of Cortland, retaining the position from 1964 to 1974. During his tenure, he remodeled the old town hall on Lattin Street, established the position of clerk-treasurer, purchased five acres for a new city well, and saw the construction of sanitary sewer lines on Fowler Street and other sewer improvements throughout the city. Thirty acres were also annexed from Fowler. This was a busy time for Cortland as the population increased. (Courtesy of Donald Jones.)

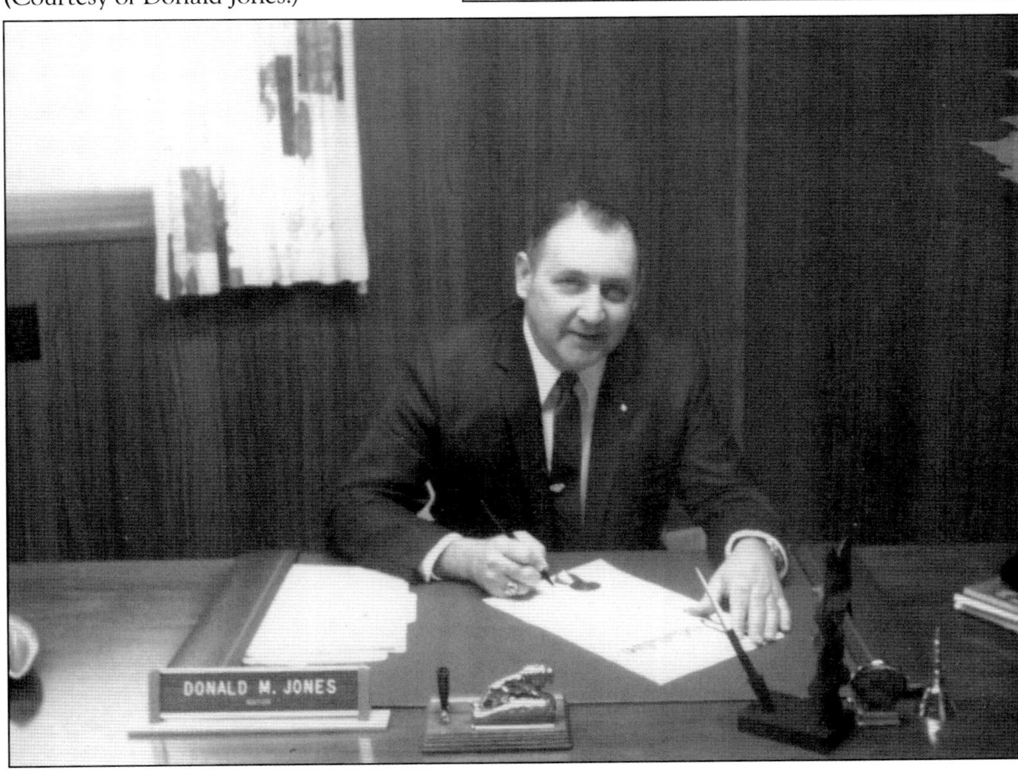

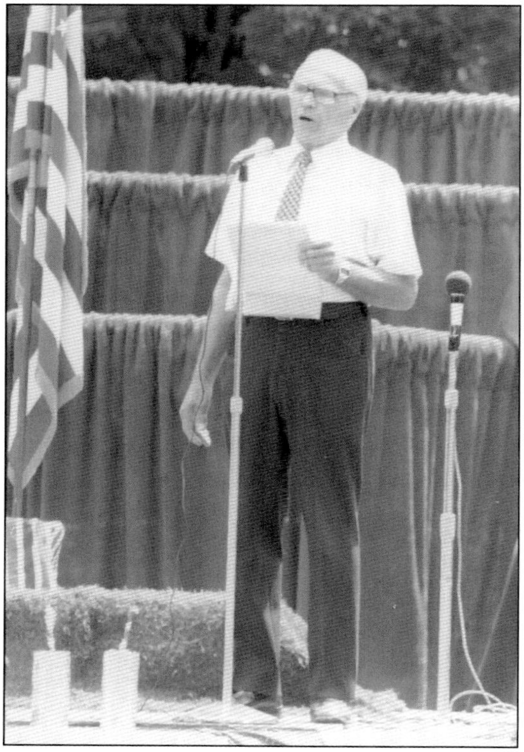

Bazetta began to grow with record construction figures in 1977. There have been many trustees over the years but few photographs. This one is of Charles Smelko as he made an announcement at the 1976 Heritage Day at Bazetta Township Park. The day celebrated the country's bicentennial and was an overwhelming success for organizers of the community picnic. (Courtesy of Carol Harrison.)

In 1974, the Bazetta Township Administration Building was constructed on Elm Road. A spacious building, it anticipated growth of the township. In 1977, ground was broken for the fire station/police department on McCleary Jacoby Road. Also, in 1977, the new township park was accepted by the trustees that opened in 1976. Bazetta continues to be one of the fastest growing townships in the county. (Courtesy of CBHS.)

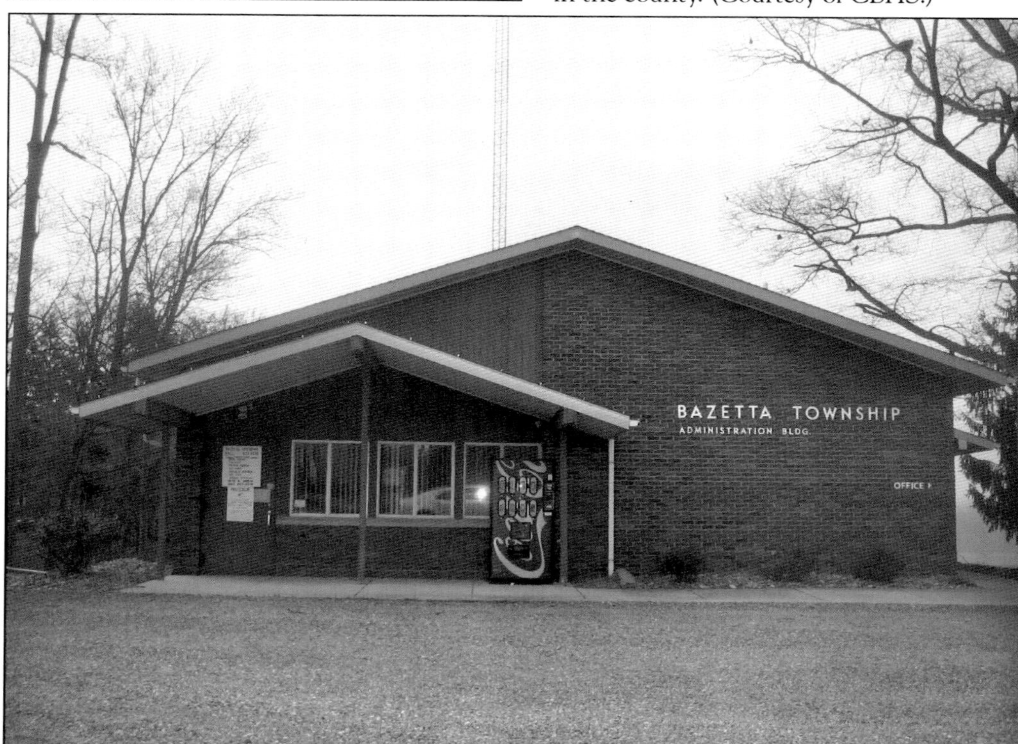

From 1978 to 1987, the mayor of Cortland was William J. Roush. As a retired superintendent of the Lakeview School District, Roush saw the effect that the increase in population had on the city. His time in office was filled with new buildings, new streets and businesses, and the transition from a village to city in 1981. He is shown here also at the 1976 Heritage Day celebration. (Courtesy of Carol Harrison.)

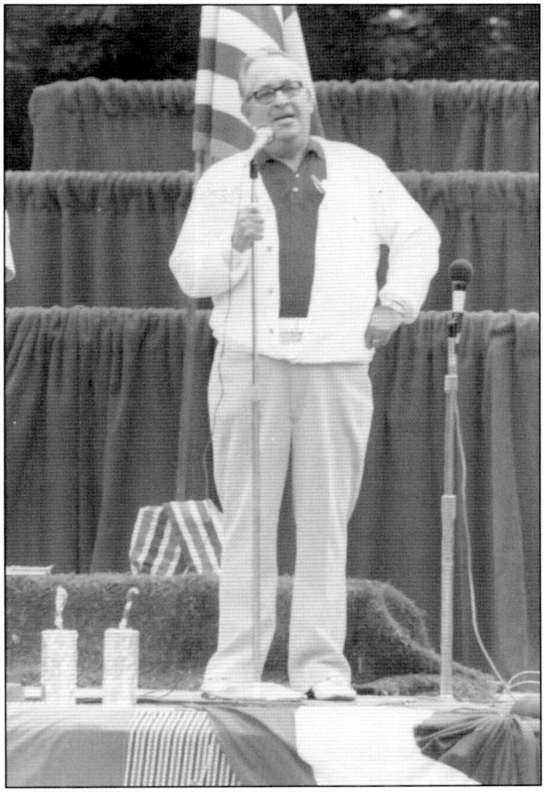

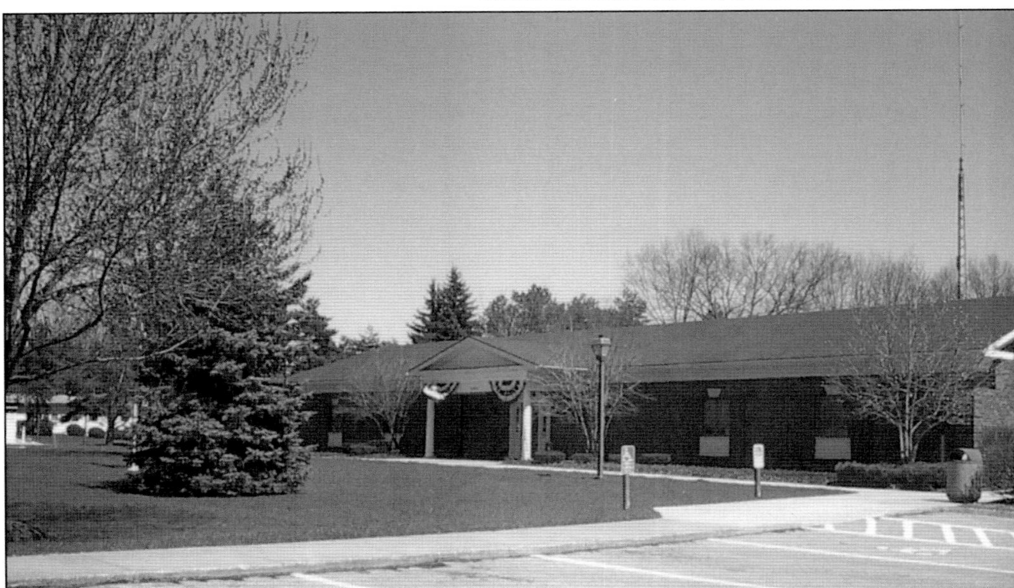

During Roush's tenure, the new Cortland City Hall was constructed at 400 North High Street in 1986. The building was designed to fit in with the historical houses nearby and to provide adequate quarters for the police department as well as city government. A new fire station was also built on Lattin Street, and the old town hall was torn down. (Courtesy of CBHS.)

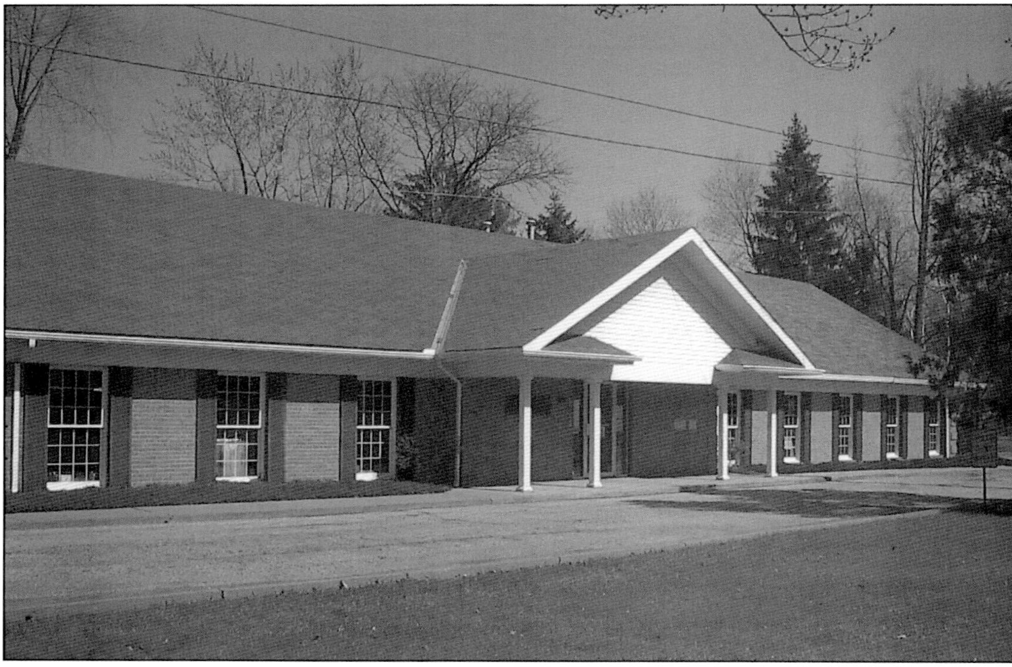

For many years, library services in Cortland were conducted in bookmobiles, an old house near the railroad tracks, the Cortland Elementary building, and the old village hall. In the 1980s, land was donated for a new library, the first built for that purpose, by Vivian Vera Viets and her sister Wilhemien. Fundraising resulted in the construction of a modern building, shown above, adjacent to the sisters' property on North High Street. Students from Cortland Elementary assisted in moving books from the old house library to the new one in 1984. Each student picked up a pile of books, marched to the new facility, and placed them on the shelves—it was quite a parade. A new, larger library opened in June 2012 on property between Lakeview Middle School and the high school. (Both, author's collection.)

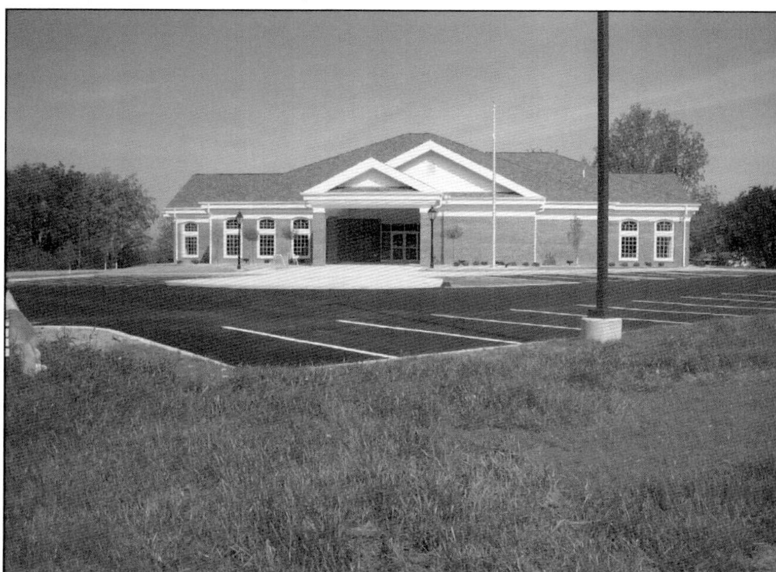

Nine

People, Homes, and Fun

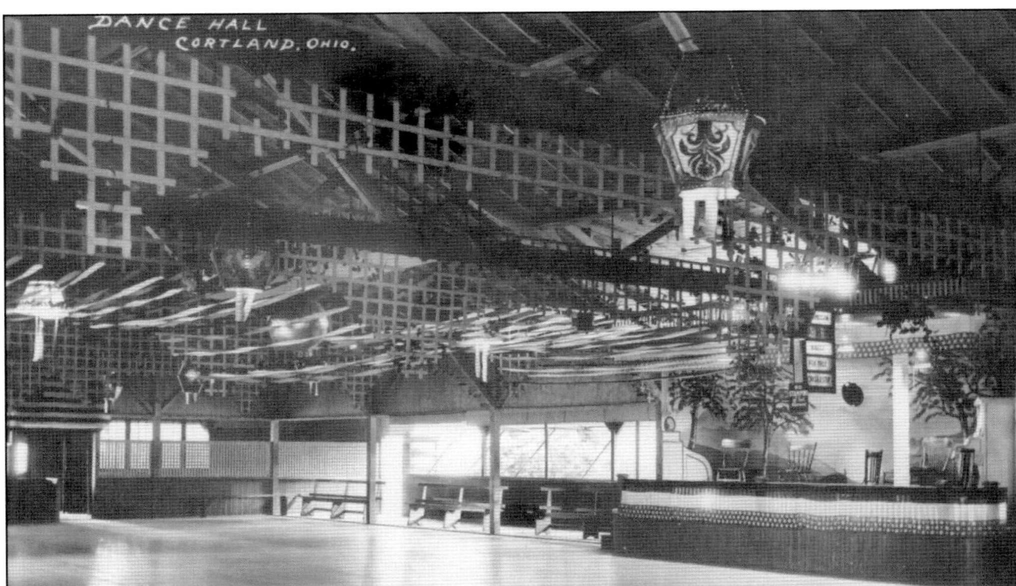

When the Edgewood Dance Hall opened in August 1921 in Cortland, where the present Cortland Roller Rink is located, it was filled to capacity. It had a large, glass-mirrored ball hanging in the middle with colored lights that shone on it for the moonlight dance. Some of the bands that played there were Paul Whitman, Guy Lombardo, Artie Shaw, and Fred Klipple of Warren. Over 200 couples could dance without crowding one another. A group of men from Warren formed the 600 Club and rented Edgewood before buying it a few years later. (Courtesy of Joe Shilling.)

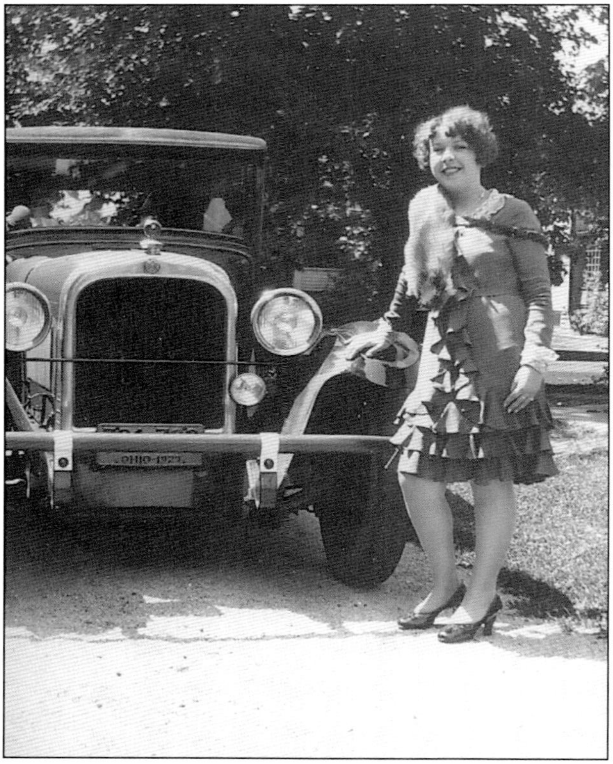

Isabelle West Hunter was 16 at the time when the Edgewood opened and this photograph was taken. Her father, William West, was a member of the 600 Club, so Isabelle felt like she was raised in a dance hall. "I danced and danced . . . and had crushes on the band players and stole a kiss behind the pot belly stove from a drummer or two. It was the best time of my life." (Courtesy of Carol Hunter Harrison.)

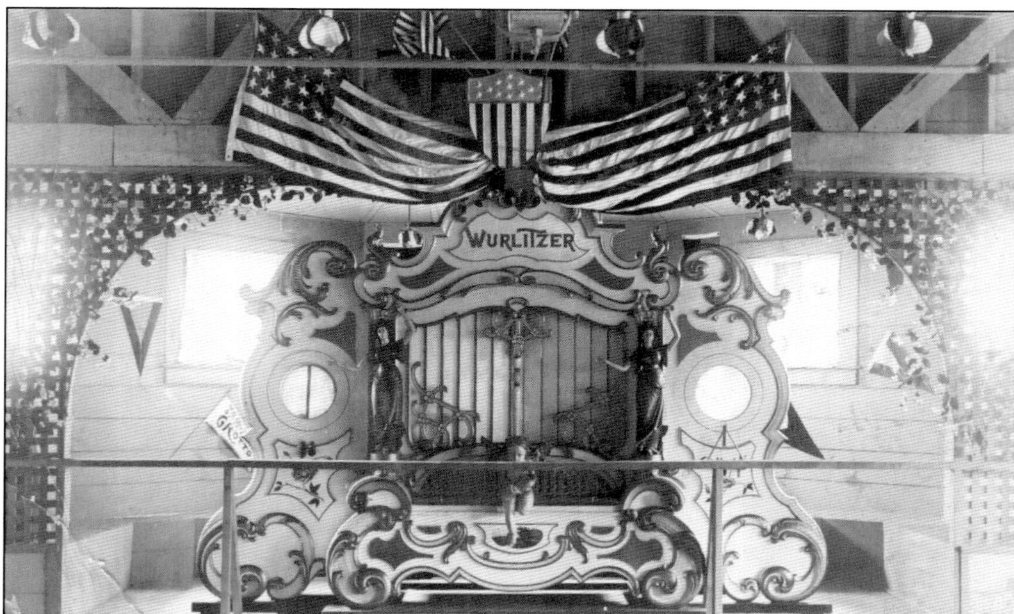

By the early 1930s, the nation was in the Depression, and the dance hall went bankrupt. When the building became the Cortland Roller Rink, a huge Wurlitzer organ, shown here, played for the skaters instead of a band as at the dance hall. Several people said that the organ could be heard all over town. (Courtesy of Mary Case.)

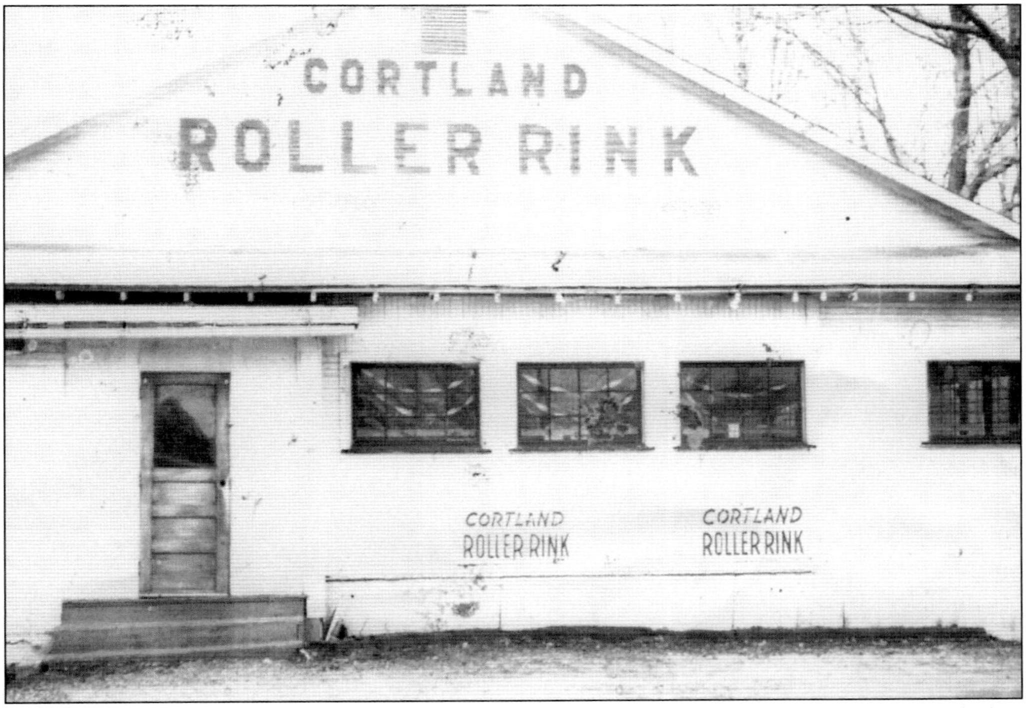

The Edgewood Dance Hall was what most people remember as the old Cortland Roller Rink that burned on June 5, 1975, on South High Street. This image dates from the 1940s. The business had several owners over the years. Jimmy DiGiacobbe, who has been the owner since before the fire, built the present rink on the same site, where it continues to be a favorite for young and old skaters. (Courtesy of Carol Hunter Harrison.)

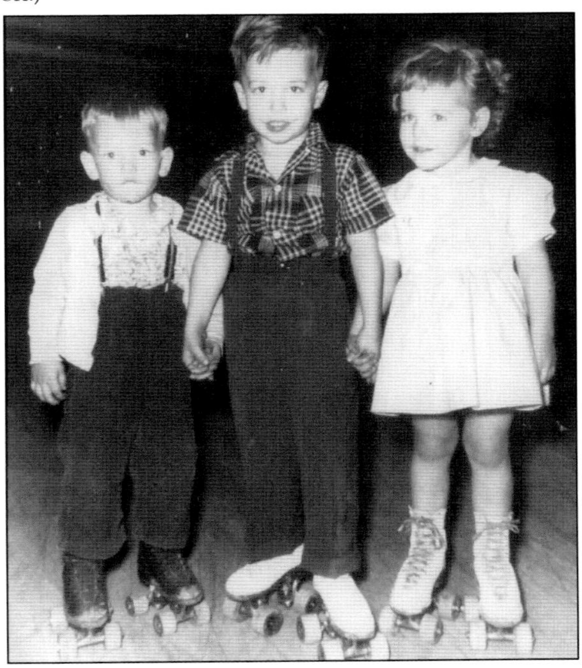

Cortland has had skating rinks from the 1870s, and they were as popular then as they are now. The first one was located on the site of Ron Miller's Barber Shop opposite the entrance to Grove Drive. Another one was on the third floor of the Arner Building, just west of the Cortland Bank on the same side of West Main Street. These are the Harned kids at the skating rink in 1954: Eddie, Roger, and Jenny Harned. Bill Harned, their father, ran the rink from 1950 to 1960. (Courtesy of William Harned.)

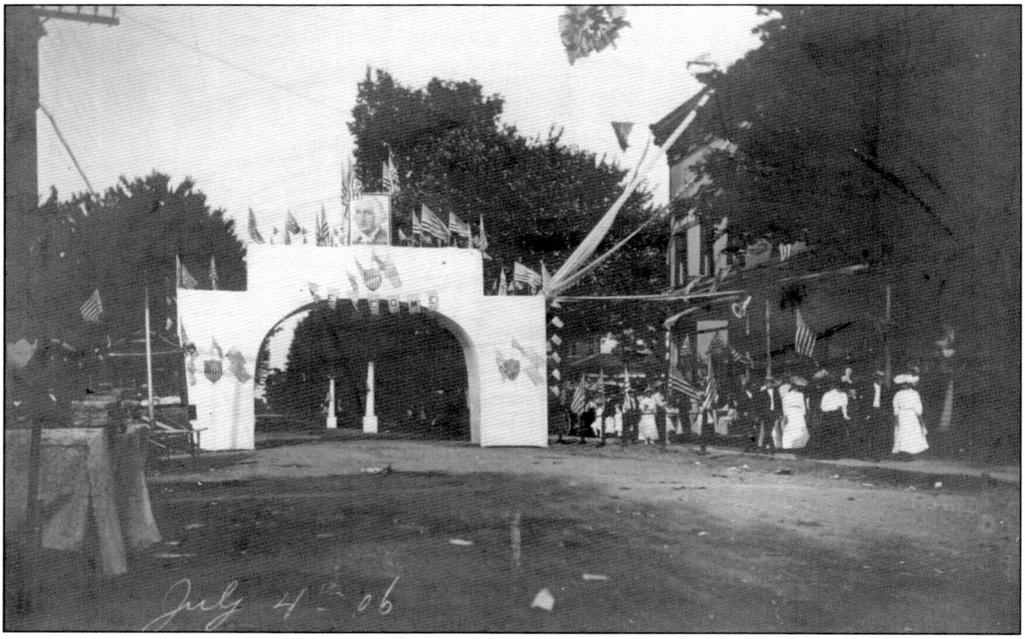

These photographs date from 1906, when the street fair was called Homecoming, typically held on or near the Fourth of July. Both images here were taken on July 4, 1906. The float in the photograph below shows part of a traditional parade. Above, ladies in white dresses and hats walk along the sidewalk, and the street is decorated with flags and an arch is over the street, a traditional element that appeared in other Homecomings. (Both, courtesy of the Gessner family.)

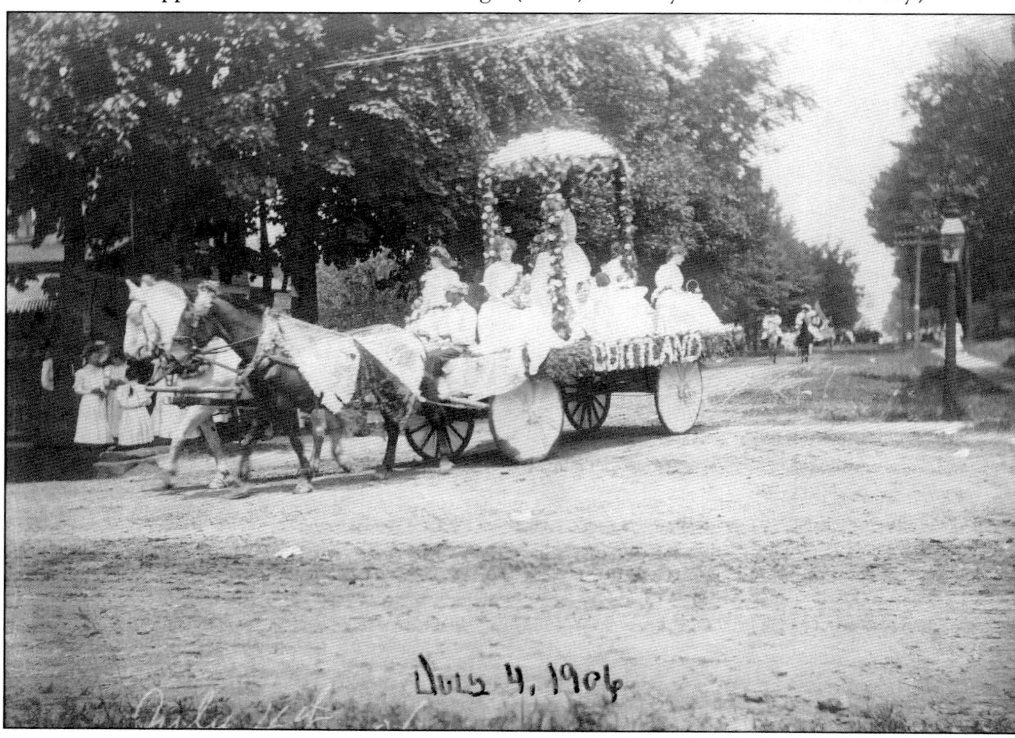

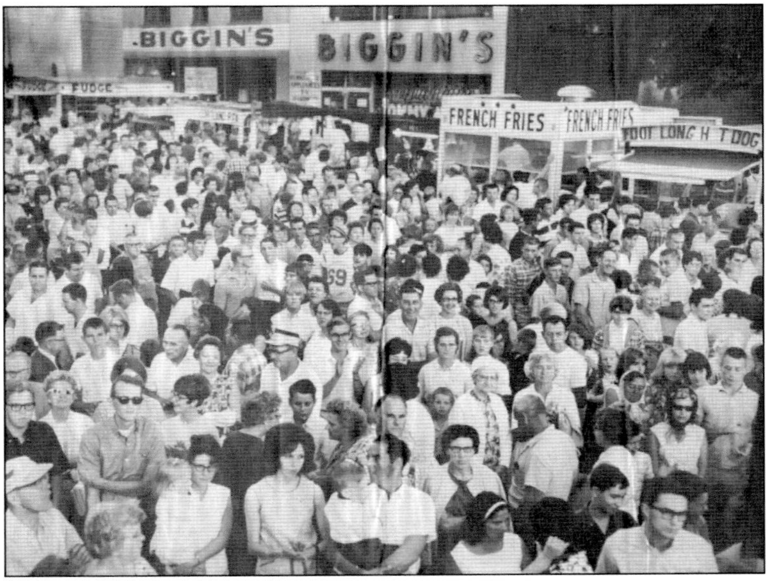

This 1966 Street Fair is quite a contrast to the one pictured on the previous page; it included vendors, rides, midway, concessions, a queen contest, and of course the traditional parade. Though the name changed to Street Fair, one thing remained the same: it was a homecoming for many former residents who returned just for the fair. (Courtesy of Don Jones.)

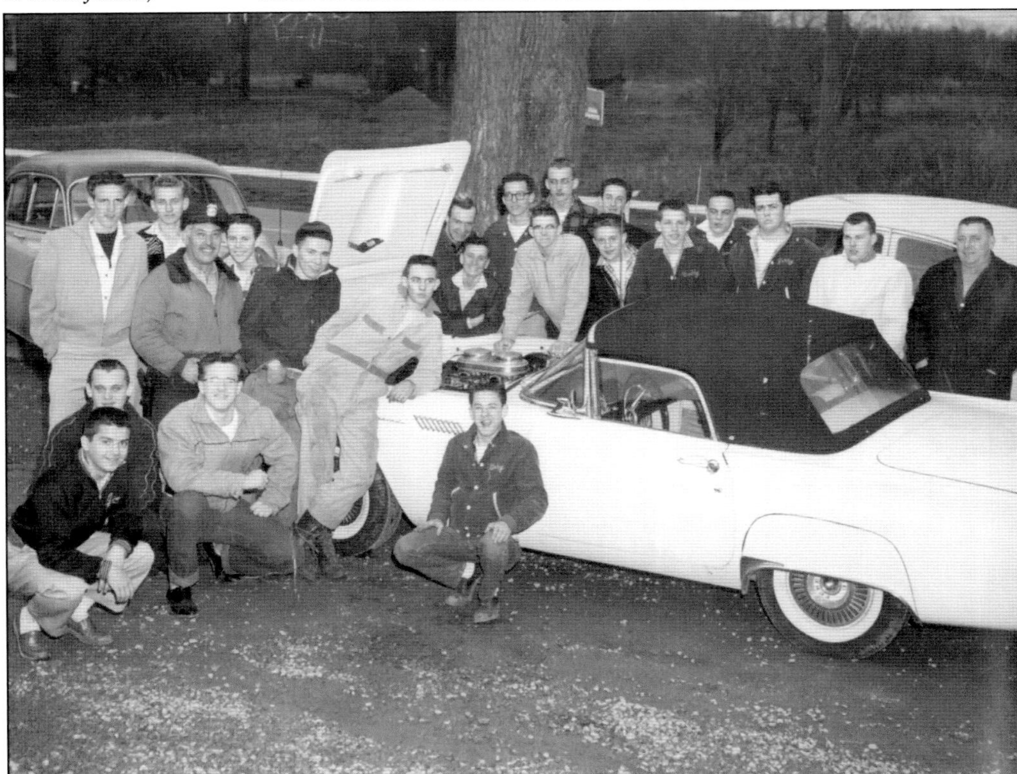

The Mosquito Lake Car Club was formed in the late 1950s and was a great experience for high school students from Cortland interested in cars. Sponsors included one of Cortland's local lawmen at the time, Mr. Orr, who kept the lads on an even keel. Still, boys will be boys and the shenanigans abounded. Gary Hunter is the boy kneeling down and leaning on the front of the car. (Courtesy of William Hallett and Gary Hunter.)

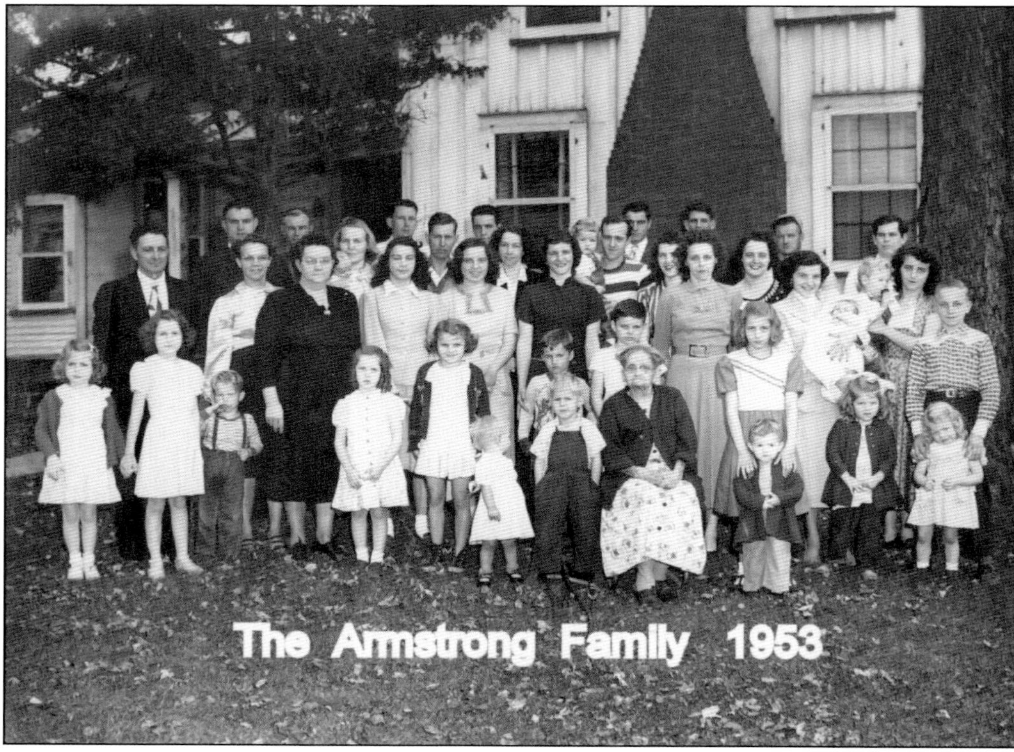

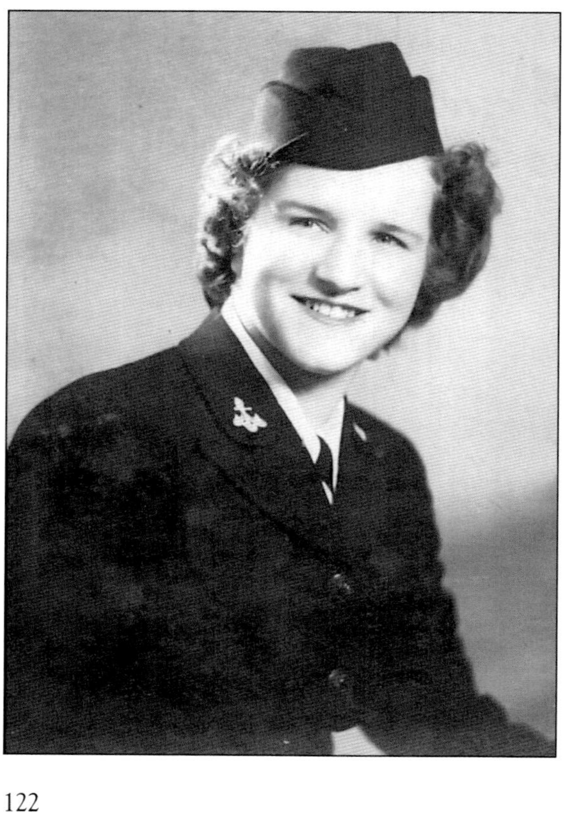

John W. and Leah Armstrong owned a farm in the northwest corner of Bazetta Township. Together they raised 16 children. John was born in 1893 and died in 1964. Leah was born 1898 and died in 1966. The family was named the largest in Trumbull County in 1953 and was featured in the *Warren Tribune*. Daughter Jewel Armstrong served in the Women's Army Corps during World War II, and is pictured to the left. (Above, courtesy of Ila Harvey; at left, Randy Reel.)

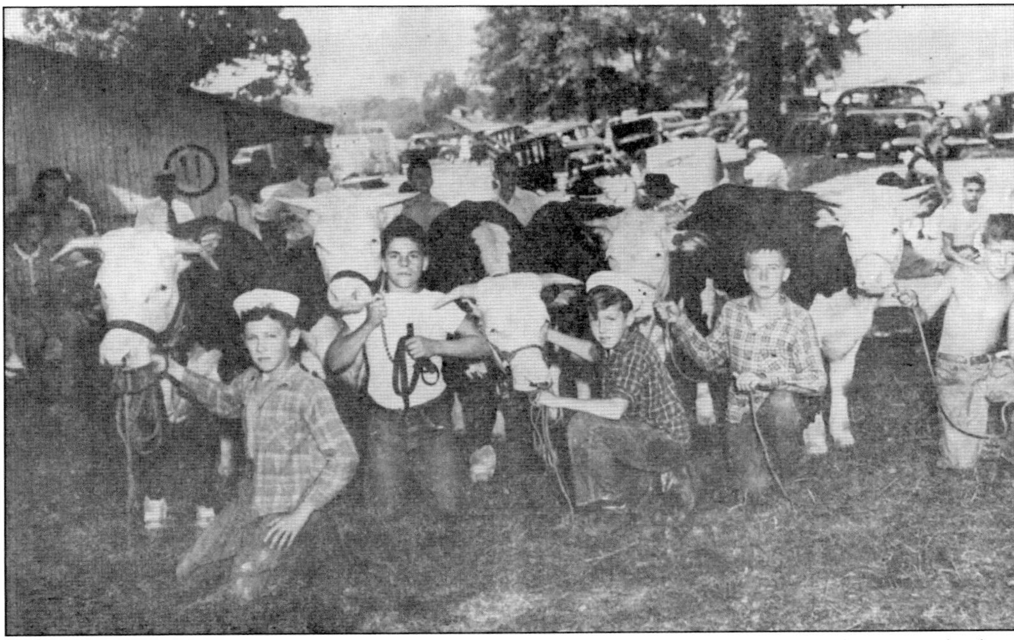

One of the new features of the 1944 Trumbull County Free Fair in Warren, Ohio, was the beef calf auction. The sale was held in the evening before the show, and all of the calves brought a good price. The calves shown in this photograph were owned by Dick Knight, Rea Knight, Neal Eaton, Jack Governor, and Jim Governor. (Courtesy of Don Murphy.)

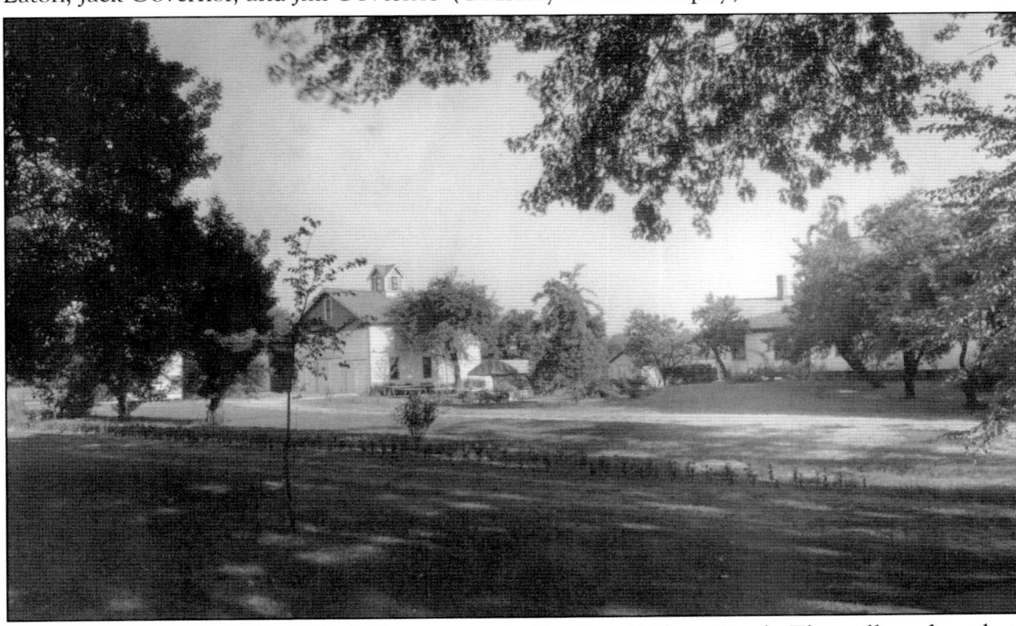

The Viets farm at 224 North High Street extended back to Walnut Creek. The millpond on their property provided water for the gristmill and ice for the summer. Tons of ice were harvested in the winter and kept in icehouses. When the pond was drained, townspeople used that area for the family cows. Part of the outline of the pond can be seen behind Rotary Park on East Main Street. (Courtesy of CBHS.)

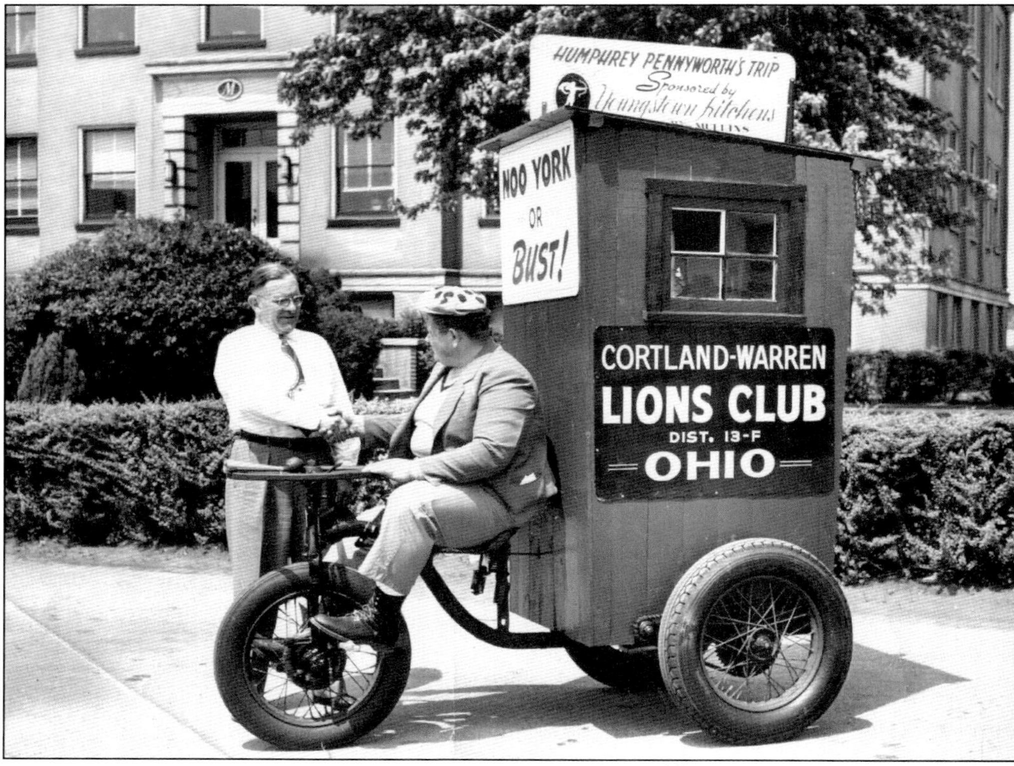

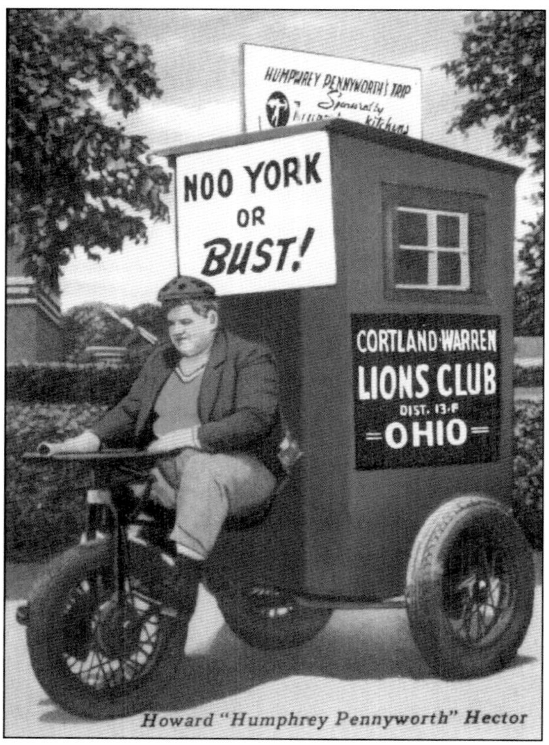

A resemblance to comic-strip character Humphrey Pennyworth in the Joe Palooka series by Ham Fisher gave Cortland's Howard Hector a certain amount of fame. In 1949, he was chosen to portray the character at the Lions Club International Convention in New York as a publicity stunt to sell US savings bonds. He soon was traveling to many towns around the country with the savings-bond message and meeting celebrities. His "Humphreymobile" was built in a Cortland welding shop from motorcycle parts, a heavy iron frame, and lumber. When Howard reached a town, the vehicle was unloaded and he drove through the town. The postcard at left commemorates the event. (Both, courtesy of CBHS.)

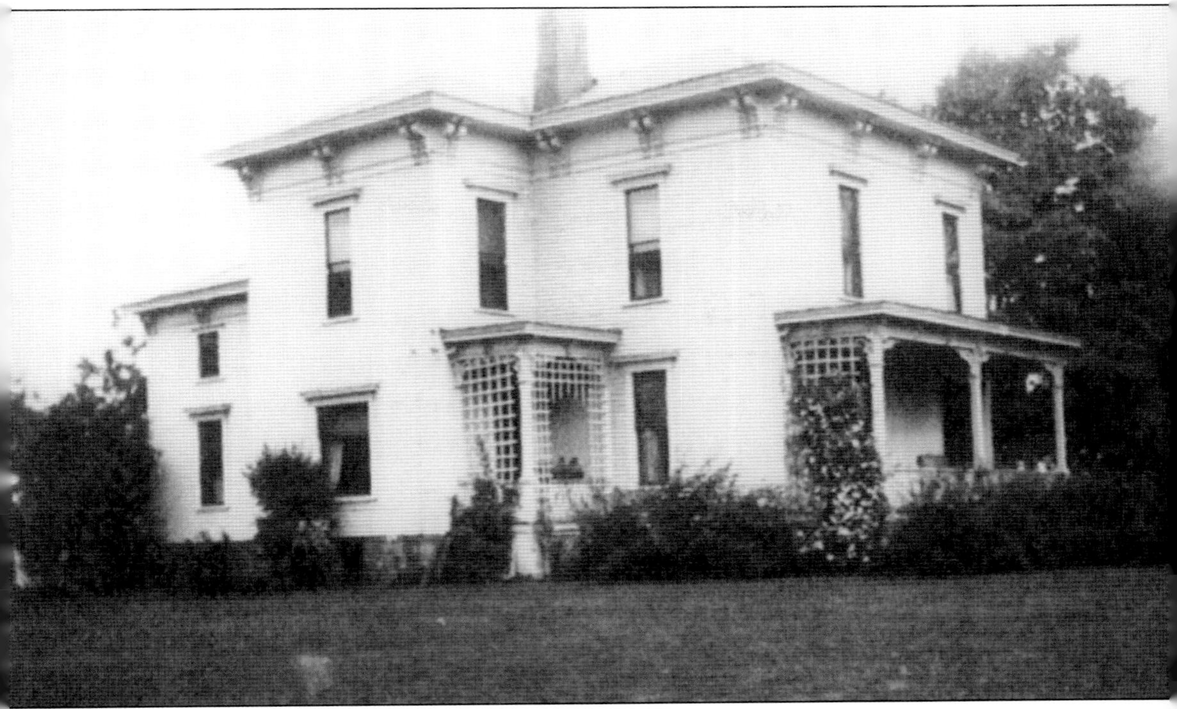

This house is the product of railroad, church, and town history all in one package. In 1863, Orrin Gates was working for the railroad but was also a Disciples Church minister. He came to East Bazetta, one of the names for the town, and stayed for six to eight years and is credited with naming the town after his hometown in New York. He bought land, known as Gates Addition, which was a rectangle bordered by Pearl Street on the north, Gates Street on the south, and between North High Street and the railroad. One of the lots he sold on High Street was purchased by Moses Bacon in 1870, who built this house. Over the years, it has had many owners and is presently being restored by Mayor Curt Moll and his wife, Gerri. (Courtesy of Curt Moll.)

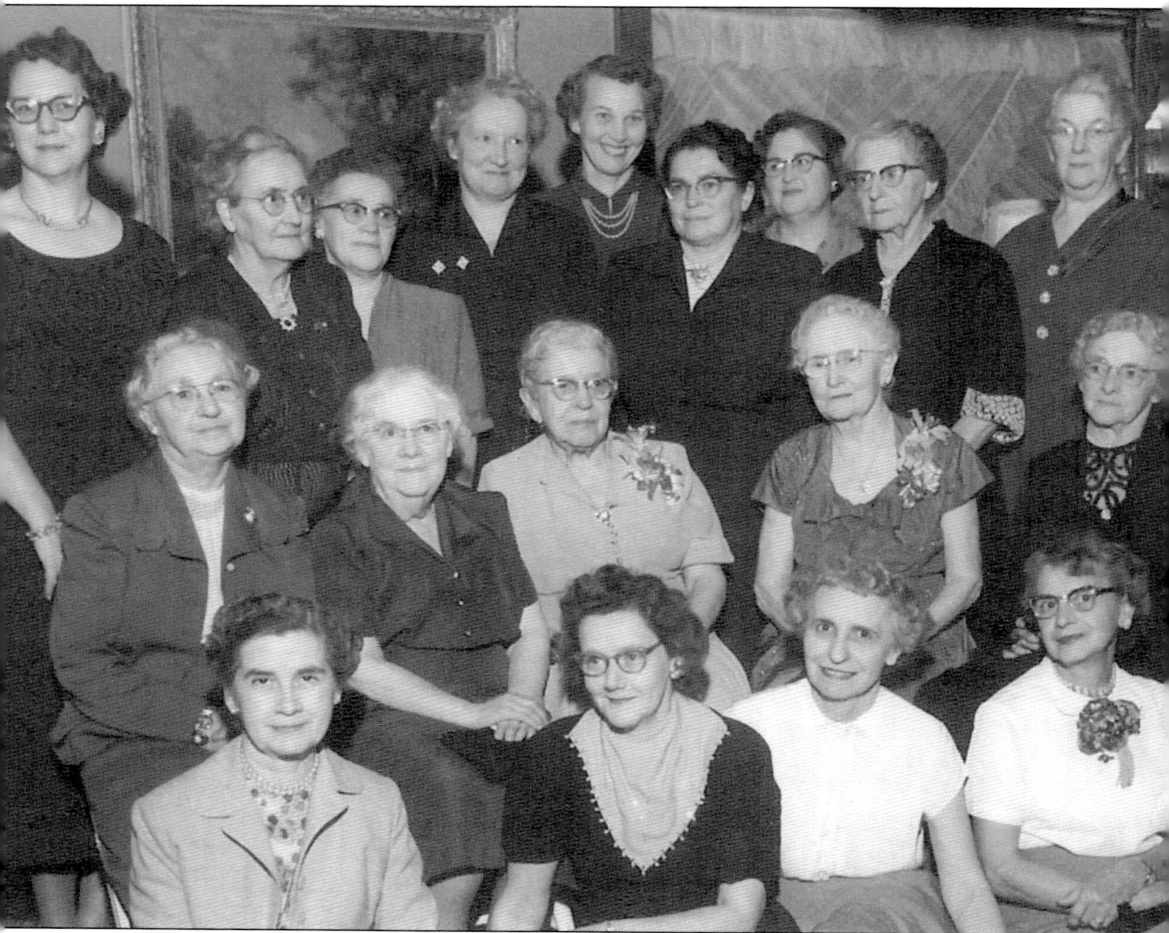

The Cortland Women's Literary Club was founded in 1904 as a way for women to get together and study literature and history. In 2004, the group met at the Viets House to celebrate the 100-year anniversary. The women who celebrated the 50-year anniversary are, from left to right, (first row, seated) Pauline Danford, Bernie Oaks, Grace Cook, and Inez Coe; (second row) Mary Retterer, Lucy Biggin, Winifred McCurley, Margaret Miller, and Bessie Bucher; (third row) Belva Burlingame, Bessie Ruiter, Cecil Marshall, Marjorie Rice, Ann Smith, Olive Cook, Altha McClellan, Kathryn Barber, and Marion Griffith. (Courtesy of CBHS.)

ABOUT THE ORGANIZATION

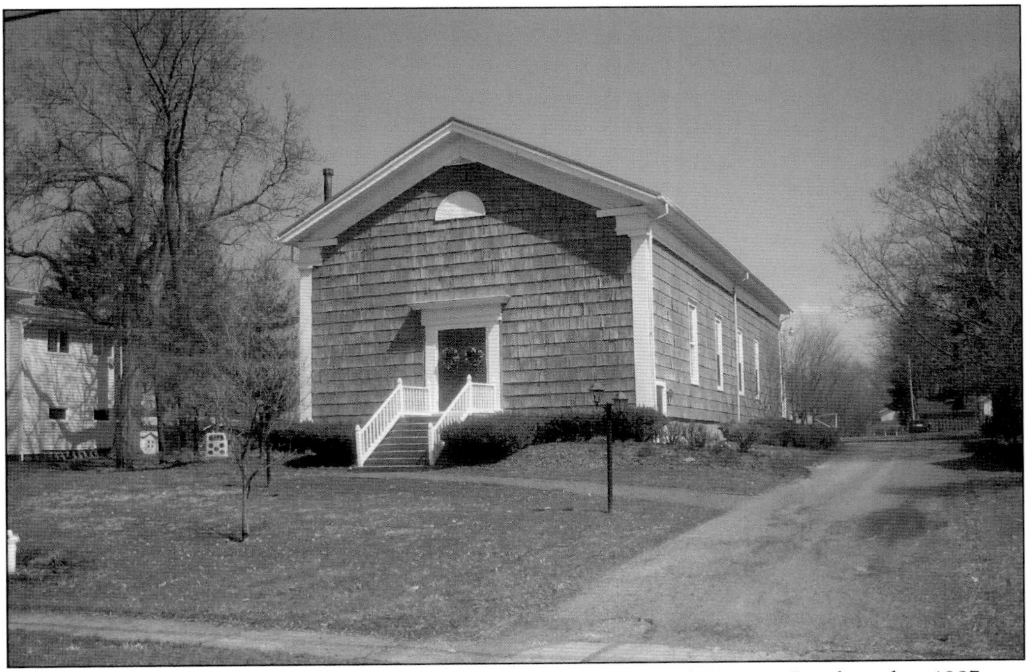

The Opera House is the home of the Cortland–Bazetta Historical Society. Purchased in 1987 as a church on a wooded hill above Walnut Run, it journeyed to High Street and spent its glory days as the Opera House and Grange Hall; the building holds the town's history in its walls. The historical society has worked very hard to preserve this building, adding a new roof, windows, furnace, air-conditioning, and paint. The downstairs is trimmed with wainscoting from the old town hall. There is a full kitchen. In 2012, the society plans to put new historically accurate siding on the exterior. The Cortland-Bazetta Historical Society was formed in 1976 as an outgrowth of the country's bicentennial celebration. Since then, the organization has offered Morning at the Museum programs, hay markets, wine tastings, art galas, garden walks, and home tours besides luncheons and sales. For membership information, look online at www.cityofcortland.org. (Author's collection.)